ADAM SHEPARD

ONE YEAR
LIVED

Content editors: Stuart Albright, Chris Hays, Jeff Wozer,
and Alexis A. Hunter
Copyeditor: Johnathan Wilber
Interior layout designers: Jay C. Polmar and Martha Delia García Márquez
Cover photos of the author at Lake Atitlán, Guatemala: Jan Laakmann
Cover designer: ImageTrance

ISBN 978-0-9796926-4-2 pbk

For book clubs, retail resale, educational institutions, gifts, or promotional use,
One Year Lived is available for 78 percent off the cover price at
www.OneYearLived.com.

For my pops, George Shepard,
a maverick who inspires me to live my life
off the beaten path.

And for Flora Herrera.

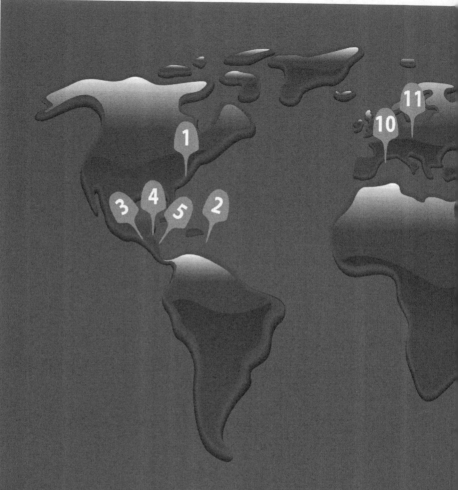

1. Raleigh, North Carolina
   (author's hometown)

2. Antigua in the Caribbean

3. Antigua, Guatemala

4. El Porvenir, Honduras

5. Puerto Cabezas, Nicaragua

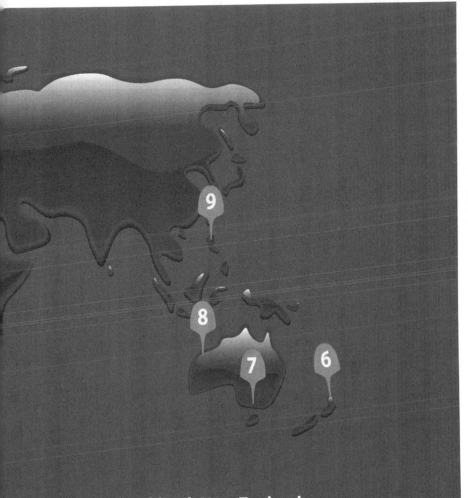

I peer up into a gray sky. I squint. I start making promises.

My pulse fights to exit through my neck and chest and wrists. I can't do this. Really? Can I? This is crazy. I can't do this. Whose idea was this anyway? Was this Ivana's idea? Dammit, this was her idea. Herein lies the consequence of running away from home and running into a Slovak girl. I dig this girl, but I don't dig this idea. My fingers tremble, and I can't seem to catch my breath, chest falling quick and uneven. This is crazy. I can't do this.

I look down over the bridge, to the left and to the right, and then up: clouds stacked upon clouds, packing the leaden sky, no sign of the sun. This isn't the proper scene for memorable moments. Where is the shine, the sparkle? I can see the start of a lake just over there, but a heavy dose of mist conceals it. They tell me that in the distance there's a wonderful view of the High Tatras mountain range. I can't see it. Below, a hundred meters of open air and a spread of green waiting for me, inviting me.

I can do this!

I turn around. They're watching. A guy in a red hooded sweatshirt. Another with a goatee, a girlfriend at his side. A lot of back-and-forth in a foreign tongue; many darting glances, bouncing from me to the platform and down to all that lies below. I know that look. Yeah, "must be a first timer" is right. Cocky bastards. I bet you were a little hesitant your first time, too.

It's been a wild journey. I've seen beautiful places. Met fascinating people. I climbed a volcano in Guatemala. Chased rambunctious children in Honduras. Dug trenches in Nicaragua. Hitchhiked in New Zealand. Castrated a bull in Australia and then fried the jewels up for dinner. Offered my naked body to a beach in the Philippines. Rode an elephant in Thailand. Visited Auschwitz. Swam in natural pools, hot and cold. Skipped rocks. Contemplated the conquest of the natives. I drank too much in Spain and not enough in Indonesia. I watched the sun rise and then set all over the world.

And now, here I stand.

Ugh. Don't pressure me. In a few minutes, another coward will be standing in my place, people, and I'm going to give that person all the time he or she needs to muster the courage—don't you worry. Don't stare at me like that. Yeah, you. I'll go when I'm ready.

I'll go when I'm ready.

Just give me a second. Jesus. Y'all don't have anywhere to be.

I'll go when I'm ready.

The cheering and clapping isn't helping. You can stop now.

I'm not ready.

Am I?

No, I'm not.

I can't do this.

My gaze rolls to Ivana. She smiles but doesn't press me. My nerves fumble my return smile. Where is our relationship headed? This is going well, right? I think it's going well. I say it's going well.

Yeah, it's going well.

But there's still no way I'm jumping off this bridge.

One of the guys says to me in broken English: "Just in case line break and you not stop before ground, we really enjoy know you."

Ugh, this is crazy.

I can't do this. I'm not ready. Man, what a horrible idea. Ugh.

Okay, that's it. I'm not ready. Unwrap the cord from my ankles. I want outta here. Let's all go have a drink and a good laugh, both at my expense. Do you offer refunds? Partial? Can I still get a T-shirt?

Ahhhhhhh. Why am I doing this! Come on, Shep.

Screw it.

I take a final, lingering look over at Ivana, her expression cheery and supportive. I spread my arms out wide above my head. I bend my knees. I rise up off of my toes. I curl my head down over the rest of my body. I dive. I soar. An exhilarated shriek explodes through my lips, prying at my clenched jaw. The world opens up. My pulse pounds even harder. I'm dropping. I'm flying. The forest widens, widens, widens—a sea of spiky green spreading beneath me. The fall lasts a day, a week, a month. Three-point-two-five seconds.

I bounce, retreat high back up toward the platform, and tumble.

The cord pulls me high, and I tumble again.

I come to rest. I look up. I can't make out the details of her face, but I know my girl's watching me, laughing that melodic laugh that infects everyone around her.

There's nowhere in the world I'd rather be.

THE LIST

I wasn't angry. I didn't hate my job. I wasn't annoyed with capitalism, and I was indifferent to materialism. I wasn't escaping emptiness, nor was I searching for meaning. I have great friends and a wonderful family. The dude two doors down invited me over for steak or pork chops—my choice—one Sunday, and I couldn't even tell you the first letter of his name. Most of my teeth are natural.

I had enjoyed some nominal success: a few books to my name, a bunch of speaking engagements across the country, a new audio program for teenagers. Sure, the producers of *The Amazing Race* had rejected all five of my applications to hotfoot around the world—all five!—and my girlfriend and I had just parted ways, but I'd whined all I could about the race, and the girl wasn't The Girl anyway.

All in all, my life was pretty fantastic.

But I felt boxed in. Look at a map, and there we are, a pin stuck in the wall. There's the United States, about twenty-four square inches' worth, and there's the rest of the world, about seventeen hundred square inches begging to be explored. I looked back, and I looked forward. This life is serious: I want the wife, I want the babies, I want the business success, and I understand the work that is required 'til the wee hours to get them. But I didn't want to leave any experience unlived before that happened.

I felt as if I was a few memories short, as if there was still time for me to go out there and get missing for a little while. Bust out the *List o' Good Times*, sell my car, store my crap, stuff a backpack, buy a small mountain of Reese's Peanut Butter Cups, and hop on a plane. Just this once.

I first started to visualize this trip when I was in high school. Back then it was a dream, like playing basketball in the NBA, although I legitimately thought I was going to play in the NBA. Then, a year or so passed, and my NBA dream morphed into the A-division in Italy. I went off to college, and my dream settled on any one of the top leagues throughout Europe. By the time I graduated from college, I would have signed with any team, anywhere. I would have lived in a tent and hunted for my own food with a blowgun. I just wanted to hoop. Then my thirty-six-hour professional basketball career in Germany came to an end, and I flew home. I left to write my first book.

My dream to travel around the world wasn't really *that* serious. Other things, domestic things, were on my mind. My first book got published; national media outlets flashed the cover on TV; I was invited to speak at a variety of venues. Then, I looked at the *List o' Good Times*:

- Run a mile on the Great Wall of China.
- Sing karaoke in a foreign language.
- Castrate a wild bull.
- Tip a crisp $100 bill on a $20 tab.
- Read the Bible.
- Handwrite a letter from the heart.
- Grow a mustache for a month.
- Cut my hair into a mullet (at a different time than growing the mustache).
- Provide a month's supply of food for an entire African village.
- Scuba dive in the Caribbean during winter.
- Watch a movie in an Asian language without subtitles.
- Pick up a hitchhiker.
- Attend the Super Bowl.
- Dress up as Batman and run around asking people abruptly if they've heard anything about a robbery in the neighborhood.

I made my list when I was a sophomore in college. The heavens had dumped a mountain of snow on us in North Andover, Massachusetts, and school had been called off. Everything was called off. Plows were barricaded in. The National Guard was on standby.

So I sat down to write. I had previously read a chapter in one of those *Chicken Soup for the Soul* books. I think it was *A Second Helping of Chicken Soup for the Grandmother's Son-in-Law's Estranged Best Friend's Dog's Wounded Right Leg for the Soul*, Revised Edition. Some elderly dude had crafted an essay about how, when he was a young lad, he'd written out a list of the things he wanted to do with his life: climb this mountain, play that instrument, learn this language, etc. And then—get this—he spent his life actually doing them rather than talking about his list at cocktail parties. "Ah, yes. Scuba diving in the Caribbean. I've got that on my bucket list."

I looked around my dorm room. I didn't have any new books to read, homework could wait, TV seemed too easy a solution at the moment.

The list seemed like a good idea at the time.

Fast-forward a few years, and there I was, approaching thirty, fast—really, really fast—the *List o' Good Times* staring back at me from the screen on my laptop, cursor blinking. One hundred forty-two items on that list. How long would this take me?

- Complete a marathon.
- Design the landscaping for my own house.
- Make a positive impact on a child's life before I have children of my own.
- Obtain minority ownership in a professional sports team.
- Fish off the coast of New Zealand.
- Learn to jump while wakeboarding.
- Anonymously buy someone's meal from across the restaurant.
- Climb Kilimanjaro.
- Smoke a Cuban in Cuba.
- Hug a koala.

- Ride an elephant.
- Bet my wad on the underdog in a cockfight.
- Learn to fly without a copilot.
- Randomly spend an hour cleaning up a littered area.
- Attend the World Cup.
- Make love on a beach.

This could take ten years, I thought. My boy Sipsey said, "Shep, this list is going to cost you three-point-four million dollars." Even if I had another fifty years or so left on this planet, depending upon a stroke of luck here or there and what those chaps in lab coats come up with, I was still far short on money. I made the determination, right then and there: two years to save and one year to be on the road. One year to get Out There, meet people, volunteer, learn, and get my heart racing a little bit. One year to read. One year to hold an impoverished kid's hand and tell her that her life can be whatever she wants it to be. One year to stand on top of a bridge, declare my dominion over the world, and jump. *Maybe I can make a small difference—in my life and the life of someone else.*

Asking yourself what you want to do before you die is a silly question, shifts focus to the wrong place. A setup for procrastination, surrendering your *List o' Good Times* to retirement. Who said anything about dying? I was healthy and capable and had no fatal diagnoses on my record. Death, still presumably far away, didn't even have a place in this conversation.

And a bucket list? To hell with a bucket list: that's not the time to start living, when your doctor announces that that black spot fastened to your lung is malignant and inoperable, and, well, you just better go ahead and make sure your will is current. A bucket list? That always makes me laugh: *Oh, shit! Now the clock is really ticking! Gotta go out and do everything I want to do before it's too late!*

This list belongs in the present. This—right now, today—*this* is our time to live, yours and mine. Quality years ahead, presumably, and we've already had some great experiences, met some great people, and created some great memories. Life is good. We ain't mad.

But I still felt boxed in. Maybe I'd gotten a little soft. Maybe I'd neglected the best parts of life. Maybe I'd become too regimented.

I needed a little perspective. I'd be home soon to find a wife and conceive kids and construct a career, but right then I wasn't worried about any of that. I needed to get out there, just for a year.

I needed a year to live.

So, here we go. You:

The high school kid with a thousand ideas for the future. Now is the time to harness your enthusiasm, start dreaming big.

The college student tossed into the blend of social and academic life, loving it but anxious about what's next. Now's the time to have your list handy.

The young professional, suffocated by a cloud of work and swearing that, "I'm missing out on something."

The older professional, thinking you've lost your window of adventure.

And the retiree, lost in reminiscence and excited to go exploring once again.

And me, sitting in the Miami airport, a mouth full of chocolate and peanut buttery goodness, ten minutes from boarding a plane to Guatemala City, about to embark on the greatest adventure of my life . . .

"It's a known fact, Phoeby, you got tuh go there tuh know there. Yo' papa and yo' mama and nobody else can't tell yuh and show yuh. Two things everybody's got tuh do fuh themselves. They got tuh go tuh God, and they got tuh find out about living fuh themselves."

—Zora Neale Hurston, *Their Eyes Were Watching God*

GUATEMALA

The Other Antigua

I wasn't supposed to be there in the first place.

As I stepped out of baggage claim, I spotted the shuttle driver standing off to the side. He held a sign with my name on it and, as I approached, tucked it under one arm in order to shake my hand.

"Welcome!" he said in Spanish.

"Welcome!" I said, returning the greeting.

He drove me out of Guatemala City in a rusty van that hacked and coughed its way from side street to main artery, bound for Antigua. It wasn't the dark of the night or the wheezing of the truck that raised my eyebrows. It was the grunginess of this world surrounding me.

Something isn't right. How did I get here?

I had committed to the trip, to a year that I'd never have back, and I'd bragged to my friends and family: "I can't be dissuaded. Get out of my way." I couldn't back out. I didn't want to become like everybody else who says they're going to take a trip like this.

Then came the question: "Where to?"

I bought a world map, spread it between the windows in my room, and peppered the drywall with the pinholes of notes posted and removed. I read this book and that blog post and—*oh, my, it says right here in this magazine that I absolutely shouldn't skip hiking through Patagonia.* I quizzed well-traveled friends about their favorite spots; I posted on Facebook, where I got thirty-eight varying responses from twenty-seven people.

- The Vatican.
- Neuschwanstein Castle in Germany.

- Machu Picchu.
- Tokyo.
- Egypt.
- Borobudur, in Magelang, Indonesia.
- Mumbai.
- Whitsunday Islands in Australia. ("And go to Whitehaven Beach and climb to the top of the hill/mountain thingy," Janelle said.)

Candace sent me a meticulously crafted e-mail on all of the highlights of Thailand, Laos, and Cambodia. Everyone recommended New Zealand.

I took it all in but maintained my discipline. In a year I could see a hundred different places, literally, or more, if I wanted. But then my trip would be watered down, wholly comprising a day-to-day existence of loading my pack and hopping on a bumpy bus or a cramped train, with little time to observe. Maybe it was more important to get to know people. The bumpy bus rides would be there, assuredly, but if I sprinted through this trip, the year would fly by, yielding a memory card bursting with the photos of this gorgeous, wide world but lacking real, meaningful experiences. A scant existence.

I wanted more than a full memory card. I wanted something deeper. So I decided to slow it down a bit—pick eight to ten countries to visit before I hit Europe for the last few months, which would likely emerge as the time for me to, in a blur, milk that overpriced Eurail pass for all I could.

So I started to shape my list. Only two things mattered at the outset: One, stay out of the Middle East. Besides the never-ending conflict from one country to the next—from Pakistan to Syria and down into Yemen—and an enthusiastic aversion for Americans, there had been a recent international incident involving three reckless, brainless hikers from the United States who'd "accidentally" crossed into Iran while sightseeing. The cab driver who dropped them off reportedly told them they shouldn't be there in the first place. "Oops," they offered to President Ahmadinejad, who wasn't exactly known for his leniency. "Just kidding." But they were accused of being spies anyway and spent several years in jail before being allowed to post the million-dollar bail.

Perhaps it was narrow-minded of me to avoid the Middle East. There are many great places to visit there, and I would like to get to those places one day. But avoiding them for now seemed sensible. (In the later months of my trip, the president of the United States issued an impromptu call for protection of all American citizens after anti-American protests started to escalate throughout parts of the Middle East and Africa. Embassies were attacked. Diplomats were killed. American flags were torn down and publicly burned and shredded.) The timing just wasn't right.

The second thing that mattered from the outset: chasing warmth. I love to ski, but this wasn't that kind of trip. Chilly, snow-covered backwoods are for young dudes, bloated with ambition and innocence and hubris; kids who scamper off to eat berries and hunt game and read classic philosophy and by and by become one with nature. They can have that. I respect them, admire them for a grit I don't possess, but that's not my style. I paid close attention to the equator and mapped out which months I should be in which hemisphere. July in Belgium is lovely; February, frigid. Plus, I didn't relish the idea of filling half my pack with a bulky parka.

Out of all of the names, all the dots littered across the map on my wall, one place seemed to linger in my mind. A place that had always struck me as exotic and sunny and begging for exploration: Antigua. Antigua, the land of smooth beaches and soft breezes and clear ocean and nearly unbroken coral.

I started mentioning to people that I was thinking about starting my trip in Antigua and then working my way from there. It looked pretty fun; the whole city sprawled on the shore, after all, and the ads splashed across the Internet suggested there would be plenty of young people and Americans to cushion my fall into the exotic. Parts of it looked a little old-school in the pictures I'd seen online, but I stood poised for a history lesson.

As it turns out, there's more than one Antigua.

There's Antigua, the land of beautiful beaches (the one I'd been hearing about from friends and family), and there's an Antigua that ain't nowhere near the coast. There's an Antigua that is new and fresh and clean, where someone will deliver your Mai Tai to your lounge chair on the beach, and there's an Antigua that's old and full of history, where you walk into a bar and order your own drink. There's an Antigua on the Caribbean, and there's an Antigua in Guatemala. The former is where you go on a cruise, and the latter is where you go for culture. I selected, signed, sealed, and paid for the latter Antigua—the landlocked Antigua—before I touched down and realized that it wasn't the Antigua everyone had been praising and gushing about.

Imagine that. Imagine getting lost on Google, discovering that Antigua also doubles as the Spanish-language-school capital of the world, showing pictures of exquisite beaches and palm trees to your friends, and buying your plane ticket to Guatemala, only to realize that there's another Antigua—the sun-soaked, dazzling Antigua next to the beach—just seven inches or so to the right on your map.

Sun and beaches and lovely ladies in bikinis in the Caribbean? Nah, I'm good. I'll take drug cartels, crumbling buildings, and three hours of rain every afternoon in Guatemala, thanks. But you enjoy yourself out there.

Then—in what would be the first of many eye-opening experiences—I walked around the wrong Antigua and discovered that it was the perfect place to begin.

Antigua, Guatemala, my home for the first month of my odyssey, is old, sure, but the colonial architecture proved a charming contrast from the new, chic, shiny buildings I was used to in North Carolina. The old buildings in North Carolina were built fifty years ago with cranes and heavy machinery; the old buildings in Antigua have been standing for half a millennium, ever since the Spanish conquered the Maya and put them to work on the other end of the whip. Every rough-edged stone was placed with care by Maya hands. As I wandered through the cobblestone pathways and trailed my fingers over the ancient stone around me, I wondered how much Maya blood had been mixed in with the mortar holding this city together. How many busted fingers and aching backs built this place? Who were the people who laid this foundation?

But that was long ago. Of the people I wove among that day—the first day I saw this other Antigua—some were young like me. Some had bright and shining eyes that greeted me kindly. Others were aging and bent men and women, their bodies malformed by years of hard labor. A few boys kicked a half-deflated soccer ball around in the shadowed alley between two streets. Their chattering conversations and frequent laughter bounced against the old walls around them before touching the sky. Before touching me, too, and bringing a smile to my face. Even in this place, there's poverty and wealth. Struggles and the joy of a game of soccer before bed.

Strict rules in this colonial town govern how much you can build, where, and with what size sign in the front. This means tranquility. This means room to walk on the sidewalk. The *narcotraficantes* are all in the mountains and up near the border with Mexico, while here in Antigua, the museums cradle the art and culture of this world: the ancient churches whose firm walls and vaulted ceilings have sheltered parishioners for hundreds of years; the dazzling fountains in the park that serenade the city with their tinkling water music; and the sweet little Maya ladies, who offer the brightest smiles in an attempt to sell their handiwork, and when that fails, carry a rebuttal to your rejection tucked in their back pockets. Sure there's poverty in Antigua, just as there's poverty in your town, but no one ever hounded me for spare change (even though I had extra money from not having touched my sunscreen fund).

I later learned most of this from Eddy, my Spanish teacher in Antigua, Guatemala. He was short, his dark face obscured by a mustache and glasses. A former soccer player, he had brainpower to match his athleticism. He would relate the history of his country alongside mine—"The capital was moved from

Antigua to Guatemala City in 1776 after Antigua was destroyed by earthquakes. 1776. The same year as the independence of the United States." I, however, couldn't have named a single significant Guatemalan date or landmark.

I was in Antigua, even if it wasn't the correct Antigua, for one reason: to get back into the Spanish game. I've always taken great pleasure in the challenge of speaking a language that isn't my own, a language that baffles English speakers on the train or plane or in the park. My brother and I worked as waiters at IHOP in high school, where we'd speak Spanish with the staff in the back of the house, learning to say things that none of our peers from the front could understand. We picked up some formal phrases—necessary things like how to locate the bathroom or how to tell someone we really like their shirt—but mostly we focused on learning how to tell a girl that she had really nice *nachas*. Things like that. My brother, Erik, amused himself by translating the English-speaking cooks and Spanish-speaking dishwashers to each other.

"Erik, could you please tell Manolo I need a large pan, two pots, and a ladle," Stanley said to my brother one morning.

"Hey, Manolo," Erik translated into Spanish, somehow straight-faced. "Stanley says to tell your mom thank you for the mint she left on the pillow this morning before she left."

The summer after my sophomore year of college, I spent a month in Seville, Spain, and a month in San Miguel de Allende, Mexico, the following summer. I loved it—speaking Spanish, visiting ancient fortresses, strolling through museums, and lying on beautiful beaches in these extraordinary, far-off lands that I'd never even heard of three months before. Before that, at Merrimack College, I learned culture and history and grammar and conjugations from Professor Brucato, even if I never understood the subjunctive or why the Spaniards would include such a dreadful thing in their language.

But I hadn't spoken more than six or seven Spanish phrases in the five years before I arrived in Antigua, and most of those included me smiling and explaining to my pops's bilingual friends that I really wasn't proficient enough to carry on any kind of serious conversation with them in Spanish. I learned to say flawlessly, "Pops just wants to make me look like an asshole by requesting that I practice with you."

And for my upcoming volunteer work in Honduras, there was technically no Spanish-language requirement. But when I wanted to have a conversation with a poor barefoot kid, speaking his or her language would be vital—I wanted to talk to him about where he came from and what he wanted to do with his future and what he could do to get there. This was important to me, and I wanted to retrieve some conversational ability. *Without* Spanish, I would have been just a happy-go-lucky white boy who came down to play for a couple months, pretending to sound like a local by adding *o*'s to the end of every word: *beero, foodo, upset stomacho.* A puppet who would soon return to his privileged, air-conditioned life. *With* Spanish, though, maybe the kids would enjoy kicking the soccer ball around and playing tag with me, and then maybe they would take me a little more serious when it came time to chat a little.

I needed a month to brush up. So I checked the appropriate boxes to sign up for the full package in Antigua, Guatemala: language classes, lodging with a Guatemalan family, meals, and a personal shuttle from the airport. After that tumultuous ride, my driver dropped me off at the house of Beatríz, my Latina mom for a month.

She said, "Welcome!"

I said, "Welcome!"

She merrily showed me her house, her little courtyard, and the shared bathroom, the entire tour in Spanish. My room, a generous room, had two wide beds with thin mattresses, a bookshelf, a desk, a small trash can, and one window illuminating the room and allowing me access to Beatríz's well-tended courtyard. She told me the times for breakfast, lunch, and dinner. She spoke English only to give me her two rules: "No drink in house. No romance in house."

I went to bed energized, head riffling through a dozen hopeful imaginings of the wonders to come in the year ahead.

Finding Fortitude

It wasn't hard for me to dream up this trip. Before I left, I went to work; I went out for beers; I went home to watch "the game" or "my show"; I went to fabulous cookouts with friends and exchanged book recommendations; I split my two weeks of vacation between the mountains and the beach. But then I realized something was missing, and my mind started to wander.

The planning for this trip wasn't a huge undertaking either. It wasn't hard to get the necessary immunizations and visas. It wasn't hard to go shopping for supplies or to load up my pack, and when it came time for me to say my final good-byes to the family, even Ma didn't shed a tear.

Indeed, the only difficult part about taking a trip like this is gathering the moxie to declare to yourself that you're actually going to do it. Everything else—the planning, the pricks in the arm, the packing, the departure at the airport—is really no sweat at all. Anybody can dream it up, but having the balls to convince myself I was actually going to follow through with my dream? Challenging. It was tough to think about everything I was giving up to take this trip: time with the family; time with friends; weddings and other special events; my savings; comfort; security; my career; and a year's worth of foregone earnings. No question it would sting to return from a trip like this jobless and broke.

I made the assertion early—perhaps to convince myself to go, and perhaps because I actually believed it—that this would be the best year of my life. I promised myself I wouldn't leave any presented experience on the table.

Don't. Leave. Anything. On. The. Table.

But questions remained: How does a person muster the courage—or recklessness—to put it all to the side for a year? To shelve responsibility? Alongside heaps of motivation—new places, new experiences, new foods—why does one decide to go and another doesn't? Whether escaping the mundane or chasing excitement, why do some people *talk* about their dream to do something anomalous and others actually *do* it?

I'm sure there are some fascinating psychological explanations, but I'm also convinced that heredity has something to do with it, whether via inspiration or out of spite. Growing up, my parents never allowed my brother and me to watch TV during the week and granted us only an hour a day on the weekends. They always encouraged us to go out and play, whether *out* was outside in the yard or outside the country.

On the other hand, many have defiantly set off into the wild to counterbalance the stiff paradigms of their upbringing. For them, it's an act of rebellion.

Many casual theories appeal to me—related to my parents, my mentors, my peers, my tolerance for risk, my persistent curiosity. Every book I've read about another castle or coastal village or fishing expedition or volunteer opportunity or run through town with a herd of bulls tight in the wake has made me want to see it all for myself. But the biggest motivation for me, the deciding factor, was my seventy-year-old self. When one hits seventy, the dust and blur of his or her life clears and reflection sets in. Looking back from that point, would I be happy with the life I'd lived, with the decisions I'd made? *Had I soaked up every moment? Did I matter? Had I made this world a little bit better?*

These aren't easy questions, the answers either crushing or uplifting.

My seventy-year-old self lives in a three-bedroom house, one-level. One of the bedrooms is an office and the other is a guest room for family. The kitchen and living room blend into one, spacious enough to allow guests the comfort to spread their wings but compact enough to keep the electric bill manageable. There is a small pool in the backyard flanked by a garden of tulips and roses and carnations and a dark green, eight-year-old Honda Accord in the driveway. He's had a hard life, but a fun life. He lives modestly, but this is how he always wanted it. He explored rather than hoarding material wealth. Maybe he reached his professional goals and maybe not, but he was sure to carve his own path. He learned and he taught, he gave affection and received it, he took some punches and threw a couple of his own.

He made some good decisions and some bad ones—like putting "grow a mullet" on his to-do list—but he never lay in wait. He always said, "Okay, that was fun," and then quickly added, "Now, what will I do next?"

Doubts attach to many decisions. Which college to attend. Career moves. Cars and houses and watches to buy. Even those lucky couples who are madly in love—who quickly resolve conflict, have fun together no matter what they're doing, converse with ease, and can't imagine spending the rest of their lives with anyone else—approach the altar and think, *Really? Is this it? Am I sure?* It's a fleeting thought, and it's more for reassurance than anything else.

Yeah, I'm sure.

It was the same with a trip like this, though admittedly on a much smaller scale than marriage. And I did have my doubts. But I owed obligation to no one, and I understood the opportunity costs. I speculated what I had the potential to gain by leaving home for a little while. I mused long over it—it consumed my thoughts and kept me up three or four nights in the process—but once I made the decision, one-hundred-percent *yes*, I bought in completely.

I had my doubts. But somehow I found my backbone. I walked onto the plane. And into the world.

Bring Your Own Badass

11:45 Thursday morning struck me full force. My head pounded, nearly erupted from conjugating irregular verbs, speculating whether to use *ser* or *estar*, cramming vocab, and trying to decode the subjunctive. *Llena el blanco con la forma correcta del verbo entre paréntesis.* 11:55. I zipped through the first three, rapid fire. 11:57. Three more. 11:59. The last four: *Llegue. Esperen. Practiquen. Salgamos.* My one-on-one session ended with Eddy, and Jan and I walked home for lunch.

Beatríz sat at the table, cheery as always, content with the work she'd put in to prepare another wonderful meal for us. *Plump*, not *fat*, is the word to describe her, and she had no shame in showing off every one of the braces on her teeth when a good story or joke was delivered.

Jan, personable and extroverted with blond hair playing around boyish features, was one of the two other boarders living with me in Beatríz's house in Antigua, Guatemala. At twenty years old, he had saved enough money to travel for six months in Central America and northern South America. The impetus of his trip, like mine, was a simple desire to see what else might be out there.

His demeanor, though, favored travel. Whereas I smile when someone smiles at me, Jan's tenderness is unprovoked and unrestrained and without motive and extends to everyone present. A hearty "Hi! How are ya!" seemed to bubble out of him without a second thought. The connector. Our second day in Antigua, we walked through the city to meet five of his new friends—Jorike, Donny, Frenchy, and two Australians—at the Gato Negro Hostel, stopping along the way to chat with two Guatemalans he'd met the day before. Jan had already amassed this group of new friends, while I'd only met the people living in the house: Jan; Anki, a boarder from the Netherlands; my new Latina mom, Beatríz; and her twenty-four-year-old daughter, who wouldn't date American men because they smell funny.

Jan was inspired by the newness of learning another language. *"Tengo una buena idea para este fin de semana,"* he declared to me as we lounged in the shade of Beatríz's courtyard.

"Bro, I get it. You're studious. But let's work on our English a little while." My smile reinforced the teasing note in my voice as I worked on peeling an orange, spewing juice all over my fingers.

"San Marcos La Laguna. It sits right on the coast of Lake Atitlán. Nothing but a bunch of natives and free-spirited hippies, hanging out on the water, a little swimming here, a couple of volcanoes to climb there. Perfect weekend trip."

I didn't need convincing. I knew better than to dash through my voyage in a blur, but I was always searching for opportunities, moments to linger in, to soak in—anything I likely couldn't get my hands on back home. We have hippies in the United States, but they don't come with volcanoes.

We raced home for a quick lunch after class Friday, caught the next thing smokin' at 12:30, and arrived in Panajachel, the port town of Lake Atitlán, a half hour past our estimated arrival time at 4:37. We were immediately bombarded by kids, arms outstretched and faces curved by big grins, wanting to carry our backpacks down to catch a boat for San Marcos. Everywhere, these kids, these sweet little gnats with giant smiles, towns full of junior wheeler-dealers.

It's a hard life in Guatemala. One either owns a corner *tienda*, slings pounds of pot up the border, or hustles single dollars from travelers. Tourists—hungry for sun, relaxation, and a little taste of flavorful culture—have forced yesterday's farmers into town to hawk trinkets.

Either way, though, outside the tourist-infected towns of Guatemala City and Antigua, natives live off the land in some fashion. Everywhere you go, chickens waddle and peck the dirt free of bugs, unaware that they'll soon be plucked, carved, battered, spiced, fried, and tucked up next to a pile of white rice and mixed veggies; oranges droop from overburdened tree branches, unenthused about the fresh-squeezed juice being served at tomorrow's breakfast; and women smack corn paste into tortillas. The simple life reigns supreme in towns where kids scurry about in shoes handed down, tattered, from older brothers and sisters, while Mom and Dad cultivate corn or coffee or soybeans or bananas in the backyard. While Mexicans immigrate to the United States to perform the jobs we've deemed below our rank, these are the Guatemalans who skip the border to the north to take the jobs Mexicans don't want.

I stood there, a bit bewildered as I stared down at the children's faces surrounding me. Their lips flapped, spilling syllables littered with *por favors* in a passionate fight to earn my business. One boy crowded in on my right. He curled his fingers around the strap of my bag and began to tug lightly. His dark eyes met mine as he boasted that he was the best hombre for the job.

I gave in, releasing my bag into his care. With a triumphant laugh, he bolted forward through the other boys and led me on my way.

Three minutes later, I tipped the kid a couple quetzales for his brief work. He grinned, content, but desiring more. Always desiring more, never enough. He trotted away to the next turista.

Jan and I hopped on a blue fiberglass boat. Its dented sides whispered of the years it had spent in service. The vehicle seated up to sixteen. There were seventeen of us, so I curled up in the bow. I pulled out twenty-five quetzales, the price quoted to us by the bus driver. Jan, proud that his half-year voyage from Guatemala to Argentina was *his* trip (he saved the money himself and politely rejected his parents' request to meet him somewhere along the way), was trying to grow up fast. At twenty, he looked twelve, and wanted to act thirty.

"*Veinte,*" he said to the captain. "*Pago veinte.*"

Anki chimed in: "And I will pay ten since I'm the first stop." Her short curly brown locks bounced around her ears with the sway of the boat.

I couldn't believe this. Negotiation? Really? *After* we got on? When you're traveling, especially to less-developed countries, you expect to get screwed. Although, you can bargain for more favorable terms to make it feel as if you're getting screwed a little less. But who negotiates *after* they're already on the boat? That's the kind of move that gets machetes pulled. With ten, maybe fifteen boats in the harbor, we could have tried to negotiate *before* loading up.

"*Veintecinco,*" the captain directed again, his tone neither agitated nor meek. He'd dealt with Jan's kind before, and he knew he had Jan in a tough spot. There were five of us together—the three of us from the language school and two Canadian women we'd adopted on the bus ride—and he knew that we weren't going to grab our bags and clamber back to the dock to save five quetzales.

"*Veinte,*" Jan persisted. He was *going* to save those sixty-three cents.

The captain huffed, ready to sling fire. He hit Jan with a string of Spanish too jumbled for any of us to interpret. It sounded as if he was pleading, but he had the clear upper hand, and Jan's twenty-five quetzales was as good as in the captain's back pocket. Jan's timing was off.

Later, we learned that, for a small fee, our bus driver had called ahead to announce our impending arrival to this particular boat captain and the captain had assembled the appropriate litter of kids to grab our bags as the wheels of the bus slowed to a stop. In reality, though, even with Guatemala's cutthroat business practices, it became evident on our return trip that all the captains had set the price together and had agreed not to negotiate with passengers. Typical lake-boat oligopoly. Twenty-five was the price.

I stood, handed the captain my fare, and resumed my position in the cramped curve of the bow. Jan ducked and paid reluctantly, but the smile on his face as he turned around told me he was secretly pleased, proud that he'd had the balls to try to bargain. *Sure, I lost*, said the smirk he wiped off his face. *But I stood up to the Man.* (Two weekends later, we went to the market in Antigua so Jan could practice his negotiating skills—not *buy* anything; just practice the art of negotiation.)

As we slowly paced from one village to the next, the boat rose and splashed back into the water, a series of jolting fiberglass-and-water kisses. Gorgeous houses of smooth sandstone, framed by terra-cotta roofs and shutters, emerged from the skirting slopes, and luxuriant vegetation crawled around them. Anki climbed out at Santa Cruz La Laguna so she could spend the weekend scuba diving. Jan, the two Canadians—a mother and daughter in her midtwenties—and I were the fourth stop. More junior hustlers at the dock, eight of them this time, two per vacationer. One pack mule and a navigator. They dropped us at our hotel, and we each pulled out bills to tip the gang.

"*Uno,*" I started to count, placing the first crumpled bill in the hand of the kid who had carried my bag.

"*Diez*," he offered, the going rate for a tip at San Marcos.

"*Dos.*" I put another in his hand, glancing into his squinting eyes.

"*Diez*," he appealed.

I had only five in my hand, so this wasn't going to end well for him. "*Tres.*"

"*Diez.*"

"*Cuatro.*"

"*Diez.*" He didn't give up easy.

"*Y cinco. Gracias por todo.*" I smiled as he wrinkled his nose good-naturedly and scurried off in search of his next target.

We settled into the hotel, the two ladies in cozy beds and Jan and I on auxiliary mattresses dusted off from the attic. This didn't bother me, and it bothered Jan less. No matter our living conditions, no matter what was on the plate in front of him, no matter the daily itinerary, he always cruised with the current. The whole month I spent with him in Guatemala, he just glided from park to restaurant, Internet café to bar, home to school, attraction to attraction—a cheesy grin stamped on his face all the damned time, saying, "This is the life," to me at least once a day. He taught me how to curse in German, his native language, which could come in handy if I ever had to deal with shady lederhosen salesmen. He showed me techniques at the Ping-Pong table. He shared travel stories and future plans. He fought for the best price. All of this with an upbeat attitude—never complained once about anything, never said a cross word about anybody, never told me to hurry my ass up in the bathroom or asked, "Why are there always little black hairs scattered about the shower floor?" It seemed impossible to ruffle him. And when it came time to lay our heads on those musty old mattresses that night in that hotel in San Marcos, that cheesy grin persevered.

More people should be like that.

We slept deeply. At five the cock-a-doodle-doo of a rooster penned not twenty feet away woke us simultaneously—all four of us. I raked my fingers across the floor in search of a shoe to use as a snooze button. "His days are numbered," Terry, the sixty-eight-year-old expat hotel owner said when we crossed paths with her later in the day. Worried that we might be a little upset about this side venture that went along with her lodging business, she added, "If you hang around long enough, we can all enjoy him together." Customer service is precious at a place like San Marcos. Each of five hotels in this little pueblo had three to five rooms, so if I wasn't happy with El Arbol, I could quickly pack my bag and skip twenty steps down the stone path to El Unicornio.

But excitement and grandeur overcame fatigue. We were, after all, about to discover for ourselves what the German explorer Alexander von Humbolt described as "the most beautiful lake in the world." We paused for breakfast at a little café. After that, we strolled to The Platform, a wooden ledge thirty feet above the lake. I tiptoed on the edge, staring down into the sparkling waters, and felt my heart tap hard and quick against my chest. "Dang, that's kind of a far drop," I muttered, pausing to stretch out and breathe deep. I took a hit from a water bottle and then lunged off the edge, the air whistling past my sweaty body. An involuntary cry ripped from my lips before the sweet, cool water absorbed me. I laughed when I resurfaced, splashing beside Jan and the younger Canadian.

Birds flew past us, staring at the mirror images of themselves in the clear turquoise water. The air was hot but not heavy; it was a relaxing day in the sun. It was a thrill, but more of a revitalizing let's-bust-out-some-cheese-and-sliced-apples-and-lay-on-the-deck-and-watch-the-volcano-in-the-distance-cough-dust kind of thrill than a Jesus-Christ-there's-a-chance-I-might-not-make-it-back-to-the-hotel-for-chips-and-guacamole-tonight one. Not much to it; not much could go wrong. The water was there five hundred years ago, and it will be there in two seconds to break your fall after your descent. Climbing the icy face of a cliff? Skydiving? Running with the bulls? Less room for error when choosing the next spot to drive the pick of your ax, or testing your rip cord, or evading rampaging bovines. My morning at The Platform, though, was leisurely and tranquil and consumed by switching my gaze from passing boats to ladies clad in two-pieces.

We napped in the afternoon back at the hostel. That evening we ate below-average brick-oven pizza for dinner and went for a couple of drinks at the Ganesh Collective, the go-to nightspot for tourists. The elevated, wooden building was owned by an American who crafted his own liquors. He'd visited Lake Atitlán five years before our arrival, immediately told his girlfriend he didn't like her anymore, signed the deed for a plot of land three days later, and vowed never to leave because "this is my home, and these are my people."

We were late to bed, but managed to wake at 2:45 the next morning. We had arranged to meet Edwin, our tour guide, at three. He showed up with bouncy enthusiasm at 3:48, assuredly, he told us in Spanish, with plenty of time to get to the top of the Indian's Nose. Time in Latin America is different than anywhere else—a suggestion more than a resolute declaration. You learn to live with sitting around waiting for forty-eight minutes.

Edwin is a badass. Two trips to the Indian's Nose ago, he was guiding a group of American tourists to the top. At the summit, they enjoyed the view, snapped some photos, built a fire, drank some coffee, had a few laughs. Then it came time to pay the "owner" of the mountain. The owner is little more than some guy who owns land in the area and possesses bigger huevos than anybody else up there. This dude, the owner of the mountain, collects a fee from each person who visits. If he knows you, you pay less. If he thinks he can get more out of you, you pay more. Kind of like your neighborhood used car salesman—just, you know, with a machete.

On this particular trip, a week before mine, Edwin paid the owner for each of the people in his flock, the same price that the people before him had paid. But the owner demanded more. Edwin and his crew stressed that they didn't have more, so the owner pulled his machete and pushed Edwin to the edge of a cliff. One of the American women, courageous but foolish, tried to intervene. Edwin tried to call her off, but it was too late: the owner shoved Edwin off the cliff.

The American woman grabbed Edwin's sweatshirt just in time. He dangled over the edge for a moment before she managed to pull him back up onto the mountain, saving him from certain death. Edwin then reached under his sweatshirt, grabbed his pistol, fired two shots in the air, and pointed it at his newfound adversary. (He must have thought his story was better with props because as he told me this part he pulled the pistol out from underneath his sweatshirt to offer me a demonstration. "Like this," he said, waving the hefty gun and making sounds like a small child.)

The owner stepped aside and allowed the group to descend the mountain. Rock beats scissors.

Edwin, all five-foot-two inches in heels of him, told me this story on the way *back* down the mountain after we had long since paid him. The presence of Edwin's friend—a certified karate instructor—further relieved any anxiety I may have held inside my chest. *"Y si mi pistola no funciona,"* Edwin said, *"sus pies funcionan."* If my gun doesn't work, his feet work.

Yeah, there are problems with thieves on that mountain and just about every other rural area of Guatemala, but that's to be expected in a country with such extreme poverty. It bothered me that criminal activity could be so, sort of, accepted. But this is a developing country, and the people there do what they have to do to hustle up a living where there's minimal opportunity. These guys don't have degrees in robberomics. They don't wake up in the morning and decide they're going to be thieves. They can't. Life as a full-time robber is just as unsustainable as life as a car thief or a drug dealer: death or prison are the only two endgames. These guys on the mountain are *part-time* robbers. They wake up, they bathe, they brush their teeth—just like you and I—they eat some Raisin Bran or whatever Wifey has prepared for them for breakfast, they grab a machete and a hoe or a shovel or a pickax, and they lumber out of the house to go cultivate some corn.

Corn. Sometimes it feels as if that's all these people have: endless fields of corn sprawling over the mountain. And an occasional pissed-off cow tied to a tree. So here this guy is, doing whatever it is he does to a corn stalk to cultivate it, and—

wouldn't ya know it—here comes a group of gringos right now! And without a guide! He starts licking his lips as he spots the cameras swaying against their hips and the wallets bulging out of their backsides. (The women in front are street savvy enough not to pack their purses on this daytrip.) He hollers to his friends, who are also cultivating corn just a ways up the mountain there— calmly whistling a tune to themselves most likely. They all grab their machetes, Guatemala's most popular accessory, and come streaming down the hillside. As a group, they relieve these tourists of their cameras and cash without hurting them. This morning they woke up harvesters, and tonight they'll take their women out drinking and dancing on the town.

This is why you must hire a dude like Edwin, his trusty pistol, and his friend's pair of Nikes. Who's to say how our morning would have ended without him?

And then, at once, silence fell upon us. Edwin paused the story he was telling, and we all turned from our perches on top of the mountain. There we saw it rise: the sun.

In the online-dating days of my past—and no doubt, future—I have asked and answered questions like, *If you could be anywhere in the world right now, where would you want to be?* or *If you had one hundred dollars left to your name and no job, how would you spend it?* As we try to work into more important matters, though, the one question that always irks me is *Do you prefer the sunrise or the sunset?* It's a silly question, boring, complex yet abstract. A stupid question. There should be no answer to *sunrise or sunset?* Each is unique, and each can be equally appreciated. Sunrises represent awakening, renewal, and hope. Sunsets represent memory, fulfillment, and worthy fatigue. One prefers a cup of tea, the other a glass of wine, but both should be respected for their unique substance, as well as their aesthetic beauty. The mere thought of pitting them against each other is ludicrous.

I'm no sunologist, though, and that morning in Central America, I'll tell you that I wasn't making comparisons between sunrises and sunsets or trying to dissect *But what does it all really mean?* We had reached the summit rather quickly—in maybe a fifty-minute climb—and had an hour to sit in absolute darkness, save clustered crumbs of light from the pueblos four thousand feet below. Just over a cloud straight ahead, streams of light started to prick our eyes, and the horizon awoke. The mammoth volcano emerged to the right; darkness lifted from the pointed hills to the left. Everything slowly turned from black to green.

Our weariness from the early-morning hike buried itself as we scrambled for our cameras. Streaks of scarlet and orange seeped through the clouds that buckled over the mountaintops, and the cool mist hanging above our heads dissipated, burned away by the rising heat of the sun. The morning chill started to break. The wind weakened, leaves paused. The last hour's idle chatter vanished.

I knew this moment. I'd never been here before, but I'd been waiting for it. Down below, way down there somewhere, separated from us by a mass of heavy green foliage, people lay fast asleep, deep in Sunday slumber. I could yell, but no one would hear me. I could boogie, but no one would see me. None of the ordinary noises from the towns—the bragging roosters or the lonely, agitated dogs—could rouse my senses back to reality. Memory remained distant as the present slowly came into focus.

I thought about my loved ones back home. In the States, my friends were rising to go to church. My mom was making an omelet. Pops leafed through a James Patterson novel and raised his coffee mug to his lips every now and again.

I never noticed how pretty the lake was, really, until that moment. On our inaugural boat ride two days prior, I spent my time struggling to calm my heavy stomach. I just wanted to get checked into a hotel so I could collapse on my very still bed. And of course the lake was striking on that clear day from the platform, but even then I'd been preoccupied with the exhilaration of climbing up and jumping again.

But this morning, I had no activity in mind. What ache my muscles retained from the climb seemed to flee as I sat on the earth and just observed. Just watched this glistening, expansive lake, sitting calm, the sun reflecting just for this group of vacationers.

No, just for me. Because in moments like this, the awe makes you forget for an instant that there are people around you. I started to wonder sappy, unimportant things like, *Why do they call it the Indian's Nose? It doesn't look like a nose. Nor an Indian. Hm. That's not what I would have named it.* Our thoughts can be flighty sometimes, our minds wandering in seemingly futile directions. My head soon cleared, though. A smile slid from cheek to cheek. I drank in the magnitude of the silent, still moment.

It was spectacular, stunning, breathtaking, without equal. In fucking Guatemala. Nobody ever talks about Guatemala unless it has something to do with civil unrest—accusations of genocide or a protest gone bad—or about how they went to the wrong Antigua. Yet there I was, in Guatemala of all places, lost in the most beautiful sunrise I have ever seen in my life.

The only thing missing at that moment—the *only* thing missing—was a girl by my side to lean over and kiss on the cheek.

Bill Clinton once visited Granada, Spain, and said that the view from Mirador de San Nicolás offered the most beautiful sunset in the world. I remember eagerly visiting Granada in college, standing at the exact same spot, watching the sun set, and thinking, *Meh, yeah. Whatever. It's all right.* Bill must have been inhaling something potent, though, if he thought that was the best sunset in the world.

So I guess sunrises and sunsets depend on perspective, but if you ever get to Guatemala, I wonder what you will think about the most amazing sunrise I've ever witnessed. Go by San Marcos La Laguna and find Edwin. Tell him Adam sent you. He'll say, "Who?" And you'll say, "Never mind." Tell him you want to climb the Indian's Nose, and you want to know how much it will cost. Regardless of the size of your party, three people or thirty, he'll quote you just about three hundred quetzales per person. Tell him he can go ahead and suck a fat one. Or you can peacefully mention that you'd like to shop around a little first. Either way, you'll get the same response. He'll say something along the lines of, "No, no. Wait a second. Let's be reasonable about this. What kind of price did you have in mind?" Cut his number in half. "One-fifty," you say. Now, he'll tell *you* to go suck a fat one, but he'll counter with two hundred. Take it. You can find someone to do it for about one-seventy or so, but they won't have Edwin's pistol or his karate-chopping friend. Edwin's your man.

Then, wake your groggy ass up early, pack two energy bars in your cargos and fill your bottle with water, and climb to the top of the Indian's Nose.

You'll see.

Fútbol Mania

Two weeks in town, and my Spanish teacher, Eddy, asked me whether I'd like to go to a soccer game.

"Sure," I said.

"I am going to need a little more enthusiasm," he said. He tilted his head down and looked at me over his glasses whenever he had something meaningful to say. "We're playing the Death. This is an important game."

I wasn't sure whether I was understanding correctly. "The team is called the Death?"

"Yes. The Death."

The winter before I left for my trip, my friend Korey invited me to come to the Back Bar in Chapel Hill to watch Carolina play Duke. "And get there early," he warned. "You know saving seats is frowned upon."

The game was at Duke, but even if it had been at the Dean Dome, I wouldn't have been able to finagle a ticket without dropping half my paycheck to sit up top. My dad's rich friend, Billy Armfield, gives us prime tickets to a couple games a year but his alumni seats, along with every other seat in the bottom half, are unavailable for the Duke-UNC game. The student campouts to get tickets—on both the Duke and UNC sides—are legendary, and ancient ushers at the Smith Center refuse to quit their jobs for fear they'll never again be able to witness Coach K's frowning mug walk into that far tunnel.

The Sox-Yankees rivalry is similar, but so many casual fans have been so drowned out by baseball's dreadfully long season that no one outside New England or New York really seems to care who won last night. They'll play fifteen or twenty more times before the playoffs. Baseball doesn't attract the sports fan who wants to just go out to the bar for some cocktails and appetizers, but I've sat down to dinner in Powell, Wyoming, and debated with Duke fans at Northwest Community College why Carolina is simply a more successful institution and they should be embarrassed to root for the Blue Devils. Powell, Wyoming. I'm good for twenty push-ups if you can find it on a map.

Football attracts the casual fan, certainly, but neither the NCAA nor the NFL has the nationwide draw of two teams that have consistently hated each other for so long. The NBA is up there, of course, but their rivalries are based more on superstar players going at one another than the actual teams themselves.

I acknowledge my Tobacco Road bias, though, so for me, Duke-Carolina, separated by a mere eight-mile stretch of 15-501, is it. Doesn't matter what the records are. I sat in that bar that night with Korey, emotions quickly cycling from cheer to jeer hinging on a defensive play or a referee's call. Two gigantic projection screens—one on either side of this expansive room—broadcast the game to the three hundred or so people packed in, mostly current students and recent alumni. And then there was the other room around the corner there. And the bar downstairs. And the Top of the Hill. And Woody's. And Four Corners. And The Library. And fifty more big screens within walking distance of the Back Bar. Korey and I, our rejection letters long since shredded, rubbed elbows that night with those bright kids with bright futures, representing devotion just as strong as theirs. My great-uncle coached the first national title team at UNC in 1924; my grandfather followed in the thirties; five guys in my family went to Carolina, starting with my great-great-grandfather in 1859; and though the admissions office took one look at my SAT scores and said, "No thanks," I still stood and wailed that night at the Back Bar as if my own brother was firing three-pointers from the corner and taking charges in the paint. You have to. If you plan to maintain your voice throughout the evening, give your seat up to a true fan and take your ass home to watch the game in your living room.

This is how soccer is in Latin America.

I arrived in Antigua as the rainy season was drawing to its slow, unpleasant close. In my effort to steer near the equator, I hadn't accounted for this. *Muahaha*, I'd thought as I scrupulously charted my course. *When those suckers back home are shoveling snow, I'll be sipping a Diet Pepsi on the beach.* But the rainy *season*? In North Carolina, it rains. So we put on a raincoat, maybe some galoshes if we're feeling trendy, and we step out into the muddied, gray world. It usually stops in an hour or so, maybe not until early afternoon if it's a *really* bad rain, but it certainly never lasts a *season.*

That last long rain of the season—the one that came and went with Tropical Depression Twelve-E—brought with it a heap of trouble, too, mostly in the form of landslides. The sturdy buildings in Antigua survived, but the crudely built shacks in the rural villages took a hard hit. Most leisure events—like the soccer game Eddy invited me to—were postponed. Without highway access, fans couldn't get to the stadium. For ten days I stayed inside and begged for the skies to clear. For ten days rain fell in sheets, and for ten days mud collapsed from the mountainside onto the highways.

For ten days I read about death. On the eighth day, I saw a photo of a single mother on the front page of the local newspaper, *Prensa Libre.* She was alone in the photo, surrounded by the coffins of all four of her sons. They were buried alive while playing in the house. I don't know how long I stared at that photo. At lunch, in Spanish, Beatríz said, "That's a great shame. I'm a nice person. I like to smile and have fun. I have a good attitude. But I don't think I'm prepared mentally to deal with a tragedy like that."

On the eleventh day, the rains subsided, as they always do. People came out of their houses, tentatively at first, anxious to release their accumulated zest for the sun. That first day after a ten-day downpour is the day to do everything you always wished you could do when the sun hid behind the tempest's fury. We hung our clothes out to dry; we sat in the park and read; we ate banana splits; we took pictures; we walked around and talked to strangers about how "I can't remember the last time we saw the sun! Ha. Ha. Ha."

Jan and I went to the market. In Central America, "the market" is swarming and hectic, although somehow orderly, almost ineffable. The air is heavy with an aroma that goes from sweet to rancid around any given corner. The noise is calm. Music hums softly from every other stall. There's no screaming, but there's the subtle badgering that comes at you from every stall: vendors aren't yelling at you to come over; they're conveying to you, relentlessly, that you're making a big mistake if you keep walking by.

Endless booths, hugged tight against their neighbors, pimp every product you could ever want to buy. Shoes. Clothes. CD players, radios, mini–kitchen grills. Pots, pans, plates, silverware. Remote controls. Lock cutters. Machetes. Luggage. CDs, DVDs, and video games. Office supplies. Books and magazines. Cell phones. Eau de toilette, eau de cologne. Hygiene products. Beef, chicken, and fish. And produce—seemingly eternal stalls packed with tomatoes and potatoes and limes and avocados and watermelons and *jocotes*. The proprietors scrape to offer you a better price than the guy three feet over. There is no Walmart. No Target. There's one supermarket across the street if you'd like to pay with Visa, but some market-goers favor the novelty of buying a sweet, fleshy pineapple from a lady whose husband or brother or cousin plucked it from the earth himself yesterday afternoon.

That Saturday, though, business slowed for a while in the afternoon as crowds of people scurried to the closest TV in the market to watch the international game of the day. I wasn't sure who was playing—it was the blue team versus the white team— but I found it amazing how everything froze, how their world stood still.

And then, at once, shouting fractured the silence as the white team roared down the field. Right, left. They passed ahead, took a hasty shot, and didn't score. More stillness. Then another advance and dozens of voices shouted around me.

Stillness. Shouting. Stillness.

The expectation, a score lurking not ten yards away, everybody in on the action, acting as if their yelling made a difference, as if they could scream their team through to victory. If I wanted to buy a cluster of bananas at that moment, I would have been out of luck. Kids elbowed their way to the front while those ill-fated people in back stretched their necks and stood on their toes.

This cycle repeated—bated silence and raucous cries. Completely empty booths pockmarked the market; men, women, and children—aged nine to sixty-five or so—huddled around various TVs. As the signal seeped into each TV, people squinted to verify what had just happened. More empty booths. More people. Gangs of people, united, spilling out of these cubicles on both sides of the alleyway all the way down the line to Antigua's main artery, so focused, so invested in the outcome of this one game. A sport! *Will our team score? Can they defend? Maintain their lead? Hold out for the victory? Is now really the best time to make that substitution? A yellow card! That's bullshit!*

Two days later, I found out that they'd been watching a game between two European teams. Half a world away yet directly linked to their lives, playing out right there in front of them on the screens in that outdoor market.

So I had an idea of what to expect when Wednesday afternoon rolled around and Eddy invited me to a real live soccer game. Wednesday. Afternoon. At three o'clock. In many respects, it's an easygoing life in Guatemala, happy people always looking for an opportunity to relax or celebrate something. It seemed like every morning I woke to the boom of nearby fireworks, until it got to the point where I expected that morning serenade. Celebrations, all of these celebrations. Relentless. These people lived to celebrate. Had a baby? Let's shoot off a bomb blast. Birthday? Bomb time. Day of the Revolution? Light the fuse. Humidity only got to 96 percent today? Bottle-rocket bonanza. "Christmas isn't a day," Eddy told me. "It's the whole month of December, always a different gala or party, and in January, we find other reasons to have parties."

So Wednesday afternoon we prepared to watch the San Carlos Death go head-to-head with our Antigua Avocados, who, along with the Canberra Big Cat Tomatoes of Australia and the Blooming Prairie High School Onions of Minnesota, make a pretty formidable guacamole.

I said to Beatríz, in Spanish, "I'm going to the game!"

And she replied: "I will save a plate of dinner for you!"

Eddy and I endured a fifty-minute chicken bus ride to join the muckle of fanatics bound for Guatemala City. The chicken bus. If you ever get to stay in Antigua for a few days, take the chicken bus. Doesn't matter where, just hop on one, get off when you feel like it, grab some lunch, and then ride one back into town. The chicken bus—nothing more than a retired American school bus that has been painted over and whose solitary rule is that there's always room for one more—is the cultural link that will briefly transport you out of the rift of the backpackers and into the orbit of the native. Three to a seat, babies and dogs welcome, often standing room only. You will thereafter appreciate every mode of transportation you ever take.

The game, between the Avocados and the Death—championed by their skeleton mascot—went just as you would think. The rippling crowds displayed all the energy and anticipation and impatience and rowdiness you would expect as a spectator of the country's chief passion. It was a live miniversion of UNC-Duke.

We, the visiting spectators, had to pay two-and-a-half times as much at the gate for our tickets, but there were twice as many of us as home team fans. Blue-collar workers, commoners, packed the seats around me, and that is precisely where you should sit when you go to a soccer game. Don't put me in the box; don't lock me up with the stoic businessmen and their muted cheers; don't give me an all-inclusive package with a commemorative program and a buffet lunch on a white cloth. Put me up in the stands, that top section there, with that group of guys who are laying Wednesday's wages on the line for a ticket, three tacos, and a frosty beer. Let me loose in the jungle. That is where we'll meet the fans who matter.

The atmosphere at a soccer game in Latin America is intense. In the States, we have the Wave. As it works its way around the stadium, people stand up and throw their arms in the air. In Guatemala, when the Wave hits you, you throw trash in the air instead, raining your neighbors with crumpled wrappers.

And everybody there is a former soccer player. When the ball zipped out of bounds, some random old guy flicked the ball up with his foot, dribbled it on his knee and then kicked it back to the linesman. He wasn't showing off. Every man, woman, and child in the stadium that day could have done the same thing.

"You want an empanada?" Eddy asked, and he went off to buy one for each of us. I turned and looked up to see a guy taking a piss at the top of the aisle by the fence. I later learned that no one had unlocked the bathroom for our side.

Half the time we yelled at the refs, and for the other half we cheered for the Avocados. In the balance, fans from both sides mocked each other. Barbed wire separated the visitors from the home team and every fan from the field. Initially you might think this is excessive, but when a goal is scored, fans from the scoring team bolt up to the opposing team's fence, grabbing their crotches and pointing fingers and telling them what they think about the shape of their heads. In the States, the Cameron Crazies can cheer as loud and as hard as they want, but they are well-behaved enough that they don't need to be separated from the opposition's fans by a steel barricade. Not so with soccer south of the border.

I thought the security guards' riot gear was a little much, but who am I to judge their tactics for impressing women? I imagine one clambering on top of a barstool, sliding back the visor on his helmet: "What, this? Oh, this is just my riot gear. I use it to protect people. Y'know, from the riots. That's what I do: I put an end to all of the riots. Anyway, can I buy you a drink?"

Yeah, the excitement for soccer, on both micro- and macro-levels, is gripping. Every advance down the field is met with the same enthusiastic ovation as the one before. Rubbish fires burn in the stands, a sort of witchcraft summoning the next score. Chants—endless chants that *everyone* knows; the persistent appeals to the referees that there's a chance they didn't get that last call exactly right. You can't keep yourself from being caught up in the passion, the fervor. The game carried no weight in my life, yet by the end of the first half, I wanted nothing more than for the Death—and their fans—to go home losers.

Eddy had given up correcting my Spanish—he was off the clock during the game—so we relaxed and had unrestrained conversations about the state of soccer in Guatemala. I learned that his country has never been to the World Cup. Imagine that. This is the passion of the people of Guatemala—they schedule their lives around the next game—and yet this tiny country has never reached the pinnacle of their beloved sport.

Eddy blames this failure on both the corruption and the players' lack of discipline. "We have unbelievable talent—guys eighteen, nineteen years old and in their early twenties—but we just don't have any kind of discipline coming from the Federation. It's incredible. And it trickles down to the players. Do you know that on the day the players were supposed to show up to sign the paperwork for the Pan-American Games," he explained, squinting and pointing his index finger at me, "the majority of the players didn't even show up?"

"What do you mean they didn't show up?" I asked. Soccer rules this country, from young kids playing pickup around the corner to finely tuned athletes getting paid to play. "Isn't this what they love to do?"

He threw his hands in the air, betraying the anguish of a guy who was very sincerely disturbed that the players chosen to represent his country could be so irresponsible. "I mean they didn't show up. They forgot about it. They were late. They spaced out, didn't write themselves a note on the fridge, whatever. And as a result, we weren't allowed to play in the Pan-American Games."

"That's crazy."

"Crazy, yes. And very important," Eddy continued. He explained the intense presidential race between Otto Peréz

Molina, who has a shady—and very likely murderous—military past and Manuel Baldizón, with his suspected connection to the drug traffickers. "The two key components of Baldizón's platform for president are his promise to show executions live on national television and his promise to get Guatemala to the World Cup."

The game ended in a tie, which wasn't the letdown you might think it was, after a controversial call went in Antigua's favor to close out the final minutes. One of our defenders stood in front of the goal on a corner kick and inadvertently blocked a certain score with his arm. The ref didn't see it, and he soon let loose his final blows of the whistle. The opposing coach was red-faced screaming; players rushed the referee; outraged fans tried to scramble onto the field, swearing they'd meet the ref in his locker room. The security guards locked the place down, took care of everything.

I sprinted a mile or so with the masses of visiting fans to catch the chicken bus home.

Winning Number, Losing Result

Despite the many, many, many mistakes I've made in my life, I don't live with regret. My disappointing college basketball career hurt me, but it also humbled me; failed businesses have broken me, but they've made me hungrier; and fumbled relationships have made me reflect on the value that someone else can bring to my life, how important it is for me to hold out until I find Her, and what I have to do to make that relationship work. I'd do it all over again. I wouldn't change a thing.

With two exceptions.

Jack was my trainer on the basketball court when I was growing up. He's a black dude with a shiny bald head, about six feet tall with a bodybuilder's physique—even now as he approaches fifty—and a gold front tooth inscribed with the letter J. He looks thirty, maybe thirty-two when he lets the dark stubble fill in on his jaw. I walked into the Garner Road YMCA just after my twelfth birthday, and the weight room attendant quickly instructed me that if I wanted to maximize my potential on the basketball court, I needed to go talk to "that fella" at the corner hoop who was putting "that other white kid" through grueling shooting drills. Jack and I shook hands, my small digits swallowed up by his. He squinted down at me, unimpressed with yet another fledgling kid who went to a Carolina game and decided that he wanted to be a basketball player when he grew up. He must have smiled on the inside, certain that I wouldn't last two weeks in his program. "Anybody can last a week if they've got any heart at all," he told me years later. "I haven't had a lot of kids make it past two weeks, though."

For six years, he put Jordan, my new best friend, and me through drill after drill after drill in the gym. Set after set after set in the weight room. He threw us on the treadmill, in the pool, and at the stairs, anything to ensure that we would outlast our opponents. Once, when Jordan and I were fourteen, Jack set us up on the stationary bikes, told us to keep it above seventy RPMs, left to eat dinner and make some phone calls to the various women he was dating at the time, and returned an hour later to retrieve our spent young legs to go play pickup. Well aware of our limited talent, he'd be damned if he ever saw us winded out there during a game.

It never occurred to us what fun our friends might be getting into after school, that we didn't have to be doing all of this conditioning. "Where did this dude go?" Jordan and I asked each other as we panted through that hour on those stationary bikes, sweat dripping to the ground off our hair. "Did he leave? I bet he left. Naw, that's craziness. He wouldn't just leave like that. Would he?" But we never thought to get off and go look for him. Jack told us to ride the bike until he got back, so Jordan and I kept our fannies on those bikes until Jack got back. We would have pedaled into a coma before we'd have been caught defying Jack's orders. We had to. No choice. Jack, the best trainer in town, offered our ticket to college, and it was inconceivable that we would do anything to disobey him.

He didn't need us, but we needed him.

Five days a week—more in the summer—Jack ran my life and he ran it ragged. Everyone else saw me as the corny white boy I was; Jack saw me as the son he never had. He taught me how to shoot, how to pass, how to be tough, how to hate losing, and how to swagger for the ladies when I was on top of my game. He knew when to cheer me on and when to cuss me out and when a simple frown and a shake of his head would do. There's no way for me to know exactly how many hours Jack put in for me. Thousands. All of the games he attended; the summer road trips he made to Charlotte or Wilmington, where he would make sure I wasn't having a milkshake or anything else heavy on game day; the time he took to sit down with me and review what I could do better the next game; and all those hours training at the Y. Thousands of hours. Thousands. And he never asked for a dime. I just reconfirmed this with my pops, certain that he must have shot Jack some cash behind my back. He. Never. Took. A. Dime.

Think about that. Here's a dude without a college diploma, constantly hustling up some second-rate day job. But after our schools let out, there he was at the Y—every day—building Jordan and me into the basketball players we would become. That's outrageous to me. I think I've done some good for society when I raise a hundred bucks to run a 5K for hunger, but this guy poured *thousands* of hours into training us and never received compensation. Never asked for it. Never hinted at it. Always bought his own lunch on the road in the summer.

Jordan played at Brown, and I got a scholarship to a small school in Massachusetts. I often wonder what would have happened if we had never met Jack, if I had never walked into the Garner Road Y that day. I know I wouldn't have graduated from college debt-free, that's for certain.

Junior year of high school, I really came into my own on the court, attracting interest from small colleges lining the Southeast Coast. Poised to take my game to the next level, I worked harder than ever with Jack. After dinner each night, I snuck outside and put up extra shots on my own, dribbling the ball up and down our cracked driveway when I was supposed to be studying world history. I added eight pounds of muscle to my frame. I changed my diet.

One afternoon in the weight room, I told Jack I needed a minute break. Sweat rolled down my brow, down my back, and dripped off my nose as I took a long, gulp from my water bottle. Jack stared at me for a moment before telling me he'd made an important contact. He asked, dark eyes glinting at me with pride, whether I'd like to play in the Chavis Summer League.

I said it was four hundred and fifty dollars, kind of expensive. He said he didn't care.

The Chavis Summer League, before it ran into trouble with the NCAA, was known in hoops circles nationwide for the talent it attracted. With the hotbed of basketball in the triangle area, players would come from NC State, Duke, and Carolina in the evening to battle one another, the local rising talent, and yesterday's legends who still had a jumper but not the step. Youngsters remained long after bedtime, calling for an autograph from Jerry Stackhouse or Johnny Dawkins or a handshake from Rasheed Wallace or Vince Carter. Poobie Chapman, whom you've never heard of, was more nightmarish to defend than Chris Corchiani, the second-leading assist man in college history. John Wall shone as one of the brightest stars in the Chavis League before ESPN knew about him, and Chucky Brown—who shares the record for playing on the most NBA teams in a career—is probably still playing in that league. Guys who you often saw only on TV in the winter—Luol Deng, David West, Flip Murray—would pop in for a random appearance at the Chavis League in the summer, and within ten minutes, you found yourself crawling over people in search of a seat.

"Yeah, I'm down," I told Jack.

"Smooth," he said. He always said "smooth." "Give me two months to get the four-fifty."

Two months later, he showed up to the gym and, grinning, announced that he had the money for the entry fee. He led me outside to his van and pulled out five rolls, bound by rubber bands—mostly fives, tens, and twenties. My throat swelled; I struggled to speak, my mouth opening and closing without producing a single word. I hugged him, holding the embrace for ten seconds. For six years he'd trained me, and for two months he'd saved all of his extra cash from delivering water jugs just so that he and I could reach our dream to play in the Chavis Summer League. He didn't go out to dinner, no fancy dates with any of his dazzling women, and now, there lay our dream in his hands, rolled up from two months in the top drawer of his dresser. "Now, we gotta find a little talent to play with us," he declared, smiling, gold tooth sparkling. "I'm not trying to go out there and get dogged."

But get dogged we did. Every night, losses. Not blowouts, just losses. We eked out one win when the other team had only five players, but other than that, we drove our way home in silence, heads hanging after every brutal game. And the natural frustration that comes with losing soon materialized: the barking at each other; the finger pointing; the ball hogging; guys showing up late for games and then not answering their phones to talk about what we could do better.

So I quit. I told Jack that I wasn't getting enough touches on offense, that we didn't have a lick of chemistry. "I hate to do this," I told him, "but I think it's best."

Silence. He didn't know what to say. He just stared at me, and eventually I had to look away.

Two roads diverged in a wood, and I . . . I took the one that the assholes take. I spit at all of those thousands of Jack's volunteer hours, and I left his team to play for another.

My second regret:

On my first full night in Antigua, Jan convinced Anki and me to head to the bar to sing karaoke in Spanish. In a stroke of monumentally poor decision making, we chose "Te Llorré un Rio," a famous song by Maná, one of Latin America's most famous musical groups. Of all time. People have been singing along to their songs for more than twenty years. Sure, it's true that you want to select a song that the crowd knows, that they can sing along with if you're absolutely horrible, but you also don't want to absolutely ruin this song—forever—for the people in the audience. I just wanted something slow. Somebody suggested "Te Lloré un Río." It sounded harmless.

I climbed up the stairs to the stage and faced the dozens of eyes staring back at me. For the next four minutes and fifty-five seconds, I wailed "Te Llorré un Río," complete with off-key notes and many mispronunciations. I survived the episode, and so did the group crowded in the bar, despite their winces and laughter.

A week later, Maná announced that they would be coming to nearby Guatemala City for one show—their only show in Guatemala—on November 2. People started talking, chirping on street corners and in travel agencies and on the radio about what a blowout event this was going to be. Ricky Martin comes to the city and he sells out the arena; Maná comes through and the entire region takes the night off.

When I mentioned their name to my dad's wife, Sharon, on the phone one evening, she lit up. "Oh, my," she said from her home in Chapel Hill, North Carolina. "I love Maná."

I did a little more research to find out what all of this commotion was about. Originating in Guadalajara, Mexico, Maná's career has spanned four decades, and they've sold over twenty-five million albums worldwide. Their music draws inspiration from rock, Latin pop, calypso, reggae, and ska. They have won three Grammy Awards, five MTV Video Music Awards Latin America, nine Billboard Latin Music Awards, and on and on. Beatríz sang Maná's songs whether the radio was on or not. She was short and she was plump and she was always prancing around that house with a broad smile that just might have cracked her entire face open at any moment. And she loved Maná.

"Meh," I said. "I'll pass for now. Save my money for something else."

For our last night in Guatemala, Jan, our two new housemates, and I met up with a mob of Swiss girls to go to El Gato Negro. The next morning I would move on to the next leg of my journey in Honduras, and Jan would hop on a bus north.

El Gato Negro was closed, so we, the whole laughing herd of us, headed across the street, back to Personajes, the bar where my journey had begun. On my first night in Guatemala, nearly my first words in Spanish had been to welcome the crowd to hear me sing. "*Bienvenidos a Personajes,*" I said with a sweeping bow. "*Somos Los Gringos.*" Later, after ruining one of their favorite songs forever, I implored them not to forget to tip their server. Nary had such a conceited white man ever stepped into that bar. At that point in my trip's early days, I wasn't sure whether I'd ever have the opportunity to bungee jump or raft or skydive, but I quickly learned that you haven't lived until you've stepped foot in a foreign country, grabbed one of their microphones, and attempted to sing one of their songs in their native tongue. My heart raced that night nearly as much as it did months later when I was in the bullring making passes with a red cape.

Dim white lights lined the ceiling of the bar, an expansive and modern place in contrast to the cobblestone streets and colonial design on the outside. During this second visit, people jammed the place, maybe a hundred and fifty or two hundred, but a hostess showed us to a table in the back. There we cramped together, shoulders upon shoulders and chuckling in spite of it all. We ordered twenty-two beers, the special. Gallo Girls, clad in the same skimpy outfits as Bud Light Girls in the States, strutted by with swag and raffle tickets. At first I didn't understand what we were signing up to win, but I didn't care. I'd take it.

"One!" the dude yelled five minutes later into the microphone from the very stage where I'd sung a month before.

"Nine!" he roared. I looked down. Still in it.

"Three!" Yes, yes. My gaze rippled over the faces packed inside. I had the first three numbers, but it looked like many others did as well.

"Zero!" he said, and the majority dropped out with deflated sighs. Ten possibilities left.

"Four!" he hollered into the microphone with feigned enthusiasm.

I walked the most arrogant walk any gringo ever made in Guatemala. I was already a pariah, the underdog by a hundred to one—*this foreigner waltzes into our town, into our bar, signs up for our raffle, and wins?*—and I pranced through that bar with my hands raised as if I'd actually earned something. I figured early on that that's what I was supposed to be doing and realized too late that I was wrong. I guess I never really understood the magnitude of what I'd won. Worse, based on our blatant entrance just five minutes before, everyone knew I was the last one to toss my name in. Dude had drawn my ticket off the top of a pile that clearly didn't get shuffled right.

Each of the two VIP concert tickets I won translated into exactly the same monthly price of a furnished room I'd seen advertised for rent at the Internet café. I don't know what VIP means in Guatemala, but for the price of two months' rent, I know they would have treated me right.

I snatched the microphone from the MC and blurted out in Spanish to the crowd: "I leave. Go Honduras Tuesday. You want buy tickets, no? Three hundred quetzales." My battered Spanish, meant to be endearing, often came off as demeaning. Even when I started to develop a firmer vocabulary and sentence structure, my gentility somehow never translated. In Honduras a month later, the cab driver quoted us three hundred lempiras; I pointed my finger at him and snarled, "No. The thing is, man, that we will pay two hundred and fifty, and that is it." Bullied, he relented with a polite, forced smile, and we rode the whole way in silence. I had negotiated—nay, strong-armed—this sweet Honduran guy out of $2.50 without a simple por favor.

My pitch to sell the tickets amused nobody at Personajes. A guy pressed through the crowd and offered me two hundred quetzales, and I took it.

We finished the beers. Jan and the Swiss girls headed two blocks up to go dancing, but the new housemates and I returned home to crash.

The next day, I was pumped to tell Beatríz, Maná's number-one fan, what had happened. She'd just prepared tea and pancakes for me (with sliced bananas in the batter). Every day she cooked these fresh, healthy, authentic Guatemalan meals for us, and cleaned our floors and our shower, and did our dishes, and washed her children's clothes, and shopped and carted her son, Bruno, to school and to dentist appointments, and weeded

the garden, and arranged flowers for her nephew's wedding, and
. . . Then, she found time to socialize with her friends. *This* was an
inspirational woman.

"You won what?" she asked, reckoning that I must have
translated incorrectly. She squinted and slanted her head to
the right.

"Tickets, for Maná. VIP!" I beamed.

She just about exploded. After the relationship we'd
established—joking at meals, going out to dinner, squirting each
other with water in the garden—she knew I was going to take
her as my date. She was my girl. When I remember Antigua, the
memory of her—her round face and laughing eyes—leap out at
me. The Indian's Nose? Learning Spanish? The soccer game? The
illuminated fountain in Central Park, the colonial buildings, and
the cobblestone streets? Of course I'll remember these things,
and I'll look fondly on those photos in thirty years. But in my
memory, Beatríz, and that smile she brought to breakfast every
morning, *is* Guatemala.

She ran, shaking her hips—sashaying mostly—around
the garden, the central area of her rented house, which was
surrounded by three bedrooms, a bathroom, and a kitchen. For
the first time around us strangers, she released her hair from
its coil. She shouted and hooted, but I didn't give her a chance to
start singing. "I sold them," I interrupted as she came to a stop. "I
couldn't go, so I sold them."

I instantly wished I hadn't told her about the tickets. She
would have shined at that concert. I pictured her getting dressed
up, maybe buying some new shoes from the market, spraying on
some perfume, her face radiating, her arms swaying in the air. Her
children and her friends and her adorable little dog made her life
great, but VIP tickets to Maná would have been once-in-a-lifetime
for her. She would have cherished that memory forever.

Her face dropped, and my stomach dropped with it as she
ducked into the kitchen. Delusion had allowed me to think that
she'd be excited for me. To her, I'll always be that sweet kid
who was friendly, returned home by curfew, cleaned my plate

after every meal, and kept my room neat. And I sold out to the first bidder.

I tell my friends that I live my life without regret. I've made a thousand blunders in my life—cheated on tests, driven after too many cocktails, tugged my checking account out of the ATM and delivered it to the blackjack table—and I'm certain that the repercussions of those experiences have made me more judicious. I vow that I won't repeat my mistakes, and I move along to unearth new ones.

But these two instances with Jack and Beatríz are different. For years, in the prime of my youth, Jack made a significant impact on my future, and for one month in the fall, Beatríz showed me that happiness can be found in simplicity. Two powerful people in my life; two different corners of the world. And I let them both down.

I thought only about myself during that summer with Jack, and I thought only about myself that night when my number came up at Personajes. Jack will never field a team in the summer league again; he did that for me. And Beatríz would have had to drop thirty days' wages to go see Maná in the VIP booth.

I stole something from Jack's spirit that summer, and in Guatemala, I denied Beatríz her opportunity to do something special.

HONDURAS

Once up on a Temple

When I crossed over the border into Honduras, I had one goal in mind: get to the ruins. Windows to the past, ruins offer a glimpse of a once-omnipotent society. It's a special experience to stand where greatness once stood, to see where ingenuity worked, to walk where nobility once walked.

Before the arrival of the Spanish, the Maya were *the* presence in Central America. They were the only civilization of the pre-Columbian Americas to fully develop a written language, and they were also known for their splendid art, elaborate architecture, and sophisticated mathematical and astronomical systems. From their inception around 1800 BC, these sharp pioneers continued to develop and grow and advance their culture until the 1500s, when Hernán Cortés figured out how to read a map and navigated his soldiers to Veracruz, Mexico, guns drawn. From there, the Spaniards worked their way north, west, and then south through Guatemala and into Honduras, a bloody march that cut down the native population of Central America by 90 percent according to some sources.

People still defend the Spanish conquest today, while others vehemently argue that the Spaniards had no right to do what they did. One side says the natives were doing just fine, hanging out and loving life, when along came Cortés and other Spanish conquistadors to murder and destroy on a very large scale. They note that the Maya calendar was once more accurate than the Gregorian one and that their hand-built temples rival Egypt's pyramids in both size and scope. Conversely, Michael Berliner of the Ayn Rand Institute makes the claim that Western civilization brought "reason, science, self-reliance, individualism, ambition, and productive achievement" to communities that represented "primitivism, mysticism, and collectivism," and to a land that was "sparsely inhabited, unused, and underdeveloped." The Maya favored simple community, and genocide and slavery brought innovation and progress.

While the Spanish colonization meant destroying almost all native expressions, rituals, texts, and art, the old stone civilizations of the Maya still left their mark at various places throughout Central America. There are many Maya today who still practice what they always have. In the United States, we forced Native Americans onto reservations where they could either choose to maintain their traditions or build casinos, and in Central America, the Maya were pushed into the mountains to live off sparse resources. They continue to craft *huipils* and necklaces and bracelets and bags and many other handmade crafts to be offered to svelte tourists at the bottom of the mountain. Native languages like Ch'ol and Kaqchikel and Mam and Q'eqchi' and K'iche' and Yucatec Maya persevere as the primary languages of millions of people in many villages in Mexico, Guatemala, Honduras, Belize, and El Salvador. Many Maya are responsible for maintaining the tourist sites where their ancestors once lived, ate, drank, worked, hunted, cultivated, created, played, and carved out dudes' beating hearts in sacrifice. I wanted to see those sites. I wanted to stand in an ancient place and feel the echoes of all those heartbeats, the echoes of a culture so vast, beautiful, and bloody all at once.

But first I needed a bicycle.

Everything is for sale in Latin America. Everything. If you forgot it at home or you need it, somebody has it, and for the right price, it can be yours. This goes for food, clothes, and any other wares you might have forgotten to pack. If you're looking for a specific item—say, a pressure washer—somebody knows the *one* person in town who has it, and then it's up to you to begin negotiations. That book on the shelf at the restaurant around the corner doesn't have a price tag, but that doesn't mean it can't be had. Jan once told me about a guy he was getting ready to travel with, Roberto from Belgium, who had six weeks of volunteer requirements he needed to complete to qualify for university graduation. After a week of working with the kids in Guatemala, Roberto paid the director one hundred quetzales ($13.07) for the printout of the six-week certificate, and he spent the next five weeks traveling around the region.

Everything is for sale in Latin America. Or rent.

So, when the lady at the travel agency in Copán told me that the slow season had struck and nobody was renting bicycles, I grinned and offered up a *gracias*. Turning, I strode out onto the cobbled streets and started playing the numbers game.

A man pedaled by slowly on his bicycle a few moments later. I trotted after him until he squeezed the handbrakes and met my stare. "Pardon me," I said in Spanish, "is your bike for rent?" *Pardon me.* That's what I said. If one's skin color doesn't shout "tourist," stiff language skills will. The Latinos in America who just learned English as their second language say, "Hi, how are you?" But when you're born in a country, you gradually learn to say, "What's happenin'?" And "Where do you think we should go tonight to enjoy ourselves?" becomes "What are we up to tonight?" "Pardon me" is the same thing. Nobody says "pardon me" in America, with the exception of convicted Wall Street criminals with powerful political friends. Still, it's one of the first things I learned to say in Spanish.

He said his bike wasn't for rent.

I shuffled two blocks down the cobblestone road to grab some lunch at a little one-room restaurant. After swallowing a mouthful of chicken and spicy beans and rice, I asked the lady cooking (and serving and cleaning) whether she knew anybody with a bike to rent. She poked her head out the door to talk to Javien.

"Javien, this guy in my restaurant, he wants to borrow your bike," she called out. "Do you want to rent it to him?"

Javien was twelve, and a hundred lempiras was twenty thousand in his world, so he was naturally excited to rent his bike for five hours. "I have to ask my mom first," he piped, already pedaling quickly down the street with a grin plastered across his face. "I'll be right back." But after the thirty minutes it took to finish our dinner, he still hadn't returned.

I tapped my fingers on the worn surface of our table. This was frustrating. Everything is for sale or rent in Latin America, I'm telling you, and it wasn't usually this difficult. I persisted. Abandoning the restaurant and any hopes of Javien returning, I crossed a few blocks to the post office, a one-room shed hugged up against the market, and asked the lone attendant if she knew the owner of that gray bike chained up right outside the door. She didn't, noting that it had been sitting there for three days, but we chatted for a minute, and she knew a guy next door at the market—the guy with the red shirt, she said—who owned a bike. I continued my search next door and found him, Oscar, cutting and weighing chicken and fish for twenty eagerly waiting hands. He was busy, hustling, likely in the mood to have someone babysit his bike while he worked. We struck our deal rather quickly.

"Hello. Uh . . . I . . . uh—dammit, how do you say it? I . . . uh . . . like your bicycle," I stammered in broken Spanish. "To rent!" I screamed, excited to find the right expression buried in the depths of so many misplaced vocabulary words. "I like your bicycle to rent! One hundred lempiras until two."

He nodded—once—smiled, and stuck out his hand as he continued listening to a lady place her order. He said nothing to me, no time for that. Chicken to chop; fish, relieved of their heads, to stuff into plastic bags. I pulled a one-hundred-lempira bill out of my wad and stuffed it in his palm. His smile widened.

It was odd, yet captivating. In the United States, this obviously doesn't happen. We have a generally honest, accountable culture in America, but I know I'd never trust some random individual who approached me at work and wanted to rent my bike. Yet, in Honduras, in Central America, as corrupt as any system in the rest of the world, Oscar trusted that I would return in five hours. He wasn't worried about the brake pads or the gears or that I might bend the front tire rim when I found some super sweet jumps to attack. He knew I'd take good care of his rusty-red bicycle with its two missing spokes, and he knew I'd be back in the afternoon.

I grabbed his bike and slowly, furtively, dodged my way through the busy market and out into the wide-open stone-cloaked streets of Copán.

At first, I didn't understand the hoopla of the ruins. "Wow," I said flatly. "Pretty neat." My thoughts shifted to what I'd packed for lunch. My gaze roved down over all those fantastic stone structures, but I still felt . . . letdown. No, *letdown* isn't the right term. The ruins met my expectations but didn't exceed them. *Satisfactory.* Gigantic stone structures rose out of the earth, staircases reached farther into the sky than I could have thrown a baseball at full throttle, and I just thought, *I mean, it's cool, but if given the chance, I think I could assemble a crew to construct that.*

There are two things to note about that attitude: First, no I couldn't. The deeper I walked into Copán, the more elaborate the structures and statues and walkways and hieroglyphs became, and the more I started to respect this marvelous construction. The season's first heavy rain would bring down the tower my team and I would construct if given the chance—even *with* an illustrated step-by-step guide.

Second, the Maya erected these edifices long ago. Really long ago. With modern machinery and a little illegal labor, we could presently put the structures up in four days, loll around on Friday morning, and then, after lunch, get an early start on our weekend trip to the lake. These folks, though, these crazy Maya mofos, had no machinery. No pulleys. They didn't even have any metal tools. Bare hands, an idea, and a prayer. They saw a pile of stones to the left and an empty field to the right, and thought, *I know what would go pretty great over there. A house! A big, stone house. And then we can put up a huge stairway and a couple altars to host ceremonies and sacrifices! Let's do it!* They didn't have plans, no blueprints to work from; no Temple Depot around the corner to help them build it. Just trial and error. Lots of trial. Surprisingly little error.

The Maya were revolutionary. They built with limestone; they developed an advanced calendar (their Ladies of the Yucatán calendar reportedly sold millions); and they made grand, colorful clothes—cornflower blue and maize yellow—from homespun yarn and intricately woven fabric. Could they have been more efficient and complex? The Spanish sure thought so, but standing there, looking at those ruins at Copán, nearly fifteen hundred years after their construction, I marveled at what they'd been able to accomplish and the role that *every* Maya played in advancing their society. Everyone got involved; everyone had a job, a responsibility. Weak links, the deficiently skilled, charged forward with lesser functions but were nevertheless industrious.

I wondered, therefore, whether they were better off than Honduran society now. Today, as we continue the hunt for perfection, we bar from our social and professional circles those who don't fit the mold; so many years ago, they welcomed one and all with open arms and offered them a purpose in the community.

It's very eerie to be in a place where so much went down so many years ago. You pay your entry fee to the ruins and you're immediately transported from the world out there on the highway, not a soccer field away, to an ancient era. A thousand years ago, on top of that scaled structure right over there, some dude stood, had some buddies brace his arms and legs, and sacrificed his body, his life to the gods. The priest cut his chest open and wiggled his fingers inside that bloody cavity before pulling out his still-thumping heart. A week later, it rained. "See?" the townspeople said, nodding as they stood smiling beneath the torrential rains. "Told you it would work."

They even combined human sacrifice with sport. *Pitz*—a popular Mesoamerican sport—involved players using their thighs or hips to navigate a nine-pound rubber ball through a ring on the other side of the field. Sometimes, opposing rulers would play against each other for rights to property or a prosperous bounty. Generally speaking, however, the tribes decapitated the losing captain and offered his various organs or blood to the gods after the game. This was the original agony of defeat. In the modern world, if a player loses, he puts on his best pouty face for the media, phones his agent (who assures him that his stats are right where they need to be), and returns to his gated community to watch a movie with his family on his plush sectional couch and big-screen 3-D TV.

But then? In the times of the Maya? Dire consequences. Can you imagine being voted to represent your team as the captain, and worse, having to give a pep talk when you were losing at halftime? "Seriously, guys," I imagine a captain saying, alternating between pleading and screaming in a desperate attempt to motivate. "Can we show a little more effort out there in the second half? Maybe play a little defense this time around? Golly. Buncha' pansies. Marhatl, what the heck, man? Get serious! Can you put the ball through the ring just *once* this afternoon? Just once? Or maybe somewhere *near* the ring? Boy, I'll tell ya. Buncha pansies. That's what you are: a bunch of goddamned pansies." He looks down, shaking his head. After a pause, he looks up. "Itzamnaj, what are you doing? Put those away. You know the rules: no effort, no orange slices at halftime! C'mon guys, focus! And Ux M'el? C'mon, Ux M'el. We go way back, you and me. We used to play *pitz* together when we were kids! I brought you a rabbit last week when Wifey was sick. Do you remember that? Yeah, you do. You remember the rabbit. Frickin' pansy. Look at you now; my seven-year-old has more powerful hips than you. Unbelievable. You all oughta take a moment to reconsider your effort before you leave this locker room. Otherwise, don't even come out at all."

Despite all this, the Maya weren't barbarians. They simply believed in sacrifice. They shot a little blessing once in a while to this god or that, but otherwise they spent their time hunting, building, or figuring out how the stars aligned.

My entry fee to Copán was three times the cost of the previous night's lodging, which seemed excessive until I began to respect the work required to maintain this epic place. So many workers meticulously, quietly chipping away at the rock to unearth a new stairwell or sculpture, a new altar or residence, careful not to damage precious artifacts. For three hours I wandered silently among the ruins, taking it all in. A heavy, touching presence settled over me. I brushed my fingers over the stones of a long-dead-man's temple. I stood alone. A tour guide would have mesmerized me with his stories and fun facts, but then I wouldn't have been able to stop, look, muse on my own terms. I craved these moments alone. Where a guided tour takes an hour and a half, I took three solo, including time to scale various platforms and to peer down across an empty *pitz* field and the Great Ballcourt—a location defined by many researchers as the most beautiful creation of the entire Classic Maya period—to chew over my own athletic career.

Marcelo, one of the groundskeepers, took a break from work to take my bare-chested picture at the summit of the royal residence. A thousand years ago, a Native American man stood shirtless at that same spot growling with his arms curved at his side. Just as I did.

The Maya scavenged and hunted. In Central America—and notably in Copán—they found rich, dark soil and a favorable climate. Greenery. So much green, blanketing the earth from edge to edge as far as I could see and extending into the sky, coating the tips of spiny branches. From the ancient woodlands surrounding the stone city, the Maya harvested food and medicinal herbs and collected wood. They hunted deer with carefully constructed weapons; they picked berries, fingers stained deep blue-black with juice; they unearthed roots, split them open, and created salve to sooth the pain of cuts and scratches. And they shared with their neighbors. "My kill is our kill; my berry collection is our berry collection; and it turns out that the roots I excavated can be used to heal your cuts, too." They traded throughout the region, from Honduras to Mexico and even with far-off Mesoamerican groups in the Caribbean.

I found, in the Royal Precinct, the most voluminous series of hieroglyphic etchings in the Maya world. The Hieroglyphic Stairway is the longest pre-Columbian hieroglyphic stairway in America and one of the Maya's most astonishing accomplishments during the Classic period. Have you ever seen these hieroglyphs? They are brilliant and completely mesmerizing. Just as ancient Maya would look with bewilderment at our modern prose, I looked at their writing system with the same confusion. Through all of these carefully etched lines and images, stories are told. Culture is preserved. History is passed forward. Beginning with the dynasty's initial leader, K'inich Yax K'uk' Mo', royal genealogy, military triumphs, and various other histories, events, and accomplishments were stamped in stone before the invention of pen and paper.

I'm not that captivated by history. Maybe that will be a rite of passage for me in the future. "Ah, yes, Stonewall Jackson," my friend Surry says to me with a glint in his eye, a story ready to fire. "There's no greater strategist in U.S. military history ... "

But now, I'm invested in the present. I'm interested but not amazed by cultural things, and when you spot me at an art gallery or history museum, you'll see a slight haze over my eyes and know that my interest is mild and that I'm at least partly putting on a show for the young lady on my arm. As yet, I'm fundamentally ignorant, though, as time passes, decreasingly apathetic regarding people in black-and-white photos whom I won't ever actually get to meet.

So let's not jump ahead and think that I've quite arrived at the point where I'm jazzed up to start reading accounts of periods past, but let's all agree that it's fascinating—nay, essential—to consider that we got where we are today because someone else came before us. Bearded dudes used to start fires by striking stone to stone, the wheelbarrow did wonders for transport (and gave us one of our most beloved Monopoly tokens), and houses stood upright with a lime base and repelled most rain with a roof of interwoven leaves and branches. The cell phone started with Alexander Graham Bell telling Mr. Watson to get his ass over here; the laptop computer once took up a full room; lead balls used to be stuffed into musket barrels; that piece of machinery that holds all of your music in your pocket began as a tower of records; and Nutella started as a hazelnut hanging from the hazel tree before somebody got the sense to make it into a delicious paste. Evolution. Progress. Modification. It started long before you and I were bulges in our mamas' bellies.

Besides, pausing to imagine what happened a thousand years ago on that stone facility over there can be pretty fun, too.

Looking back raises the question of what our lives can be like moving forward. What will they say about us in fifty years, a hundred years, a thousand years? Next year, next month? Will they revere us or scorn us? Are they proud of our accomplishments or resentful that we could have done more? Are they inspired by our passion or baffled by our passivity? The Maya came together to build an elaborate, extraordinary community and have been effectively moving forward for the five hundred years or so since they—and every other native group in the Americas—were pushed into the mountains. But that doesn't mean the next five hundred years are a gimme, as we are always faced with a new set of challenges and problems with which to contend. Right? Even the Maya, the revolutionary and gumptious Maya, struggled with overpopulation and overhunting and drought and wars as their empire—this empire where I stood—started to weaken, even before the gun-toting Spanish hit the shores of America. The Maya made a thousand mistakes, surely, just as they did a thousand things right, but the point is that they did *something*. And their legacy is planted in history as a result.

Honduras Child Alliance

I don't love kids. I'm never the life of the party when kids are around. I'm usually standing in the corner and hoping they don't decide to bring their jabbering language and grubby fingers my way. And likewise, they never jump to attention upon my arrival—it's as if they know there are better, more willing targets for their wild affection and energy. "What are you even talking about, bambino?" I ask them. "I don't get it. Whatever. Call me when you've learned a couple three-syllable words and you're reading books that don't have pictures in them."

Kids want to play. They want to run toward things and away from things and throw things and catch things and construct things out of beads and yarn and tell knock-knock jokes that I have to pretend are clever. "Ah! I get it! Because the cow says 'moo,' and he interrupts you before you're done talking. I like that one. Good one. The interrupting cow. Moo. Yeah . . . Another one? Man, I'd love to hear another one, but I think I hear my . . . uh"—cough—"calling. Besides, a good comedian always ends on his best joke, right?" And they never rest. Man, kids never rest. Their feet run for as long as their little mouths do, and it's just exhausting. I don't have time for them. I'm growing up and away from juvenile behavior and toward scholarship, and I have better things to do. Yeah, scholarship. That's my excuse. I'm too scholarly to be bothered with this immaturity.

Besides, these are other people's children. *Where are their parents? They should be around here somewhere.* I'm not getting paid to babysit.

My brother, Erik, though? He'll make a great father one day. He bounces into a five-year-old's birthday party with a lively grin, arms in the air, and voice pitched with excitement. Hours later, he exits, head ducked. Utterly spent but happy nonetheless. He's always the center of attention, crowds aged two to sixty-two, but he specializes in youngsters. He's the godfather of three children from three different families and counting. He once built a customized easel from scratch for one of their birthdays. An easel that you paint on. From scratch. All of that throwing and catching and running and constructing and pausing to tell jokes? That's him. They adjourn just long enough for a noisy round of cookies or cake, if tendered, and then they're off again.

"Just stick 'em in the basement," my mom always says. "And we'll grab 'em when it's time to leave." Set 'em and forget 'em. Throwing, catching, running, constructing, jokes. Throwing, catching, running, constructing, jokes.

"Where's Erik going?" I heard a boy say once to his mom as my family left their house. "He's not leaving, is he?" He delivered the words with a pleading, dejected tone, his entire face already sinking into a full-lipped pout. "Is he leaving?" His mom's affirmation of Erik's departure sent the poor kid off wailing to his room.

It's always been like that, since I was six and Erik was five. And for whatever reason, he is never the one to get hurt. I am. He'll be caked in mud or building a makeshift sled or bundled up in camo to lead a gang off into the woods to go exploring, and I'm headed to the hospital with a cut on my forehead. Sixteen stitches required, just because I didn't want to be left out. Gravity doesn't apply to Erik, but it hammers me every time. I should have been on the front stoop reading or out back shooting hoops or, y'know, socializing with the other scholars in the vicinity, but instead I'm lumbering off to the hospital pressing a bloody rag above my eye.

Yeah, *love* is a strong word, so it's tough for me to tell you that I love kids. Mostly, that's because I generally don't even like them. I don't *dislike* them necessarily; I'm just indifferent. They can have their little games, and I'll have my conversations on current events and lands journeyed. We'll go to our separate corners and reconvene when it's time for cookies, milk, and Ritalin.

But this trip around the world wasn't about me. It was about the places I'd see and the people I'd meet. When I googled "volunteer in Latin America," I arrived at essentially the last affordable place to volunteer. Honduras Child Alliance is an organization devoted to advancing the lives of the youth of El Porvenir, that little town on the Caribbean coast where I decided to hang my hat for two months. The organization's vacation activities program gives kids a positive outlet for all their energy during those three months that school is out of session.

El porvenir means "the future" in English. In the States, and in every other developed country across the world, children are the future, sure, but there's opportunity there that doesn't necessarily exist everywhere. And in the States, even if we completely screw up our lives in the early years, there's almost always time to recover:

Don't want to go to class now? No problem! You can get your GED on the cheap whenever you're ready.

Don't feel like working now? Sounds great! There's plenty of time to gain experience when you're older. And besides, with a little grit, you can start your own small business anytime.

Wanna smoke a little crack? Steal a car? Rob the corner minimart? Go for it! The state will pay for your rehab program or a shiny diploma while you're in prison spending your nights trying to figure out how to make a shiv out of a melon rind.

In Honduras, though, the children are the future to the extent that the adults—once children with promise—aren't progressing the country forward. Honduras counted on those bright children slipping through the cracks to be their next innovators. Bright children fall away in the States, and there are plenty of others to stand up in their place; we'll do just fine with crews of free-spirited genius heroin addicts roaming the streets. There are no second chances in Honduras, however, and even the first chance doesn't look very encouraging. Even the kids who make it, the ones who finish high school and go off to college—the state pays for classes only up to the sixth grade—find their way right back to their hometown to hawk chocolate-covered bananas or man the local seafood market, occupations that didn't require an education in the first place. Clerking at the bank is the goal, but those limited positions fill quickly.

I can't change any of that, though. What I can do is run and throw and catch and construct. And read. After living in Honduras for a week, I found myself struggling to develop a daily routine. I didn't have the lay of the town—I was following other volunteers wherever they went—and I knew only a few kids by name. We had just returned to the church from a morning spent playing outside, the whole group was strewn across the concrete floor around me—sweaty, every one of them—and here was my orientation: Erlin, all four and a half feet, eighty pounds of Erlin, sat near my lap, beseeching me to read the book again, the first time this had happened to me since my arrival in El Porvenir. Story time can be fun, but it's never quite as fun as soccer or Steal the Bacon or jumping rope or races. For them, story time is the brief-as-we-can-make-it gateway from snack time to time back out on the field.

But here they were, ordering another reading. *"Otra vez!"* they all shouted, one on top of the other. *"Otra vez!"*

I read my favorite book from when I was a child, *Love You Forever*, and my heart was spirited. The book's most popular verse translates the same into Spanish as I'm sure it must to every language in the world.

> *I'll love you forever,*
> *I'll like you for always,*
> *As long as I'm living,*
> *My baby you'll be.*

We'd read ten children's classics to them so far over the weeks—*Curious George, Dr. Seuss, Clifford the Big Red Dog*—all to applause, but this was the first one they asked me to repeat. And this was certainly the first and only one where they chimed in on the chorus, lifting their voices with mine.

> *Para siempre te amaré,*
> *Para siempre te querré,*
> *Mientras en mí haya vida,*
> *Siempre serás mi bebé.*

This was why I went to Honduras. I didn't go to sightsee or to relax, lounging on a sandy beach. I wasn't on vacation. I was there to spend hours on Sunday planning an entertaining and enriching itinerary for the kids' week. I flew 1722 miles and bumped elbows with other travelers in cramped buses and boats, all to run and catch and construct. And for those moments when Erlin requested a story again. Maybe I'd enjoy myself and maybe not, I thought, but I arrived in Honduras with the singular intent to engage a couple of kids—not ten or twenty, necessarily—to tell a boy or girl, or two or three, that there was more out there than selling chocolate-covered bananas and working fish stalls in the market. That there was opportunity waiting for them, that they'd better get their shit together if they ever want to taste the life that lay on the other side of the fence. That if they stayed in school, studied a little extra, developed an entrepreneurial mind, and maybe learned English, they had a shot.

They say "okay!" but it was hard for us volunteers to compete with their often strained home life. Mom and Dad didn't emphasize or enforce school by day and study by night. Five-year-old Daniella, with her little pigtails bouncing on either side of her round cheeks, came in crying after lunch because her mom hit her. Luis missed three days in a row, because his dad dictated work to be done. Jenifer brought her pants-less baby brother—pecker pointing to the sky—to class, because, well, "there's nowhere else for him to go, and I want to be here for the activities program." These kids' vocabularies were weak. They were starved for affection and attention. Their parents loved them, but love takes different forms in different cultures.

But the kids didn't complain, and they certainly weren't sentenced to distressed childhoods. Some of them knew they were poor, but everybody was poor, so what? Mostly, they couldn't understand that they were likely cycling through a state of perpetual poverty. They stumbled over bottles and wrappers in the streets, dropped firecrackers in passing, and played soccer in bare feet, because that was normal. They didn't fully understand the answers to their inquiries about the destitute life in the States. "Hold up, you mean to tell me that our counterparts to the north eat three hearty meals a day and have free access to the Internet at public libraries? Well, ain't that a little unfair." To them, all of the people wearing business suits and driving in glossy cars lived on an island called Hollywood. Talk of millionaires was assuredly sarcastic, as if someone could ever actually obtain that much money. This was all they knew—dusty streets and soccer in bare feet—and they would have had to know better to be upset about it.

For the most part, these kids didn't have time to think about what their lives *could* be like because they were too busy being a pain in my ass, just like a couple of the children I knew back home. They ran around when you told them it was not time to run around. They clapped and sang and talked during quiet time. They were outside when it was time to be inside, inside when it was time to be outside, and over there at the field when none of the volunteers had even mentioned one word about migrating in that direction. They paid attention when it suited their needs, and they made three bracelets when we clearly set the allotment at two. And they constantly made fun of my pronunciation.

"*Frijoles*," I'd say, and they'd laugh.

"It's *frijoles*," they'd chant.

"That's what I said. *Frijoles*."

Laughter. "*Escucha, Adán. Frijoles*."

"Right. *Frijoles*."

Laughter.

I'd keep my face very straight, adopting a look of innocent confusion. "What? *Frijoles*."

"*Adán! Frijoles!*"

I'd ask them whether they use *champoo* to *watch* their hair when they were taking *chowers*.

Sometimes jokes and laughter filled our days together, and sometimes we had to send the villains home to do a whole bunch of nothing for their break from school. Some days I was the hero they all gathered around, and some days kids refused to sit next to me in the circle. One day after snack time, Hector threw his empty paper plate on the ground. He glared up at me and called me an *hijo de puta* for not giving him seconds. Turning, he stomped out, knowing he was going to be sent home anyway.

I deserved every bit of trouble they gave me, though. The ghost of my schooldays past must have hitched a ride on my journey to Central America. I was a lovable little pupil in kindergarten. But after playtime ended and the time to actually learn something rolled around in the first grade, I never gave my teachers a break. All the way through. In the eleventh grade, we had to do ten-minute presentations about a social topic of our own selection. Ashley Foor wrote S-E-X in big letters on the board in an effort to grab everyone's attention, strode to the podium, and—chin raised high and with a small smile—declared, "I am going to speak about saving virginity for marriage." She made an eloquent and compelling presentation on this topic. Then, when my turn came to present, I wrote S-E-X in big letters on the board, mimicked her confident walk up to the podium, and proceeded to give a lecture on the evolution of the basketball shoe. Chuck Taylors to present. I showed a video of an interview I did at a local shoe store—me standing between two black dudes—and I called it my Oreo-cookie interview. I had a fake cell phone in my pocket as I stood in front of the class, and I made it ring halfway through my presentation, pretending to tell my classmate Kareem's mom that "I can't talk just now, babe, but I'm looking forward to seeing you tonight, if only you could please wear that red nightie that you know I like." I then called back to Ashley's presentation, making a remark or two about the absurd idea of saving yourself for marriage: "Where will you get your creativity from, if not a few preliminary romps?" I demanded, heroically. "And God help you if you get to your wedding night, and your partner is bad in bed. What then?" I threw my arms up in puzzlement as a series of muffled laughs rippled through my juvenile audience. "What will you do then, I ask you all? Why not try it before you buy it?" And then there was something more about the evolution of the basketball shoe.

My teachers—Ms. Armstrong and Ms. Campbell—sat silent at the back of the room, expecting something like this, clicking five points off my grade at a time, finally cutting me off and inviting me to spend the duration of the class in the hallway. Good for them; what a jerk I was, that desperado making a mockery of their classroom. I would have appealed to bring back corporal punishment if I were either one of them.

I spent two months in Honduras rounding up those rascals. And maybe that was the commencement of a lifelong effort to atone for the terror I was all the way up until I skittered off to college and got serious.

But maybe I'm exaggerating how tough it was to control those little darlings down in Honduras. Even among this roguery, every day was fresh and exciting for all of us. We sent the baddies home, and the rest of us read books. We made bracelets out of beads and string, and then I helped tie them around the kids' tiny wrists. We learned how to run the diamond of the kickball field counterclockwise and how to throw the ball at an opposing player to get an out. (If only their proficiency with their hands matched that of their feet.) We dodged horseshit as we rounded the bases and paused momentarily for the cows when it was their turn to graze through. We crafted the solar system out of papier-mâché. We drew. We painted. We sang. We ran dizzy bat races, no doubt a first in El Porvenir. We ate bananas and pineapple or rice and beans on a tortilla during snack time. We played with puppets, the children giggling hysterically about the characters having the same broken, mispronounced Spanish that I myself used. We went to the beach and learned to Slip 'n Slide on a flimsy clear tarp that John managed to scrounge up. We stayed in to do our stretching exercises and learn English phrases when it poured, but played outside in a drizzle.

These kids were tough, and they were competitive. We played Steal the Bacon, and that plastic bottle in the middle mattered. They wanted that bottle. They needed that bottle. They focused everything they had on that bottle. They scratched for that bottle. They plotted to get the bottle. Tempers rose. Nothing else in the world mattered except latching their fragile fingers onto that bottle.

I think we lose some of that enthusiasm as we grow older.

These kids were witty, too, just like the nine-year-old class clowns back home. One day, we were doing an opening circle exercise, each person describing their hero. Some proudly declared their mom, their dad, or a grandparent their hero. Others, a famous soccer player or historical figure. Luis said the Incredible Hulk.

"Okay," I said, probing further, "but why the Incredible Hulk?"

"Because I'm like him. Most of the time, he's a normal guy. But he can always get angry, and his muscles puff up." He pushed his shirt up to his shoulder to expose his flexed right bicep.

His sister, Esther, hollered from across the room. "Look at you, Luis! You don't have any muscles!"

"That's because right now I'm normal," he shot back. "Don't make me angry."

I made the beans for their snack one Wednesday. Unanimously, the kids decided my beans were . . . less than delicious. "Terrible," they said to me, no hesitation. "Too dry. No flavor. They smell rotten. Did you use chicken stock . . . ? Water . . . ? You just used water . . . ? Who taught you that?" Do you have any idea how bad your beans have to be for the gracious poor kids of Honduras to detest them? Nauseated from hunger, they still turned down my beans. Ivana, a gorgeous volunteer from Slovakia, made beans the following week, and they couldn't get enough, but mine went virtually uneaten.

The girls taught me how to string a proper bracelet, and the boys taught me how to work my way around a defender. I showed the girls how to do a push-up and a sit-up the right way, and I showed the boys how to do a chest bump after a score. I showed everybody how guys dance in the States.

For two months, I got to know Kevin. And Esther. And Keni. And Yolani. Lisbeth, tall and gangly for her age, begged me to sit next to her during story time. Breny laughed at my pronunciation every time I spoke. Pretty much every time I saw him, Daniel asked when we were going outside. Suany just wanted to make necklaces, her fingertips nimbly shifting through the beads to find the perfect color combination. Herles just wanted to play soccer. Carlos asked when we were going for a ride in the airplane. Tapping on my arm like a little woodpecker, Javier pestered me for leftover snacks, and Oscar didn't say five words as long as I knew him.

Everybody has their favorites, just as so many of my teachers along the way picked me and my little band as their least favorites. For me, my favorite from the beginning was Luis. Curious and mischievous, he also minded when I told him to put his breeches in his seat and listen up or else I'd make him eat my beans.

Once I'd surveyed the lay of the town and developed a daily routine—bike to the church for morning activities, walk to Oscar's living-room gym to lift weights during the lunch hour, return to the church for afternoon activities, bike home, make guacamole, read, eat, relax, go to bed—Luis started creeping in my shadow during the day. I'd arrive early to find Luis sitting on the step of the church, waiting for me. He was only thirteen but he was already making attempts to impress the ladies by spiking his hair, keeping his teeth white, and wearing a dab of cologne that he scavenged from who knows where.

"Adán," he'd ask in Spanish as he scampered a few steps behind me on our way back from playing outside. "Is every road paved in your town back home?"

"Sure is," I'd say to him, and he'd reply with a smile and an "Eschúchele." Listen to this guy. He always said, "Listen to this guy."

"And a lot of people have cars?" he'd ask.

"At least one per family," I'd tell him, pacing slowly so he could keep up.

"Escúchele. And your mustache. All the other volunteers are growing mustaches for the month of November. Why does your face have only about six hairs?"

He inquired about snow and skiing and what I did for work and how much money I made per day and whether I had a closet full of clothes back home or just the two shirts I always wore in Honduras. "Escúchele." He asked me about my girlfriend, referencing scripture. "It says Adán y Eva, man. But I never see you with any Eva." Curiosity filled his eyes as he skipped over a puddle in the street.

"I'm still looking for her. She's missing. Let me know if you find her."

And that's how it started, right there on that grungy road with Luis. "Adán sin Eva" quickly spread across town as my new nickname—Adam Without Eve—and for six weeks, inquiries came at me from the street sides of this small town from people I'd never met. "Dónde está Eva?"

I told them I'd located forty-seven Evas online, but none of them had returned my e-mails. I told them she was on her way, not ten minutes behind me. I told them she was at home cooking. I told them she says hi.

They'd pass me walking to the store with Ivana. *"Ay! Adán sin Eva. Pero, Adán con Ivana!"* Ivana and I had been hanging out a bit, and that was great. I was working my game. Now these adorable little children were mocking me around every corner.

Biking the last leg to the church, I sped down the thoroughfare in approach. Ahead, all my little tykes stood on the steps of the church. As soon as I pulled up, they cried in unison, *"Adán sin Eva!"* I glared at Luis, since he'd started this *"Adán sin Eva"* business. He just laughed. A few of the kids would run to me and valet my bike, asking about Eva. "She ate some bad fruit," I told them. "So, she's at home sick today. She offered some to me, and it was tempting, but I didn't take it." We'd hug, high-five, unlock the church, and get started on the day's activities.

Then came the last day before Christmas break. We threw a party with food and games and a piñata, and we made paper snowflakes and greeting cards for our parents. Anthony stared up at me, and asked, *"Adán,* instead of eating my lunch, can I wrap it up and take it home to my mom after the party?"

All the planning, all the rounding up, all the times I waited patiently for them to quiet down, all the lectures, all the energy I expended making the round-trip by bike—twice a day each way—all the money I spent on little artsy knickknacks, all the lice that Sarah found in her hair, us demanding her to return to the volunteer house to boil her sheets and towels and all her clothes, all the effort just might have been worth it.

When I'm seventy, my grandchildren, all six or seven of them, will sit around my La-Z-Boy at Christmas, and they will want to hear stories about my one-year journey. The aroma of a honey-glazed ham and turkey and green-bean casserole and stuffing and cheesy hash browns and mashed potatoes drifts softly into the living room from grandma's kitchen. Two pies—pecan, my favorite, and pumpkin, which I don't care for—are cooling out back on the screened-in porch. And my grandchildren will ask me questions.

"Why is it," one of them will ask looking at an old photo, probably one of me casually posing with my muscles flexed atop a Maya ruin, "that you used to be young and handsome and now you're old and wrinkled?"

"This is the circle of life," I will tell them, before mentioning that their bodies are already slowly beginning to shrink and wrinkle like fallen leaves and they will look like me soon enough. "Right there around the eyes, the creases," I will point out to whichever one of those impish little nippers posed the question in the first place. "I see you've already gotten a head start."

"Did you meet the Dalai Lama?" they will ask. "Did you buy anything for Grandma? Like a scarf or something? Did you see any Asian people? I mean, like, *real* Asian people. Not like the ones with funny accents that we have in the United States."

I'll try not to be the contemptuous old man, but I'll have to wonder whether there's *any* creativity to *any* of these inquiries or whether a few of my grandkids will need to be tested for learning disabilities.

Then, a raised hand from the corner will catch my attention. One shy grandchild will sit alone, having sat silently this entire time. When our eyes meet, he'll wait, hand still raised, for me to acknowledge him. *Good Lord, son. You needn't raise your hand to speak in this household.* I'll point to him.

"What is the one place you enjoyed the most during your journey?" he'll ask, and I'll be curious why it takes the most intelligent ones so much time to gather the moxie to be more outgoing. *Why are you sitting in the corner?* I'll wonder. *Please don't sit in the corner. Are you listening to the rest of these questions? You really are the only hope for this family.*

This question, though, about the one place I enjoyed the most will be a question I've long pondered. The one place. Maybe it won't be fair for me to think about these things, since I'll have enjoyed the trip as a whole, and every individual spot from start to finish will have been new and exciting and held its own flavor, and besides, our greatest adventures are the next ones—whether those adventures are a segment of a 'round-the-world trip or just hoping to finish dinner without our teeth falling out. Great places we've been, great places we will revisit, great new places still left for us to discover. Right? Nevertheless, though, we all have that special place in our past. Maybe it's a moment, or maybe it's a location—maybe it's a particular look in a woman's eyes or maybe it's watching the sunrise over an unfamiliar and exotic horizon. It's useless, perhaps, to hope to return there, but maybe it's enough to have a picture painted, etched forever, in our minds. That one place; that special place.

"Honduras," I'll say, and this will grab everyone's attention. They'll all scoff at me. "Honduras!" they'll yell, looking one to the other as if I can't possibly be serious. *He must be kidding, this antique of a man.* "Honduras?" they'll ask again, just to make sure they heard me correctly. "You fought bulls in Nicaragua and rode an elephant in Thailand and hiked Abel Tasman in New Zealand and bungee jumped in Slovakia, and you're telling us the place you enjoyed the most was Honduras?" They haven't heard favorable reports from anywhere in Central America and especially not from Honduras.

"Yes," I'll say. I settle down into my chair. "Honduras." But I won't explain it to them. They won't understand; no elaboration will be sufficiently convincing. Somehow, such experiences shed merit as they pass from occurrence to anecdote. "You'll just have to go see it for yourself," I'll tell them.

Honduras.

I don't necessarily have a particular affection for Honduras as a country, nor would I even put it on a top one hundred list of vacation destinations (save for the Bay Islands). But when people ask me the one place where I wish I could have frozen time, I will tell them to put me back on that field with those children in Honduras. Those children, one or two wearing a pair of shoes, a couple in bare feet, most of them in sandals. The sun searing my neck, salty sweat draining into my scratches and cuts and scabbed mosquito bites, burning like flowing lava. A dehydration headache and a stuffy nose lingering from the germs streaming through the air and passing from hand to hand.

It's three o'clock, an hour shy of close-up time. I'm exhausted, muscles groaning and begging me to lie down and be still. Two sessions of activities with the kids; weightlifting during the lunch break. The soccer field is that vast blend of trampled grass pounded into the mud with net-less goals gaping to the north and south.

Carlos, eight years old, zips over to me with a wide smile that can't possibly be replicated. He looks up and into my eyes. He makes his appeal. *"Adán!"* he pleads. Man, that smile. *"Adán! Avión!"* He raises his arms up to me. It's airplane time; three o'clock is always airplane time, and as soon as he mentions this, the herd drops the soccer ball they've been kicking among themselves and thunders toward me. Assembling around me, they cheer one another on while awaiting their turn.

One after another, I hoist them up by their waists, grunt as I stretch my arms over my head, and sail them through the air. I run fast, careful to keep from slipping in the muddy grass. I make each flight as thrilling as I can while keeping a little gas in the tank for the next flyer. They open up wide, arms and legs extended to capacity, and they set themselves free. These kids had a small lunch at home, maybe a little rice and beans, and some beans and pineapple will be served for dinner. Their dads cherish them but work too long and too hard to have any energy to play with them at night, and their moms will have a list of chores that continue long into the evening. They'll sleep three or four to a room, sharing hard, scratchy, fifteen-year-old mattresses, and they'll wish their parents could afford just one more fan to keep the sweat from beading all over their bodies while they sleep. But right now? Right now, right at that moment out on that field, they're soaring through the air, no worries. The breeze plays across their faces; the air welcomes and embraces them and makes them forget. One after the other.

"Adán! Avión! Vamos!"

I extend my own arms up, lift them over my head. I slow down, searching for that second and third and fourth wind, but they want me to pick the speed back up. *"Más rápido!"* they chant, and who am I to take them for a ride in a puddle jumper when they clearly signed up for a ride on an F-15? I pick up speed.

"Más rápido!" they scream. *"Más rápido!"*

We soar from one end of the field to the other and back. Again and again, one plane at a time, twenty little birds following behind, their laughter echoing through the soccer field and bouncing off the trees and cracked plaster and wooden homes around us. Everybody is smiling now, eager for their turn. I've caught my next wind. They want to dive—y'know this business of flying in a straight line is fun enough but still not quite as fun as finding a wild current to jolt this plane from the ground to the sky.

So we catch a drift. We swoop and we soar. We're at the mercy of that burst of air now; it's out of my control. They laugh and bellow for more. And life is good.

I wish this moment would never end.

But it does. Just like that, we have to go inside for story time. This frustrates them for five seconds or so—they'll play airplane until next Tuesday if given the chance—but they quickly get excited about which story we'll be reading. To which land will we travel today? Will Dr. Seuss be there? Curious George? That fierce dragon from yesterday's tale? The ugly duckling? There'll be more time to fly in the *avión* tomorrow.

Yeah, Honduras. Sitting there at seventy, I'm imagining that my life will have mattered to somebody, if no one more than my family. It will have been a great life, and if I keep walking my two miles a day and taking my cholesterol medication religiously, and if that savage dog next door doesn't dig his way out of his backyard and kill me first, maybe I'll squeak out some more years. I should probably go easy on the whiskey, though, and the second helpings at the dessert bar aren't helping. But looking back on my year, that great year I had in my twenties, if given the opportunity to pick one place to which I can return, I'll want to be back on that field in

Honduras. Miserably hot, no water in sight, shade an illusion, no air conditioning to look forward to; and I couldn't possibly have cared any less. I just wanted to see those kids' eyes sparkle.

I just wanted to take them for one more ride in an airplane.

High Stakes

'm a risk taker, a competitor, a man of highs and lows who thrives in the extremes. This attitude has served me well in entrepreneurial environments and on the basketball court, as well as when faced with stressful decisions. This attitude prompted me to decide to take this trip in the first place; it led me to Guatemala and Honduras, sent me jumping from The Platform, laid me down to watch the sunrise, and gave me the opportunity to impact the lives of some wonderful, beautiful children.

But this attitude is also why I've had a few troubling rounds with the casinos.

Spring break of my freshman year in college, my good friends Dave and Brian convinced me—without much effort—that we should hop across I-90 to spend the weekend at Turning Stone Casino in Verona, New York. Turning Stone is littered with restaurants, an arcade, a confectionery shop, a comedy club, a showroom, a beautiful golf course, and an incredible spa, but these attractions barely entered my mind. Only one thought, one fact, loomed there, casting a delightful shadow over me—Turning Stone is one of the rare casinos in America where you don't have to be twenty-one to sit down to play blackjack.

The walk inside depressed me. Higher-end gamblers shuffled their chips at tables down in Connecticut at Mohegan Sun or Foxwoods (or smartly avoided casinos altogether), but in this blue-collar country in midstate New York, grizzled, tired machinists, farmers, and repairmen spent their days sweating and their evenings hunched over the roulette table, betting diaper and dinner money on a few flashing revolutions of the wheel. We were sweet-smelling kids with straight teeth, clean Oxfords on our backs, and lots of potential cultivating back at our

$40,000-per-year college. I turned to Dave and muttered, in jest, "Ha. If I ever turn into one of these mothers . . . "

I won a few hundred at the blackjack table the first day, but two hours into our second day, I blew all of my winnings plus the four hundred I had brought. I was playing with five hundred dollars recently milked from an ATM machine that Turning Stone offers "right over there in the corner, baby." Over the course of the next hour, I let that five hundred slip through my fingers and found myself playing with another five hundred, all of this drawn from another credit card. When Dave and Brian told me that it was about time to wrap up and head home, my spirits called for another trip to the ATM. "Last one," Dave said with a smirk, as if he had witnessed this type of behavior before. He and Brian nursed bubbly cups of Coke while watching over my shoulder, having retired their own fruitless attempts for the night.

So I played on and lost another five hundred and we stood up to leave. Dave walked in front of me and Brian behind, escorting me out of the casino as though they could foresee another bad decision.

Just as we turned the corner around a row of slot machines, I (no kidding) faked right, cut left, and sprinted back to the ATM, dodging someone's lovable little old grandma on the way and using her as a screen. Drawing out money with a plastic card and betting with little plastic chips, I lost the sense that this was real money. That I was really gambling myself deeper and deeper into a hole. This wasn't food money or clothes money or school-supply money or car-repair money; these were abstract funds. And once I was sitting at that table waiting anxiously for the dealer to flip over the next cards, the idea that I had nearly zero control of the game was lost on me. After every loss, I kept telling myself I could beat this game if I played just one more time, just one more hand, just one more ATM withdrawal. I just knew I could. By the time Dave and Brian caught up to me, I had already punched in my PIN and $1000 was *flit-flit-flitting* its way out of the machine and into my waiting hand. Another grand. This was big money for a kid on scholarship whose account balance had been limited to what few dollars remained from cutting grass last summer.

That first trip to Turning Stone ended just as you'd expect. I lost that last $1,000 and rode home in a car with Dave, Brian, and remorse. In the wake of the flashing lights, electrifying sounds of the cards flicking out across the green table, and the steady hum of chattering voices, everything felt so silent and . . . empty.

Despite all I lost, the lesson didn't stick, didn't burrow into me.

I began to conspire against the casinos, develop schemes to get my money back. And then some. *Ocean's Eleven* minus ten. Adam versus the Native Americans to avenge his financial Little Bighorn. I knew I was smart. I knew I could out-think the casinos. I could beat the game.

But over the next three years, Brian and Dave and I taking on the world, I lost around $8,000, money I didn't even have. (As an upperclassmen, I made $224 every two weeks as a resident advisor.) During those three years, I also walked into Citizens Bank to take out a five-figure cash advance on seven credit cards to buy a sure-thing penny stock that went under eight months after I bought it (and recommended it to my friends Brett and Korran). I reasoned that I had worked hard on the basketball court and in the weight room to earn my college tuition with my own sweat and strength, so why not play a little?

Carrying the weight of that kind of debt on my shoulders, I graduated. I kept my shoulders straight as I walked across the platform, but it was all a masquerade. I had fallen into a pit of debt, the kind of debt that offers neither a favorable interest rate nor the opportunity to defer payments until six months after graduation. The kind of debt that holds your diploma hostage. Walking across the stage, all my friends received lovely leather-bound booklets with their diplomas proudly displayed inside; I got a lovely leather-bound booklet with a letter typed in boldface ordering me across campus to pay the $412.38 balance on my account if I ever wanted to see my diploma alive again.

But the worst still lay ahead.

I vowed to stay away from the casinos and clean up the six-foot deep hole that had become my financial life. But it only takes one wad of cash, one gluttonous split-second decision, and one win for it all to slip through your hands. The casinos count on the hope brought out by an encouraging victory once in a while. Three years out of college, after my first book enjoyed a little success, I was debt-free and had $10,000 cash tucked away in my desk. At the time, I flew for free as a wheelchair attendant at Raleigh-Durham Airport. So, lying in bed one night I orchestrated my master plan. I would fly up to Philly the next morning, drive to Atlantic City, double my money or not, and return home.

And it worked. Within thirty minutes, I took Trump Plaza for $10,000 in pink chips, cashed them in, and flew home. It was a great trip. As I soared thousands of miles above the ground, I really felt how high up I was. My cheeks were probably brightly flushed. I'm certain my eyes glittered. I looked around at other passengers and thought it a shame that they couldn't enjoy life as I was. It's hard to describe the rush of a moment like that—the way your heart pounds almost painfully against your chest. A good kind of pain. I was on a high; life was good.

Three months later, Justin and Ryan invited me back up to Atlantic City.

This story is gloomily predictable. Justin and Ryan and I reached Atlantic City on a Saturday night, gambled for a while, knocked back some rum and Cokes for a while, and danced for a while, all within reach of a blackjack table. When Ryan and Justin retreated to the room, I lingered at the tables. Hours ticked by in that cavernous room. By six o'clock Sunday morning, my debit card was declining even the smallest withdrawals, and I was on the phone with some lady at Bank of America in Pakistan or India pleading with her that I was the real Adam Shepard and that she should release my funds. She explained repeatedly that she didn't have the power to do that—no one did on Sunday—so I would have to wait until Monday. I was already down a few grand, plus the few grand they'd allowed me to tug out of the ATM, and I was asking for the rest. But she said I had to wait. So I waited. But not long.

By Monday at 10:30 A.M., my bank account was empty. I had blown the final $9,000 or so in my checking account, in my travel fund, and I was furious at myself—not for losing, but for being such a lazy, irresponsible, greedy piece of shit to sit down like that in the first place.

When I pulled out of the haze—that almost zombielike state of desire for the thrill of the game—when I realized what I'd done, I dropped my head in my hands. I sat on the edge of my chair as the hubbub roared on around me. Dozens, maybe hundreds, more men and women around me were caught up in the thrill of it. While I was just waking up. Waking up to realize what I'd done and what I'd lost.

I called my pops and met with him Tuesday for lunch. I confessed what I'd done. Spilled the truth about everything that had happened over the previous years. He conveyed his disappointment with a few soft words and a furrowed brow that shook me deeper than if he'd screamed obscenities. I've rarely responded to his wrath—and he's rarely offered it—but those couple of times he has shared his disappointment have changed my life.

In one short weekend, I lost two years' worth of savings, and a year's worth of opportunities to see the world.

But instead of shriveling up, instead of giving up, I got back to work. I started saving. I never sat down at a table game again, and thanks to a teary-eyed promise to my father, I never will.

And that decision, that promise, put me in a position to be on the dance floor in Honduras with a beautiful girl from across the world.

I Think I'd Better Go Get John

As I stepped down a blank street in Honduras, my stomach rumbled. It's hard to ignore that kind of protest. I headed to the corner and binged on *pasteles*, those delectable Honduran minicalzones stuffed with meat and potatoes. I scarfed down six, wiping the grease from my face to my shirt.

I showered and did my hair up nice. It was my second Saturday in Honduras, and I was geeked for a night out on the town. With a single girl to single guy ratio of four volunteers to one, I had my sights set on one thing: meeting Ivana on the dance floor.

Back home in the States, my friend Korey glided from bar to bar along Franklin Street's main corridor, peered up at the stars, and wondered whether I was having as much fun as he was; Tony raised a toast to my trip and all of the sightly young lasses I was destined to woo; Brian typed out an e-mail to remind me that, no matter the hemisphere, the less I said to a girl at the bar, the better.

In Honduras, Chris liked my odds; Danny pondered his own play for the evening; John didn't care either way.

The homies. See, when I started planning my trip, I made some good decisions, had some fairly perceptive foresight, and I made a few mistakes, didn't think some things through as thoroughly as I should have. I did make one very good decision, though: I decided not to plan my journey too strictly. If I was having a great time in Nicaragua, I was going to hang my hat for a little longer, whereas if I was bored in New Zealand, I could pack my stuff inside of ten minutes and hop on a plane to another destination. Lake Atitlán in Guatemala, for example, was a spontaneous weekend trip, and I was able to make a last-minute decision to spend an extra day in Copán before meeting my volunteer group in Honduras.

In El Porvenir, we sat for a dinner of fried chicken at Juaquin's, and everybody welcomed me with cheer. Belinda studied computer science at UNC. Jennifer hailed from Ohio. Sarah from Virginia. Many were European. Between mouthfuls of chicken, they filled me in on what to expect over the next months. Sometimes with laughter, sometimes with earnestness, they told stories of which volunteer to call if I needed something fixed and who had the most creative game ideas for the children.

Less than a week passed before I was working out with John and Chris. Bro time. We'd push ourselves through these tough workouts in the basement of the big blue beach house— P90X Legs and Back, Kenpo X, Bi's and Tri's. Of course, all this was mostly a cover to allow us to really get in touch with our virility. Passersby could sense the bromance kindling. All this time we had to spend around women—the ratio didn't favor guy time. We talked all of this guy talk, used deep voices, and gave each other fist-pounds after a good set and talked about how our pecs were sore from the workout that we'd crushed the day before. Then we would heap big-ass piles of pasta onto our plates and watch *Bloodsport*—in which Jean-Claude Van Damme's acting chops, incredibly, make Chuck Norris look like Robert De Niro—and continued to talk, mostly with our mouths full, about nutrition and health and techniques for gaining muscle and losing fat.

"A gram of protein for each pound you weigh," Chris said, speaking with experience. His physique, stout and well formed, hadn't changed much since his college days as a wrestler.

"Yeah," I replied. "Tuna, chicken, peanut butter."

"We'll start making milkshakes," John added. A former football player, he was tall and sturdy, but fleshy around the middle. Over the course of his time in Honduras, he eventually lost twenty-five pounds and looked almost literally like a new man. He added, "I don't know if they'll have tubs of protein powder here, but I've seen bags of powdered milk that could suffice."

And we'd all grunt our approval.

These guys were amusing, always entertaining. Their motivation to travel, like mine, was not an escape or a search necessarily but just a desire to take a moment to see what else was going on in the world.

After midnight, John frequently shuffled through the living room on his way to or from Jennifer's room, wearing nothing but a pair of four-leaf-clover boxers.

"John!" I would proclaim. "Where are your pants, kid? Your pants, man. They're missing! Where are they?"

He would pause and look at me seriously. "Adam, I will tell you this, sir. That is a fair question, my friend." He'd cock his head back to stare up at the ceiling in puzzlement, deep in speculation. "A very fair question, I'll tell you." More speculation as he rubbed the stubble on his chin. "I'll get back to you. Be right back." And then he would scramble off into Jennifer's room until the sun rose.

Meanwhile, Chris had a way of challenging my ability to think critically. In searching for the next horizon he'd left behind his life as an attorney in Vegas. Every other morning I had a different philosophical discussion with him, and in the early evening, reflection. I mostly listened, Chris probably having read five or six books to each of my one over the last ten years. He opened up, hands waving enthusiastically, on American political strategies, social ethics, and his future professional possibilities without having to join the nine-to-five grind. We discussed the best locations to meet women, and we debated the merits of Jesse Ventura's *American Conspiracies*, all the while chowing down a high-protein meal.

It took delicate practice to find the balance between seeing as much as possible and sprinting through this trip. Before leaving home, even after committing to being adaptable, I still had a rough itinerary of the places I wanted to visit and a general idea of what pace I wanted to maintain on my journey. But when I relayed my forecasted itinerary to my friend Scott McKaig back home, he objected.

"Shep, the world has one hundred and ninety-seven million–ish square miles. The countries where you're going in Central America are less than one one-hundredth of one percent of that area. Why so long in one place? Also, no South America? Chile? Argentina? Brazil? You're not going to meet any Brazilian women? And no Africa? At all? That's a tremendous place. Give me Egypt, at least. The pyramids! Jesus. You're racist."

I told him I was excited to one day visit Africa and South America and Eastern Australia and the spots in Asia and Europe and everywhere else that I planned to skip on this trip, but I couldn't see it all, not all at once.

Before I left, I talked to friends and family—heck, even strangers—about my destinations. Some people offered great recommendations; others voiced their disbelief that I was going to spend a full year abroad and I wasn't going to Machu Picchu. Or the Taj Mahal. Or the Great Wall. Or Fiji. Or England. Or Greece. "You're going to miss Scandinavia altogether?" Anki asked, puzzled, back in Guatemala. "You're going to be in Europe and you can't just go up there for a week? Shame."

But this was my trip. I had to do it the way I thought best.

You cram a thousand people in a room, and you're going to receive a thousand different itineraries, all passionately voiced. Even then, those itineraries aren't going to play out as prescribed. That's the beauty of travel in the first place—that we get to create our own journey, and even with all of our planning, we still don't know what's going to happen. The road that lies ahead of the traveler is marvelously shadowed, and that mystery gives each trip an even stronger feeling of adventure. Then, when it's all over, you swap stories with the understanding that someone may take you up on your recommendations or they may forge their very own path instead. Just as you did.

Scott made an interesting point, however, about the duration of time I'd budgeted each place. A month in Guatemala; two months in Honduras; a month in Nicaragua; a month in Costa Rica; a month in New Zealand; a month in Australia; two months in Asia; two months working around Western and Central Europe; my last month in Italy. I could have bought a bus pass and seen thirty hot spots and every country in South America in three months.

But there are vast differences between being a tourist and a traveler. A tourist passes through momentarily for a few snapshots and a ride on the town's zip line, while a traveler hangs around a bit longer to get to know the place more affectionately. The traveler wanders up and down side streets and back alleys, poking their head into every crevice of a city. Neither one is better than the other. Some places I'm a tourist, and others I'm a traveler. I enjoy getting lost and I likewise don't mind ordering a package deal and hopping on a bus for a day, crowded between a bunch of visor-wearing, fanny-packed retirees desiring to learn about history and culture. Two days in Copán sated my appetite for Maya ruins, but I needed a month to really appreciate Beatríz and Antigua the way I did.

I'll never be Honduran. I could lose six inches off my height, crop my hair and dye it black, learn to roll my r's, master the Bachata, and open a produce stand out of the back of my pickup truck on the curve leading into La Ceiba, and I'd still be a North Carolinian. I dip my toes into someone else's world, try on their culture and lifestyle, and return it on departure. This is okay.

But along the way, I can meet John and Chris and Jose, and perhaps shake their hands longer than "How ya doin'?," "Where ya from?," and "Where ya headed?" This, after all, is how you find the best bars, restaurants, and other spots off the Gringo Trail.

Danny, a native Honduran, guided a group of us outsiders to the uppermost waterfall of Pico Bonito, pausing along the way to educate us on the flora and fauna and to entice us to eat termites—Honduras's version of trail mix.

"They feed on wood," I told him.

"They taste like carrots," he declared, swallowing a pinch of ten.

"Really? Hm. Cool. Hey, you know what else tastes like a carrot?" I asked, grinning. "A carrot."

"Protein," he reasoned, eyebrow arched toward his scalp.

I spent four minutes chewing through a finger full of termites. (When one eats a termite, he or she ought to give it a head start on digestion.)

Danny spent his Saturday leading us up a mountain to a vacant swimming hole. An eighty-foot waterfall crashed just on the other side of those boulders, a football toss away. He brought us to this wonderful, remote place all in exchange for, well, nothing. He didn't have to do that. But he got to know us, tendered his friendship, and was proud to show us bits of his country.

None of this would have happened, though, if I'd been passing from one bus stop to the next.

And we didn't shave. Lucky for me, I arrived in El Porvenir, Honduras, just in time to spread my wings of brotherhood with No Shave November. No Shave November, or Movember, started as a way to raise money and bring awareness to a variety of men's health issues. Over time, it morphed into something cool to do, a way to pass time as winter dawns and an excuse—as if you'd need one—to throw a party once the skin above everyone's lip has filled in. Besides, there's never a reason to let your facial hair run wild just for fun. You should always have someone by your side for that adventure.

Spending an entire month gearing up for the Mustachio Bashio is just as nerdy as it sounds, bearing in mind the two byproducts of sporting whiskers: One, you don't have to buy razors or blades. And two, you're going to save money on condoms, because if you have a mustache, you can go ahead and forget about talking to women for a while. Male birth control. These are the two understood consequences of growing a mustache, and you take them with something of a resigned grin—much like the first time your parents forced you to go to camp for the week, because, well, after it's over with, you realize you had a great time canoeing in lakes and playing dodge ball, and you didn't feel the least remorse for the week missed playing video games as you thought you would. All things have opportunity costs, even mustaches.

So there I was at our house, meters from the sands of the beach. A sofa and two loveseats polka-dotted a big living room that blended into the kitchen. Five or six chairs huddled around a dining room table, and on the far wall, a TV sat enthroned by stacks of books on either side. I sported a ten-day-old spotty goatee. The sound of crashing waves flowed through the screened-in porch and into the living room, where the lot of us volunteers had assembled. John told a quick story, and everybody laughed. Chris added a quip; more laughter.

I sprawled out on the sofa, intoxicating myself for courage. Watching Ivana from across the room, I plotted my first move. I always plot. And I have no moves. All the volunteers enjoyed a little preparty as the night kicked off, nursing beer bottles and frolicking about the beach house, one of three gathering spots in our little town and definitely the most popular. Ivana flashed glances at me from her perch on one of the loveseats. I couldn't read these glances. She was glancing at everyone: men and women, tall and short, full beards and peppered cheeks.

She moved to the kitchen to wash the dishes we'd accumulated over the past two days. Still lounging, I watched her from behind. I already knew of her flowing blonde hair and spectacular brown eyes and slight, graceful physique. But as I sat there watching her, she kept smiling this wide smile, this seemingly exaggerated smile as she spoke with the other volunteers. Her hands sunk deep in sudsy water; she nodded and laughed and shook her head in agreement. She said, "You're kidding! I've been there, too! I loved it!" Then, "Oh, wow. And he lives in Iowa? I definitely want to see pictures later."

What's my play here, I thought. *Do I go with the Israel-Palestine conflict on the Gaza Strip or stick with something safer like pop culture?*

"Dishes," I said aloud.

I grabbed Chris's and my dishes and made my move.

"Here's another couple of plates," I offered gallantly, as if to say that I had collected those dishes all by my very self. None of these were her dishes. This wasn't even her house. She lived down the street, where she had her own dishes. Why was she doing our dishes?

"Oh, thank you," she said with her Eastern European cheer.

I leaned against the counter. "I could help, if you'd like."

"No, that's okay. You don't look like you would be very good at doing dishes," she said with a laugh. "But I'd love if you would stay and talk to me."

I didn't understand. This had to be flirting, surely, but I'd never been great at picking up on flirting. "Or, y' know," I replied, "I could dry. THE DISHES. AFTER YOU WASH THEM." I often underestimated her level of English as I came to know her—she spoke eight languages of various proficiency, and with volunteers in our group from all over the world, I didn't know which language had Ivana's attention at any given moment. So I would do what we all do when a foreigner doesn't understand what we're saying: we slow down and yell at them. "I SAID I CAN DRY THE DISHES AFTER YOU WASH THEM," I repeated.

"But we don't need to dry them," she noted, motioning with her left hand. "I just set them in this bin to dry."

"Yeah, that's what I was saying. You hand them to me, and I can set them in the bin." Really, I just wanted to whisk Ivana out to the beach to hold her hand in mine, and I was struggling not to blurt out anything random like "cuddle" or "pretty eyes" or "God, *I-vana* lie on the couch and embrace you in my arms until morning."

So we washed dishes together. She scrubbed them with a ragged cloth and then rinsed them before handing them over. I proceeded to awkwardly move them six inches to the right, setting them in the rack she could have easily reached. We made small talk—mostly about dishes—and I wished I had *one* ounce of skill with women.

She said that this was the start of her second month in Honduras, and her plan was to do a full five months of volunteering with children before heading home to Slovakia. "I graduated from college in June," she added. "I've been saving my money for a long time to take this trip to Central America."

We also took a minute to compare El Porvenir, a small town of seven thousand people and only six or seven two-story houses, with the towns where we came from. El P. is mostly run-down and lacking resources, upshots of an eon of poverty. Houses are concrete shacks—three bedrooms for the *narcos* and the town's aristocracy, two for those with good jobs, one for the fieldworkers. Grass grows sporadically, but there's always a cow dawdling nearby to devour it. The streets are dusty or simply made of dirt. Skirting horse muck becomes a mere formality after being in town for two days. A forty-minute bus ride to La Ceiba is required if you're in search of shopping centers, but El P. has corner *pulperías* selling produce, sauces, spices, tampons, beer, toothpaste, toilet paper, cigarettes, Snickers, diapers, and hair gel. Cars and trucks occasionally drift by in puffs of choking engine exhaust, but it's mostly by foot or bike that people travel in town. Walking about, I often passed a goat ranging on the road or a horse tied to a tree, both claiming living space among four or five chickens per house. Pigs wallowed in backyards, their angry squeals drifting down the street and into town. The people of El Porvenir don't tell stories about what life was like growing up on a farm; their world *is* a farm.

The focus of the town, the center plaza is, of course, the soccer field. Everybody gathers around the soccer field at night to watch the year-round recreational games and to drink a couple of Salvavidas and generally just be tranquil and jolly. That's where you bump into your neighbor; or your aunt; or most certainly, your buddies whom you haven't seen since yesterday.

In the States, there isn't a single place in town where everybody congregates. Which is good and bad, I suppose. I dig the intimate vibe of El Porvenir, but at the same time, with one central social hub, personal business rides the gossip train from one edge of town to the other in just a matter of minutes, and there is little real privacy.

Over the first week of being in El P., my thoughts on living there evolved two times:

Holy shit, I said from the onset. *I could never live like this. This is crazy! Cows trampling down the road? Seriously?*

Then, I made peace with the cows, and the town started to grow on me. *I mean it's not so bad. Very peaceful. Simple. Borders the sea. I could live like this. Yeah, I could definitely live like this.*

Then hot, sticky nights ticked by, and I rationalized, *Okay, I could* live like this. *I mean, it is* possible. *But who would want to live like this when I've got alternatives? I'm telling you, Ma, I could live like this, but after a couple of months here, I'll take back my air-conditioning and energy-efficient washing machines.*

I figured that the only nuisance, really, were the stray dogs, but I tolerated them as the idols I perceived them to be. Besides, I'd already reasoned that in my next life I was coming back as one of them anyway. Everywhere, these stray dogs, and no manner of policing them. They trotted down the dusty street and in and out of strangers' backyards, overlong nails clicking against the wooden and concrete porches. They just existed in their own little aloof world, alongside but segregated from the people of El Porvenir. And that world, for them, was idyllic.

Hm. What do I feel like doing right now? a stray dog in Honduras—Victor we'll call him—asks himself. *Hm. I'm just not sure. Oh, I know! I'm hungry! I think I'll eat something.* So Victor scavenges for something to eat. No problem. (Many stray dogs are emaciated and skeletal, no doubt, but then some plump dog steals down the street with a chicken in his mouth. I would be that dog.) Victor then wanders around aimlessly for ten minutes. *Hm. Now, what do I want to do? Let me think. Let me think. I know! I'd like to go to the bathroom.* So Victor takes a crap, wherever he happens to be at the moment. This is *his* world, and his world is a bathroom, too. *All right, feeling good. Feeling good.* Again he circles the village aimlessly for ten minutes but grows restless. *Gosh,* now *what is there to do?* he asks himself. *Oh, I know! I think I'd like to make some love. Yeah, that's it. Make some love, doggy-style.* He looks around. *But to whom shall I make love?* He peers down the street. Well, lookie there! It's his girlfriend, Katrina! Victor approaches her. She bats her eyes. She's been waiting for him, knows what's coming next. Doesn't matter who's watching. They're stray dogs in Honduras; they can do whatever they please, wherever they please. Victor and his girlfriend get it on for ten minutes. *Now what?* he asks himself rhetorically, for he already knows the answer. *Why it's nap time, of course! And darn it if I'm not going to make my bed over here under the shade of this tree, because this town is my town, and in my town, I get to eat, shit, sleep, and fornicate on my own terms.*

Now that is the life. Sure, my life span as a dog is going to be eighteen months or so before I'm stoned to death by the owner of that chicken in my mouth, but that's going to be a glorious eighteen months. And besides, after my dog life, I'll come back as a ninja anyway, and then I'm looking at a lifespan of at least three hundred years.

Placing plates and forks into the bin, I stammered through all of my thoughts on stray dogs with Ivana. She simulated interest, looking as if she was wondering why, if karma was real, my bumbling presence served as the reward for her voluntarily washing someone else's dishes.

But the night was young, as they say. The preparty wrapped up, cabs arrived, and we headed to the club. I don't love spending time on a crowded dance floor, but I played along. I bought four drinks and set them in front of myself, Anna, John, and Danny. I acted the part of Tom Sawyer playing with the other kids across the yard in an effort to get Becky Thatcher's attention. Showing off, I call it. This was my move. Don't buy Ivana a drink; let her buy her own drink. That'll win her heart. Go get 'em, champ.

I stepped outside to the patio to hang with Chris and John, who also didn't like the idea of dancing without women. Let the girls dance in their little Girl Circles. Ivana came around, and we started chatting again. My second chance. I don't remember exactly what I said, but it wasn't a complete fail, because the next moment found me on the dance floor with her. This was a sure enough female repellent, but if she was going to eventually find out that I dance as if a swarm of mosquitoes is attacking my lower back, then we might as well get it out from the kickoff.

We danced. I managed to step out of my self-consciousness enough to enjoy the way she moved—graceful swaying and spinning to spicy tunes pumped out by two tiny speakers by the bar. She gave me two songs and then pulled me out into the chilly rain to talk. She said she liked the rain. The water pouring from a leaden sky plastered my yellow shirt against my body and had the same effect on her blouse. My skin tingled. I could see fifteen feet ahead, but not twenty. Lights shone faintly in the distance, probably a lamp in someone's bedroom.

We were alone. Ivana's sunny blonde hair darkened and clumped, strands clinging to her face and neck. She wore no makeup; there was no mascara trail running down her cheeks. I was cold and wet and shivering, a pathetic little puppy. But she was smiling as she leaned against the railing, and there was nowhere in the world I wanted to be more at that moment than right there in the eye of the storm chatting with quite literally the most beautiful girl I have ever seen in person. It was euphoric, that moment.

Part of me thought: *Kiss her! Do it! Now! This is your shot! Seize the motherfucking day, baby!*

And the other part of me thought: *Seriously, dude. Look at you. You are bloody mad if you think she's going to kiss you back.*

And then the first part of me thought of the second part: *You're an ass.*

I glanced at my watch. Eighteen minutes we had been out there in the rain. Eighteen minutes. This had to be a test of some sort, a standoff to see whether I would duck back inside first. We spoke of the world, of places traveled and destinations desired. The rain let up, and we headed back in for more dancing, a good sign that she wasn't irritated by my stiff movements.

I had another drink as the two o'clock hour approached. Six of us caught two cabs home. Anna sat behind the driver, Ivana in the middle, and I settled in on the right. I pulled out my camera and curled my left arm around Ivana's neck. I held the camera out in front of us, kissed her on the cheek, and snapped a photo. Another of my moves. *Screw it. What is she going to do? Tell John and Chris what a creep I am? Let's go ahead and get it all out there.*

She smiled. I grinned. We asked the cab to stop at a street vendor for *baleadas*—folded tortillas stuffed with beef, beans, eggs, and cheese—and I bought one for everyone. Big spender. Slightly intoxicated and heavily enamored, I would have emptied my pockets at Ivana's request. Lord knows I'd emptied them for less appealing gambles.

We were back at her house by 2:30, but she'd forgotten her key so we couldn't get in. We talked outside, sitting on the padded porch swing, while we waited for someone to return. At 3:30, everyone else came home, and we all spilled inside. The spot I'd staked on the couch was immediately revoked. I wasn't going to walk home that late in Honduras, so I'd planned to sleep on the couch, but Carly, little Carly from Canada who shared a room with Ivana, was having none of that. She'd had at least a quarter of her body weight in rum and Cokes—light on the Coke—and she was adamant, with a dose of militancy, about crashing on the couch so she could watch a movie as she fell asleep.

Delighted at the opportunity to move closer to Ivana, I collapsed on Carly's bed, five feet away from Ivana's bed. I'd been assertive but not aggressive that night, and I never got the kiss. I would have traded twenty kisses with twenty pretty girls for one kiss with Ivana that night. She was funny and peppy and unassuming and compassionate. She did *our* dishes, a house full of dishes that weren't even hers. But the kiss never happened, and I drifted off, defeated but buoyant, just before five in the morning.

At 5:30, Ivana woke me up. "Adam!" she whispered urgently. "Adam!"

I cracked my eyes open and groaned. Blinking my vision clear, I propped myself up on one elbow. Ivana was clearly flustered, worried about something. She said there was a guy outside her window and she edged out of her blankets and closer to me. I sat up. Rubbed the grit from my eyes. My foggy, sleep-deprived mind figured this must be a ruse, Ivana making her move on me, clever girl. But I was wrong, and her wide eyes and pale face showed that she actually did think there was a guy outside of her window. I uttered one word: "okay." I let out a single, sardonic laugh. I mean, there was a dude outside her window. Okay. But she was serious and clearly shaken. I said nothing more. From there, we simply dissected the expressions on each other's mugs. She seemed to be thinking, *What can you do about it?* My exact thoughts were: *Are you kidding me! I already bought* baleadas! *And now this man out there? What . . .uh . . . what do you want me to do about this exactly, babe? You want me to go out there? Like, outside? And* talk *to this man? Really? I already bought* baleadas! Sensing—from just my sarcastically raised brow—my utter lack of masculinity, she nodded and remarked, "I think I'd better go get John."

I'll pause here, as you have to understand one thing before you judge me. The violence in Honduras is bad. Really bad. Honduras consistently ranks in the top three in the world for murders per capita. As I sat up in Carly's bed, all tangled in pink sheets, I couldn't help but recall that Honduras was—and had been for a while—the reigning champion of murders in the world, in fact, with the United Nations reporting more annual murders per hundred thousand (eighty-six) in Honduras than any other country on the globe.

Eighty-six out of one hundred thousand. Not far from one in a thousand. That's a staggering number. Consider that the odds of playing in the NBA are about one out of seventy thousand. If, for my ninth birthday party, I asked for a basketball and declared,

"I'm going to play in the NBA, daddy, just like Michael Jordan!" he would have said, "Go for it, son. Work real hard in the gym, eat your green beans, be nice to your mother, and you can do it." But the reality is that I had a much (much!) better chance of taking a bullet to the chest when I visited Honduras as a twenty-nine-year-old. Pops should have bought me a set of body armor for my birthday.

And the region where I lived was as dangerous as anywhere in the country. Five of the fifty-eight nights I stayed in El Porvenir, I heard gunshots cracking through the night. The restaurant two-and-a-half blocks from our house, Juaquin's, was robbed one Thursday at noon—at *noon*—and the owner's son drew his own gun and fired down the street as the robber skedaddled. (Coincidentally, a woman named Maura currently owned the restaurant, as Juaquin had been murdered two years prior. She couldn't find it in her heart to change the name.)

We had been warned not to walk around after dark. Charlie, one of Honduras Child Alliance's directors, had warned us not to check our e-mail at the El Porvenir Inn—the only hotel in town and one of two places to use the Internet—because he'd heard that one of Honduras's biggest drug dealers was staying there. "Yeah, okay, sounds good, Charlie," I remarked with rolling eyes, but four days later, that drug dealer was gunned down along with his three cronies in the middle of a party.

Two days before I arrived in El Porvenir, they found a body diced into pieces in the pineapple fields and could only identify it by the clothes that the guy was wearing the day he disappeared.

On December 15 at ten o'clock in the morning, the lot of us volunteers and children alike cowered together behind a barricade in the church after hearing two rapid-fire gunshots that couldn't have been ninety yards away. My heart pounded as I spread my arms around a few of the kids, keeping them low and trying to reassure them. They just blinked back at me, sadly rather used to this sort of event. Moments later, we watched a truck full of police officers whiz by.

Four days after that, right before Christmas recess, the brother of one of our kids was murdered. The killers sent one of his eyeballs to his family.

And on and on, to say nothing of the armed robberies and sexual assaults that are the backwash of a poverty-stricken country with an anemic educational system. In Raleigh, North Carolina, if there's a killing, you can bet on comprehensive local coverage of the investigation, the trial, and the aftermath. In Honduras, the newspapers couldn't keep up with it all, so they quit trying. Even if nearly all of this bloodshed is related to gangs or narcotics, El Porvenir is a town of just seven thousand people, too few for so much violence, and no one is safe from the crossfire.

So, there I was, having heard and lived through so many of these stories already, when Ivana woke me with this business about a guy outside her window. "Okay" seemed a fair response. Barbed wire laced the top of the concrete walls barricading the house. Besides, even if this shadow man had worked his way through that obstruction, sturdy, steel bars were bolted over every door and window, completely securing the house against intruders. This man was not getting in.

Ivana had nevertheless diagnosed my expression and made her decision. "I think I'd better go get John," she said, averting her gaze. *I think I'd better go get a man.*

She crept out of the room and down the hallway to knock on John's door. John emerged a moment later in his drawers, alert because he'd been watching a movie with Jennifer. He paused to put on his chain mail and to grab his lance. Here I was trying to slyly put the moves on Ivana when John came prancing out atop his white stallion. What a jerk! He popped the door open to go outside, I mean without *any* hesitation. And he was tender, as well: he was gently trying to explain to Ivana about the monsters under her bed and the bogeyman, while also getting in the right mindset to take care of the man, that phantom man, on the other side of Ivana's window. "It's okay, Ivana," he murmured, understanding and sympathy in his tone. He laid one gentle hand on her shoulder. "I have nightmares, too, from time to time. I'll go have a look, and

we'll get this resolved. It's going to be all right." *This motherfucker.*
Eight or nine hours I put in trying to woo Ivana, and in ninety
seconds this worm had slithered in to show her what I was lacking.

He flipped on the exterior lights and stepped into the open.
I knelt in the doorway, taking as long as I could to tie my shoes.
I was probably twenty steps or so behind him as he turned the
corner. A fraction of a second later, he started screaming at a dude,
who was, in fact, right outside of Ivana's bedroom window. There
was actually a dude. *Interesting.* I froze, and my sphincter muscle
tightened while John strong-armed this guy. John confessed to
us later that he'd thought Ivana was crying wolf, again, yet there
he was—this man, this drunk swaying man—right outside our
window, having worked his way through quite a challenging
barricade. It was very bizarre.

So John, our gallant hero, sprang from around the corner,
pushing and screaming at this dude. And dig this: all of a sudden,
his Spanish was fluent. He knew *exactly* what to say to this guy—
his sentence structure, his conjugation, everything was flawless.
He formed all twenty-two words of his vocabulary into completely
coherent sentences and let this fellow know he had best not come
back 'round these parts ever again. Jennifer stood in the front
doorway, gripping a knife from the kitchen—this blade must have
been at least nine inches, a minimachete—and she screamed:
"You don't want me to come out there!" John pushed the guy out.
One hundred percent valor.

Moving forward from that cowardly night, my reputation slowly
continued to slump with the fellas. Sunday afternoon, we went
into La Ceiba—Chris, John, and I—to watch football, but I
couldn't understand all the football jargon. I just sat there and
repeated what everyone said. Chris would say something about
the Packers' secondary tackling the other football men, and I
would just say, "Yeah, yeah, that crazy secondary with their crazy
tackles. Peyton Manning, making passes. And running the ball.
Passes. And y'know, the touchdowns, of course. Ha, the secondary.
Budweiser. Craziness."

The workouts and dinners lasted the duration of my stay in Honduras, but as much as I learned from Danny and John and Chris, and as much fun as we had, I couldn't be taken seriously by these guys. Or Ivana.

I had truly lived up to my new name: Adam Without Eve.

But I persisted. I lost Ivana that night with one word—*okay*—and worked for nearly two months to get her back. She gave me plenty of chances: we rode bikes together to admire the sunrise over the pineapple fields; we ate *jocotes* in the park under a hazy afternoon sky; I walked her to Kinder, her volunteering site, and if she had a stack of books, I would have carried those, too; we sat on her stoop and talked; she sang.

She was witty and clever and fit and vibrant and inquisitive. The kids blitzed their way to her whenever she entered the room. She was fun and she was focused and she was relaxed amid turbulence. She listened. She was passionate, and she was kind. Confident. Humble.

I remember when one of the volunteers was sick and dragging from her bedroom to the bathroom like a zombie. Ivana came home from a long day of working with the children, took a look at her, and immediately left for the corner store. She said: "I think she needs some dinner." Ivana spent an hour in the kitchen cooking this wonderful meal for her. She organized it beautifully on a plate, knocked on her door, and gave it to her, and then she and I went over to the beach house to watch a movie. Nothing more was mentioned about it. Ivana hadn't made this dinner because she wanted to be recognized or to put a down payment on a future return favor. Her friend simply needed a meal, so Ivana made one.

I listened to her talking on the phone one day. Her friend Adel, back in Slovakia, had passed some kind of major exam, and upon hearing this news, Ivana immediately called her. "This is crazy!" she screamed into the phone. They spoke for fifteen minutes, jabbering syllables of a language I did not know. But I didn't need to know Slovak in order to understand Ivana's enthusiasm. She laughed, bringing a flush of color to her cheeks. She sat up, then stood, then paced from one end of the living room to the next, all the while waving her hands. She *really* cared; she expressed a genuine happiness for Adel, excitement for what this would mean for her friend's burgeoning career. When a friend gets married or has a baby, you buy them a rice cooker or knit them some booties and wish them well; but there was a level of sincerity, of loyalty, to this phone call that I hadn't seen many places.

One morning, Ivana said to me, "Okay, so you can't cook. How about you buy the food? I will cook it. And I will train you on the dishes."

In return, I said awkward things, and she wondered whether I was kidding or serious.

I tried, but my game continued to fall flat. I longed to return to that dance club. Wanted to go back to standing in the rain. Why hadn't I kissed her then? Thousands of miles from home in a foreign and often dangerous world—why couldn't I just have taken one more chance, one more risk? My cowardice might have leapfrogged me into the friend zone.

Worse, I had to struggle with the realization that I just might not have been good enough for this girl. For me, there was an instant attraction, and I thought how awesome it was that I could meet such a wonderful young lady in a place so different from my home, but she acted as if I was just another guy along the way. Here she was, the girl worth writing home about, and here I was, fumbling the ball. The idea that I might not be good enough for her was a tough one for me to swallow.

But I stuck with it, and she hung around. We sat on the beach; we watched soccer in the square; we went through a stack of movies; we delivered meals to Astrid's mom in the slums; we ran; I bought food, she cooked, I ate.

She taught me how to cut a pineapple without wasting any, and I taught her slang in English. We tossed kids around during the day and taught English to adults by night.

And then we kissed.

It was drizzling the first time. I walked her home one night after all the volunteers had gotten together for dinner. I had no coat or umbrella, but this wasn't a messy or chilly rain. She walked under the big tree in front of her house, and I followed. She smiled, and I wanted to kiss her. None of this was unusual: it rained almost every day in Honduras; I often forgot to bring a coat or umbrella; and the desire to kiss her had been present since that first night in the beach house doing dishes.

Unusual, though, was that I garnered the courage to actually do it. Even more unusual, she kissed me back.

And no one shot off any fireworks in the background. The planets did not align, and the skies did not burst open. It was just two silly gringos standing alone on a gravel road in the rain. But, for me, it was pretty great.

There were more kisses. There was hand-holding. There were smiles exchanged across rooms.

And there were letters. On day three in El Porvenir, I wrote my first note to Ivana, but I didn't give it to her until weeks later, just before I left Honduras. I wrote pages about all her stunning qualities: that she can hold a conversation with anyone in the room; that she had already seen so much in her life yet still found simple pleasures in everyday occurrences; that she sat down to study Spanish for an hour despite her desire to be out playing; that she was confident enough to stand by an unpopular view and that she was humble enough to admit when she was wrong.

I wrote how happy I was to have been able to get to know her, and then I closed it:

There is no concealed purpose or agenda for this note. I just want you to know that I'm really glad to have met you. If you maintain the same attitude, you're going to do great things in your life, and I'm excited for you. It would be nice for our paths to cross again one day, but failing that, I wish you the best in everything you do.

I came to Honduras to enjoy my independence; to read and write and call my parents every couple of days and sit down in a comfy chair with a glass of wine to think. I came to El Porvenir to volunteer with a great organization and then move along. I did not come to El P. to woo women.

I was baffled on so many levels, but mostly I couldn't tell whether Ivana had serious feelings for me or whether I was the fling with that one American kid back in Honduras. I couldn't tell where this was going. I struggled with the idea that I'd found a fantastic girl but maybe it was only starting to go well because she knew she didn't have to take things seriously. That this would all be over soon. That we would soon go our separate ways, ensuring that no commitment was necessary. That maybe she saw me as worthy enough for a walk on the beach, but nothing long-term. That I had met my match, but the feelings were not reciprocal.

I needed answers. The idea that I might not ever see her again after Honduras didn't sit well with me.

"What are you going to do after Honduras?" I asked her one day while we were checking our e-mail on Charlie's tiled front porch. There were a high ceiling above us and tall pillars around us.

"What do you mean? Where am I going to go or what am I going to do with my life?"

"Go. Where are you going to go?"

"Home. To Slovakia."

"Oh," I said. "Cool."

We sat in silence for three or four minutes. Charlie's dog, Mocha, moseyed over looking for a rub behind his ears.

"I'm going to go to Nicaragua and then to New Zealand, probably," I told her. Our relationship had been intimate for a while, but I wanted to veer away from "this one cute girl I knew once when I was in my twenties and volunteering in Honduras" and toward "there's a chance you're the girl for me, so let's go ahead and chat for a minute about the next step."

"Oh," she said. "Cool."

Two more minutes of silence. This wasn't going well. She left the front porch and went to the bathroom. She came back.

"Oh, hi," I said. "I was just looking up some things online here about New Zealand. For instance, did you know that there are nine sheep to every one human in New Zealand? Also, for each person who lives there, the country produces one hundred kilograms of butter and sixty-five kilograms of cheese each year. That's a lot of dairy. Also, Sir Edmund Hillary is from there. He climbed Mount Everest. And, now this is exciting, there are no snakes in the whole country. No snakes. Hm. Really fascinating stuff going on there in the country of the Kiwis. That's what the people are called. Kiwis. Not like the fruit, though. Like the bird. There's the kiwifruit, which you already know about, but there's also a kiwi bird. Fat little fella, with an elongated beak and—"

"Elongated?"

"Yeah, long."

She was busy crafting an e-mail to her mom, and the topic of New Zealand rested for the balance of the day. The next day, late morning, I considered my next move. I wanted to maximize my opportunity. When the ice cream truck went by, I said to her, "Hey babe, we could get some ice cream?" And she said, "No thanks. It's loaded with sugar, and sugar turns to fat. I don't want to get fat. But thank you, though."

Later, in the afternoon, back on Charlie's front porch, I got out of my chair and took a step toward her for a kiss.

"Honey, what is that on your lip?" she asked.

"A cold sore."

"A cold sore? You mean, like herpes?"

"Well, I mean. Yeah. I guess. I mean, I guess. Yeah. Kinda like herpes."

"Oh, okay. It's kind of sickening."

"Well, I mean, it could be worse."

"It gets worse?"

"Well, I mean—"

"Maybe we don't kiss for a while."

So many things had been going right for me, but I just couldn't catch the break I wanted at that moment: to find the right time to invite her to travel with me. So I just came out with it. We were sitting at the small table just outside of Charlie's front door. Ivana had her hair set in two hanging braids. The sun was bright, but the day was pleasant rather than hot and sticky. I blurted out, "Y'know, I was thinking you could come to New Zealand, too."

What is this? What are we? Are we dating? Are we friends with benefits? Are my benefits getting ready to be revoked? Good Lord, this is an awkward defining-the-relationship-type conversation, jumping directly into, "Hey, when we leave this region, let's go ahead and spend literally every minute of every day together nowhere near any of our friends and family and just kind of see how it goes."

"To New Zealand?" she asked.

"Right."

"To do what?"

"New Zealand."

She thought about this for a minute. We shot a few cracks to ease the tone of the conversation, but then I smiled. "I'm serious," I said. "You should come with me."

"This is a big decision," she said as we looked out onto the dusty streets of El Porvenir. "A very big decision."

"Yeah, of course it is. Take all the time you need."

She looked apprehensive, but I couldn't tell whether she was worried about our budding relationship or about how she would be able to afford more travel.

"You'd still be technically on your way home," I noted. "We'd just make some stops along the way."

She ducked back to her computer and said, "I'm going to need some time to think about it."

Border Jam

So I finished volunteering in Honduras. The next stop beckoned, and besides, this country I'd spent the past two months in was becoming increasingly dangerous. Peace Corps volunteers had been beaten and robbed over the last couple of years, two of them killed. Then, one more was shot in the arm during a routine bus robbery, and the director of the Peace Corps, completely fed up, ordered the extraction of all of their volunteers from Honduras.

I took a ferry to Útila, one of the Bay Islands snuggled in the Caribbean, and after four days, earned my scuba certification. I started introducing myself in social settings as "Adam Shepard, certified scuba diver."

Then I caught the bus for Nicaragua. An oversold bus schedule left me stranded in Tegucigalpa for a three-day layover. Tegucigalpa: the Honduran capital, the pit of the earth and don't let anyone tell you otherwise. If you ever find yourself mad at your life, fly down to Tegus, that bustling, decrepit place, and you'll come to appreciate everything you have back home. The people are nice enough, but you'll have a hard time noticing them over the odious city landscape—the dilapidated buildings almost leaning against one another as they decay, the grimy sidewalks, the pungent market stalls.

Then, to escalate my troubles, as I finally crossed the border from Honduras to Nicaragua, the immigration official at the window frowned and signaled me to a back room. Confused, I followed him back to a cramped office. He preferred to remain standing as he informed me that I'd overstayed my visa by five days. Despite his otherwise aggravated tone, I caught a flicker of sympathy on his face as I stared down the barrel of a very fat fine.

"You understand," he said with a sigh, a placid demeanor now, frowning down at my passport as if it was just as much at fault as I was, "that this is a very big problem."

There were no shady side rooms with men wearing latex gloves; he wasn't going to lock me up in a dank prison cell for the weekend or call in his superiors to give me a shakedown. His tired eyes said he knew I wasn't deliberately doing anything illegal; he knew my pack wasn't stuffed with sacks of marijuana. But matter-of-factly, I'd overstayed my welcome. I'd misunderstood the CA-4 alliance among Honduras, Nicaragua, El Salvador, and Guatemala, and I'd been in the region five days past the allotted ninety.

"Hm. I don't understand," I said sincerely, leaning forward and pointing to my passport. I was prepared to pay a fine and any other punishment as long as I could understand what I'd done wrong. "I was in Guatemala for thirty days, and then I came into Honduras. I thought my ninety days started over when I entered Honduras."

Fidgeting with the shiny badge attached to his breast pocket, he explained the precise legalities of the CA-4 alliance, and I pondered about how the precise legalities of the CA-4 alliance were a bunch of bullshit. But so are all short-term tourist visas. "Get serious!" I wanted to scream. "I'm spending my money here, fine sir! So you want to limit my time and how much money I can spend here? I'm having fun! You want me to take my money elsewhere? Get serious." I was baffled. I stared out the window at a flat, dry land giving way to rolling hills demanding yet more exploration. I blew a frustrated sigh through my lips. *Why do they want me to leave? Do they think I'm going to hang out too long in Central America because I'm illicitly stealing someone's job?*

"I'm an American citizen," I said, searching for some tactic that would get me out of this dingy back room. "Does that count for something?"

He said, "Buddy, your mom smells like the poo of an African gray parrot, and your dad herds Peruvian goats for a living. I don't give a turd if you are the most valuable batsman on Sri Lanka's national cricket team. You have violated the CA-4." At least that's what he might have said. I couldn't be sure. Dozens of Spanish syllables rolled off his tongue at a blistering pace, and I'm best with the slow-motion variety of Spanish.

I told him he had to ease up if we had any chance of sorting this out. Or, at the very least, provide subtitles.

"Well," I offered. "I'm not sure exactly what to do. I obviously didn't understand the rule here, and for that I'm sorry."

I'm sorry. That's what I said. *I'm sorry.* As if I'd dribbled mustard from my hot dog over the bleachers' edge and onto his crisp, clean replica jersey at a soccer game. *I'll pay for the dry cleaning, sir. I'm sorry.* This hombre, as affably as possible, was explaining to me that I'd broken international law, and I shot him a little "whoopsy daisy."

"Yes, I understand that you're sorry," he pronounced with authority, "but you have to understand that this is a very big problem." These security people live to give others a hard time. This is how it is all over the world, of course, but Latinos love being hard on Americans especially, because our visa policies for them are much, much stricter than the CA-4 is for us.

But I'd broken the rules, and this was a problem. "A very big problem," he kept telling me. I limped along in conversation, steadily: "Well, I do understand that, but I'm not sure exactly what to do here. It appears that my options are limited." I wasn't mad or hostile. My tone, though laced with suppressed frustration, came out as calm as I could make it. I knew this wasn't going to end well for me, but I also knew it wasn't going to end with me sitting in a cell with a hole as a toilet, fighting for elbow room amid a gang of smutty outlaws. I'd resigned myself to the hefty penalty that loomed ahead, money shaved from my funds, which would likely land in the border official's motor scooter fund, and then I'd be on my way. A day ruined, a lesson learned. "I thought I understood the law here," I continued, "but I guess I didn't. Listen, I feel bad. All I wanted to do was come to Honduras and visit and be a volunteer, and—"

"Volunteer? You've been volunteering?"

"Yes, sir. Two months in El Porvenir, and now I'm going down to volunteer in Puerto Cabezas, Nicaragua."

"Well, son," he said, nodding. "All I can say is thank you for the service you have done for my country." He reached his calloused hand out to shake mine. He scribbled something in my passport—which I couldn't read then, nor can I now—signed it, and ambled off to help the next person in line.

I couldn't believe it. The nominal per capita GDP in Honduras is just over 4 percent of what it is in the United States. Four percent! Put another way, it takes a Honduran citizen twenty-five years to earn an average U.S. citizen's annual salary. That guy, that pudgy junior-grade border patrol agent, with his glossy badge and his fancy pleated pants and his lazy Friday nights at home with TV dinners, could have eaten heartily for three weeks on the money he knows I was getting ready to pull out of my pocket. And nobody would have known.

But he didn't care about that. He smiled, shook my hand, and he let me go.

NICARAGUA

That One Dude

The summer after my sophomore year of college, I studied abroad in Seville, Spain, for a month. I was with a group of friends in an elegant downtown shopping district one Saturday afternoon. There was a homeless guy sitting off to the right, who was missing a leg below the knee. He had a basket and a sign that proclaimed SAVING FOR A FERRARI. ALMOST THERE. PLEASE HELP. I tossed in a few pesetas.

Then, another guy ambled by. His shorts were tattered at the bottoms, his shirt was holey. He had an untidy beard and stringy black hair. He looked as if he hadn't showered since Tuesday morning.

He had a daypack behind him and a camera—a really nice camera—strapped around his neck. He was looking around with the wonderment of a mime inside a real box, yet he was moving as if he had somewhere to be. I watched him until he turned the corner and was out of sight.

What is he looking at? I wondered. *Where has he been, and more important, where is he going?*

I value a daily bath, but I want to be that dude otherwise. Much like the first time one sees a guy strumming a guitar and determines to be a musician or goes to see *Batman* and immediately runs home to sketch plans for a Halloween costume, this guy inspired me.

Ever since that Saturday, I have striven to live my life pleased with my station and always anticipating the next destination.

Straight from California!

"**F**uck it," I said. "Give me the *sombra*."

I reached for the red cloth—nay *snatched* for the red cloth. I wanted in. These brave guys, juvenile to grizzly, bolting into the ring, teasing and taunting this wild bull, a balancing act between valor and a gutted belly. I had scouted enough. I snatched my improvised red sombra. I peered up into the crowd of spectators: a gang of teenagers, some whipping their shirts in circles above their heads, a family—mom, dad, daughter—a group of ladies dressed in pink and yellow sundresses, another gang of teenagers. Seven hundred people, at least—eight hundred, more likely. I lowered myself from the support of the bleachers. I sucked in a deep breath. I strode out into the sphere of fervor. And I stood, legs braced and every muscle ready for action. Six feet away, this great hulking beast stood in a similar stance, head low, horns tilted toward my chest. He scraped the earth with one hoof, hugging and snorting like something out of a nightmare.

As a twenty-year-old in southern Spain, I traveled on the weekends with the twelve other students studying abroad from Merrimack College. We visited all the usual hotspots beyond our base of Seville: Granada, Málaga, Cadiz, Córdoba, Ronda, and Matalascañas.

One weekend we traveled to the oldest bullring in the world to witness a bullfight. At first it was gripping: the atmosphere created by a thousand voices lifted in cheer and taunting, the excitement raised by the danger of the dance. But as the event trudged along, I began to sense that it was all counterfeit, forged. The bull thunders into the ring, pissed and confused. He tosses his head, mighty horns and all, back and forth—hunting for blood. They haven't fed him for a couple of days. No water either. Sometimes they tie string around his balls to rile him up even more. A matador taunts him with a red cape, swirling it in flourishes and then letting it hang down for the bull's furious charge. The beast charges straight through, spinning back when he realizes it's not a person—or anything else he can gore for that matter—and he snorts, confused and pissed again. Rinse, repeat three or four times. Toreros dance about on graceful feet, taunting the bull. They prick him with lances as the matador steps out of the arena to grab some chips and a Coke. He returns, cape in hand, for a few more passes with the bull. Finally, as the bull tires and weakens from the matador's numerous passes and the toreros' incessant taunting, the matador drives a sword—a barbaric move, I dare say—deep into the bull's back, just on the other side of his neck. With an agonized bellow, the bull stumbles first to his knees and then onto his side. Dead by the hand of the matador. Often matadors aren't able to drive the sword into the exact right place and a second sword is required. It's a messy affair.

Then the matador circles the ring to cheers and applause. He bows, proud grin firmly in place, as he collects bouquets of roses tossed from the audience.

This is all admirable and valiant—so say southern Spaniards— but the bull never has a chance. From the beginning, you *know* that the matador carries a distinct advantage over the bull, and you *know* that the bull will die. It's six against one. You know that the toreros stand ready to assist the matador and that if anything goes wrong, which basically never happens, the toreros will step in to save the day. The matador will return home with the prettiest girl in the land, and the bull will go home to accompany a plate of rice and veggies. There's little room for alternate endings to this long-practiced game. It's a good show, I suppose, but it reminds me more of professional wrestling's folding chairs than the bare knuckles of ultimate fighting.

In Nicaragua, though, they've got it right.

After my hiccup at the border, I had a feeling that Nicaragua was going to present a rousing experience. Upon my arrival at Ometepe Island, the largest island on Central America's largest lake, Jhonas asked me whether I'd like to ride on top of the bus instead of down below, and I leapt right up there with him. And it naturally turned out to be the best bus ride of my life. At one of the stops, I tore eighty córdobas out of my pocket, and the guy in the orange hat up top with us swooped into a store. He reappeared a few moments later balancing four beers in his arms, one for each of us riding topside. I don't love beer, don't even like it really, but I'm telling you there's something liberating about riding on the roof of a bus on a sunny day, ducking under occasional tree branches and sipping a cold drink.

Jhonas: the worst trail guide in the Western Hemisphere, maybe the world, and also my most vital companion in Nicaragua. He was the guy to know in town. I met him in transition to Finca Magdalena, where I stayed for my eight days on Ometepe, and he had invited me to follow him up Volcán Maderas.

He was short, trim, and agile—three quality traits in a hiking guide—and cordial as anyone I'd encountered in Nicaragua. "Tomorrow, we go. You and me," he said, in English, smiling. "I have man from England and German, also. It be fun."

I wanted to relax, but I needed a workout, so I casually agreed to climb. For the next forty-eight hours, I stood just behind his right shoulder as we skipped from one adventure to the next. We rifled through town to find a replacement for my broken bag just in time to catch the bus to Balgüe. After relinquishing our throne at the top of the bus and dropping my things in my room, we walked twenty minutes to the Festival del Niño de Dios. As I've said before, Christmastime is one long party in Central America. Many workers get an extra month's paycheck in December as an end-of-year bonus, and nearly every man in rural Nicaragua starts drinking on December 1 and doesn't stop until a final weekend in January when everything is laid on the table for one ultimate weekend fiesta, an unadulterated blowout: fireworks, food, booze, dancing, games.

And bullfighting.

"Ah," I remarked to Jhonas as we watched the first few cycles of bulls, "this is the right kind of bullfighting." He tilted his head at me, not understanding. He didn't know any different. This was the only bullfighting he knew. In Spain, *matador* translates literally as *killer*. In Nicaragua, *torero* means *I can't afford a shiny sword and*

that tight matador's uniform, nor do I really want to deal with the
messy cleanup of dragging a slain bull out of the ring, so I'm just
going to stand here and flirt with him a little with this red cloth.
Nicaraguans choose simplicity over grandeur. One of the toreros
wore sandals. And this makes for a more authentic experience.
Fewer rules, less restraint. More recklessness, less certainty.
Exactly how it should be: a bull and a dude with a section of red
cloth. Fate hangs in the balance. *No, no. Just wait. Let's see what*
happens here. This is going to get good.

Out back and out of sight of the audience, cowboys infuriate
the bull before his entrance to the ring. "Bravo," they say, as in, "Hey
there, buddy. You might want to wait for the next one. This bull
is too bravo for you." So, after the bull has been transformed into
a stubborn, angry whirlwind of hooves and horns, it takes three
horsemen to drag him into the ring by three ropes tied around
his neck. As you can imagine, this upsets him even more. He digs
his hooves into the soft soil, creating deep ruts as the mounted
cowboys drag him forward. He thrashes his horns against the side
of the gate, a rattling sound that echoes up into the stands where
the audience sits almost breathless. In the ring now, the bull's black
eyes roll left to right in confusion. He wants blood. To show the
crowd that they're really going to piss him off, the cowboys tie the
bull taut to a post—by his neck again—so they can saddle him up.

By this time, the bull is raging. He bucks furiously, trying
anything to break free from restraint. Laughing, the cowboys
dodge his flailing hooves. The post groans as the bull throws
his weight away from it again and again. I begin to wonder how
long that piece of wood can withstand the bull's assault before it
cracks and lets the beast loose. The anticipation thickens among
the audience. I feel it passing through me, contagious.

Every bull is new, after all, and anything can happen. If you
go skydiving, you'll scream and plummet thousands of feet, but
nothing bad is really going to happen. The parachute is one pull
away, so enjoy your flight. Bungee jumping? Same thing: accidents
are rare. So you just enjoy the view. And the whiplash. And on and
on, from rafting to skiing to paragliding to wakeboarding to any

other leisure activity through the wilderness where you're trying to become more skillful with each Saturday afternoon.

But bullfighting on Ometepe Island? Those guys got it right. Put it down with BASE jumping and free-climbing, although short of Philippe Petit pacing a tightrope from the roof of one Twin Tower to the other without a safety harness. Excitement correlates with increased negligence and lack of regulation, as anything can—and inevitably does—happen. In that world, only three things exist: a bull, a ring, and you. And you don't want to be the one-in-single-digit statistic being dragged out of the arena, serenaded by a gasping crowd.

So some ballsy Nicaraguan guy crawls out of a bottle of rum, throws a few prayers at the sky, and clumsily scrambles onto the bull's back. The cowboys pull their knots free and scatter. The bull tears away from the post, off on an eight- or ten- or twenty- or thirty-second rampage. He bucks wildly, this way and that. His hooves tear up the earth around him. He spins left then right. Saliva flies from his mouth. Still kicking savagely with the power of a thousand pounds of muscle—making every attempt to dispatch this strange creature on his back. Eventually, he tires, the speed of his bucking cyclone lessens. The rodeo rider dismounts to the crowd's screaming ovation, and then the real fun begins.

Three or four guys swoop into the middle of the circle with red capes in their hands, enticing the bull with a little game of Catch Me If You Can. They brace themselves, feet planted wide in front of the bull with their red sombras, hoping the beast will charge. When he does, they leap or twist away, scrambling around and sometimes over one another to dodge his horns. Sometimes, these toreros don't even wait for the bull to charge. They lurch at *him*. I don't even know the goal. Not die, probably. Entertain the masses and don't die. Because if a dude gets gored out there on Ometepe, the primitive care at the "hospital" might keep him alive long enough to transfer him somewhere that can offer the care he really needs. Or it might not. So yeah, the goal for these guys is to tap the bull's head with their cloths, slap him on his backside maybe. And not die.

Bulls are violent animals, and they aren't very bright. A perilous combination. They rush hard, heads ducked down, and in one rapid-fire spasm of muscles, ram their heads upward in an attempt to gut stomachs and spill intestines. If their horns don't meet flesh after four or five yards, they seem to forget where they are. They stop, raise their heads, and turn to find the next potential victim. The bull is confused, and he's infuriated, sides heaving as he struggles to orient himself to the toreros' changing positions. "Who are all these people?" he's asking himself. "Where am I?" He lowers his head and charges, and then does it all over again. Exhaustion begins to slow him, and he stalks around for three seconds, shaking his massive head and spewing foamy drool in a five-foot radius. He looks to the left and to the right. Four, five seconds. Then he gets another wind—you can see it in the way he raises his head again, the way he trots back into the game—and resets for another pass.

The fans can't keep themselves seated, hyped with anticipation, bellowing with delight, poised for electrifying moments. It's easy to be caught in their midst, completely overtaken by the insanity and the heart-pounding near misses of the bull's sweeping horns.

And it's every man for himself, as it should be. *We aren't a team. Tonight, we drink and dance, but right now, in this ring, I don't know you. You want to be in here, fine, but you're on your own. I got my back, and you got your back.*

On bull number three of our first day, I spotted a drunk guy dancing in the corner of the ring. A lot of drunk guys filled the ring, but this was the babbling guy you see downtown on Friday night, shirt unbuttoned, chest and stomach exposed— the guy who wakes up the next morning with a neck tattoo of Mr. Rogers.

He danced for two or three minutes while the cowboys were out back readying the bull. They brought the beast in and secured his neck to the post, as before. The rider mounted him. They let the bull loose. And don't you know, the drunk dancer stumbled over to the bull to say, "Hi, how are ya, amigo?" No sombra, no protection, no athletic ability or sharp instinct to aid him when the bull charged.

And charge the bull did; stuck his head down, bolted forward, found the drunk guy, wrapped his horns around him, lifted up, and hurled him 360 degrees over his back like a rag doll.

What happened next is what makes bullfighting in Nicaragua bullfighting in Nicaragua: one of the toreros raced over to the drunk's side and dragged him by the arm away from the bull. Three other guys rushed over, each to a limb, and they tossed him facedown under the stands—out of the ring and into infamy. There, they left the drunk guy, static, limp and motionless, and returned to the action—out of sight and out of mind. *Maybe he's alive, maybe not; but he's not our problem.*

"That is what I like to see!" Jhonas beamed as he called out to me over the gasps of the crowd. "That is bullfighting!"

I was equal parts horrified and emboldened. I wanted to give it a go. I could pay a tour company to take me on a plethora of great adventures, but how often does one find an opportunity to step inside a bullring? A *real* bullring.

I remember a story my pops told me years ago of the early days of his marriage to my mom. He, my mom, and their dog Gypsy were coming south from West Yellowstone, Montana, into Yellowstone National Park and had stopped near a lake to let Gypsy run. It was the only time on the trip that Gypsy didn't come right back. So when she returned about five minutes later, Pops was impatient to get started. Just as they got loaded up and started the car, Ma said "Stop! I want to take a picture of that moose!" Pops told her the moose had been relocated all over the park. "You'll get a dozen better shots," he said. And they never saw another one.

This is our moment, right now. Our identities are the sum of the little pieces we gather along the course of our lives, of experiences either chosen or bestowed upon us by force. Some call it destiny. Others, hubris.

"Why couldn't I have met Ivana today?" I mumbled. I started scheming. "I want to go in there," I yelled to Jhonas over the roar of the crowd. "Inside the ring."

"No, you don't."

"Yes, I do."

"No, you don't."

"Yes, I'm telling you, I do."

"No, I'm telling you, you do not." I could see the mirth slipping off his face as he realized I was serious.

"I do."

"You don't."

We were reliving Tom Sawyer's first encounter with a stranger in the street, the fledgling newcomer to the neighborhood, as they childishly and eternally argued about who could lick whom.

I let the matter rest for a spell. I bought dinner and numerous beers for Jhonas. I retired for the night, still scheming. I woke up and climbed Volcán Maderas with our group of four, the whole time slyly mentioning to Jhonas that we should go in the ring that afternoon, that Sunday afternoon, the last day of the last party of the season. He started to cave.

"This dangerous," he explained. "This serious. Dangerous and serious. I do not understand why you want to do this."

"I don't either, man, but you've got to understand that I don't get an opportunity to do this very often. Step in the ring with a bull? This will be great!"

He squinted at me and returned to talking about the girl from the night before, the one he was trying to have a go with.

I informed him that he was making dangerous pursuits himself. "You talking about that French girl?" I asked him as we settled next to a tree for a moment's rest. "The one in that pink dress?"

"Yes."

"The big one?"

"Yes."

"Bro, you're five-two, a hundred and forty pounds, maybe," I told him. "She is five-eleven, 'bout two twenty. She will crush you, homes. Absolutely devour you. You wouldn't know where to start. I favor my odds in the ring with a bull." Besides, ninety minutes from home, he was spending his nights in a hammock strung up between two trees. What was his plan of action exactly? A romp on the hammock? Her place, in the dorm with five other people?

I could see that he was already relenting on my quest to get in the ring. We finished the climb, that long, miserable, satisfying climb, and descended into town. I continued to ply him with beers—a couple tall, two-liter bottles all to himself. I pumped him full of chicken and rice and fries. I slipped him a handful of córdobas so he could buy a ride home if the buses were no longer running. We brainstormed ideas for a sombra.

"A towel?" he asked, leaning back in his chair. "A shirt? A blanket?"

"Yeah, yeah," I replied. These were good ideas, but where could we find a red towel or shirt or blanket? It was a Sunday afternoon in a village on Ometepe Island—all the city's inhabitants had shut their lives down to come watch the bullfight.

"We can ask one of the toreros in the ring to use theirs," he said after shoveling in another mouthful of chicken.

"That's your idea?" I inquired. "Just ask nicely, 'Hey, man, could I pretty please borrow your sombra for a minute to go screw with that bull?' Borrow a sombra? That's your idea? Really?"

I spotted a red tablecloth at one of the tables behind me.

"One question," I muttered in Spanish to the lady running the restaurant. "I would like to buy that red tablecloth. How much is it?" Whatever number came out of her mouth next was soon going to be hers. Expenses mustn't be spared for once-in-a-lifetime experiences. She could have named my watch and my left shoe as her price, and I would have pretended to think about it two seconds before handing them over.

She didn't understand. "The tablecloth?" she asked.

"Yes. How much?"

"*Veinte,*" she said. "*Veinte córdobas.*"

I paid her and tipped her. I made Jhonas fat and happy for ten dollars, and for less than a dollar, I'd secured my red sombra. We finished eating and mustering courage as the four o'clock start time neared. We headed over to the ring, the longest seventy-meter walk of my life. The sun blazed above us as I poised myself to forget how worn-down my body was from the volcano climb. Jhonas followed sluggishly behind me, full of food and beer. When we reached the ring, he started talking to his buddy at the gate to the corral.

"Veinte córdobas para el gringo," they commanded.

Another ninety American cents to enter the ring, fifty cents cheaper than it cost to sit in the stands as a spectator. *Suckers.*

But that is why I needed Jhonas on my side. He was absolutely a horrible trail guide. Horrible, I'm telling you. For the first hour up Maderas—a straight hour as we began our ascent—he babbled on and on about that French girl as we passed petroglyphs and monkeys and cool-looking plants without a word of explanation. "Tell me one thing about this mountain," I wanted to say. *"One* thing." But I kept my mouth shut, succumbing to my fate.

But when it came to getting in the ring, he was the man I needed. On day one, he'd plucked me out of a crowd, the outlander whom he could easily convince to climb the mountain, and now he served as my ticket into the ring. Everything may be for sale in Central America, but this was unique: on that day, I couldn't just start asking favors from any guy. I couldn't sneak into the ring from the bleachers. I couldn't bribe the gatekeeper, and I most certainly couldn't petition for my own entrance into the arena. Can you imagine that conversation?

"Hey . . . uh . . . hi, there, I'm Adam Shepard. I'm not one of your kind of people, that's true, but . . . uh . . . and y'know . . . hm . . . I would like to—y'know—well . . . see, I just bought this red tablecloth, and . . . " It would be like asking to play Augusta National because I brought my own clubs.

Jhonas was the guy to know, my ticket in, just as I was his ticket to an afternoon of food and drink. I think we made a fair trade.

We slowly, steadfastly walked through the corral (it's amazing how calm a bull can be one minute and how irritated the next) and into the ring just in time for the first bull of the day to be lassoed and dragged back out of the ring. The announcer shouted across the rickety wooden arena in Spanish: "Yes, ladies and gentleman! Yes, yes, yes! Hey, hey, hey! Watch out! The next bull is fiercer than the first! More powerful! More angry! More dangerous! Yes! Yes! Yes! And admission is cheap! Yes, ladies and gentlemen! Thirty córdobas for adults, twenty for children! Yes! Yes! Yes! Hey! Hey! Hey!" Moments later and repeatedly throughout the evening: "Don't go anywhere, ladies and gentleman! That's right! Stay in your seats! The last bull of the evening comes from San Francisco! It cost us millions of dollars to bring him here! Millions of dollars! Hey! Hey! Hey! Yes! Yes! Yes! Millions of dollars!"

The whole time, nonstop, this announcer chattered on. Fireworks boomed and sizzled outside the stadium, their brilliant colors lost to the blue of the late afternoon's sky. The crowd *ooh*ed and *ahh*ed, an obnoxious out-of-tune band screeched through its cacophonic sets, and the announcer blared in my ear. Then, a bull readied to clear his way through the ring. It was a lot. Tension and excitement boiled in my stomach. My head started to vibrate. I gripped my red *sombra* with shaking fingers.

They let the second bull loose.

Now, you've got to understand what was going on in my head at this point. I'm not tough. I know I'm not. And everybody around me is constantly reminding me that I'm not tough:

"Shep!" my college basketball coach would yell across the court, many, many times, red-faced and veins bulging. "Didn't I tell you to trade your lingerie in for some real drawers! Softie! That kid is soft," he'd mumble to no one in particular, storming away. "Softie." So many times.

When assembling backup for a fight, my friends always said, "Naw, I got this one, man."

Beautiful, wonderful women look at me in moments of turmoil and say things like, "I think I'd better go get John."

So I'm not tough. And it bothers me. I want to be tough. I want to be respected on the basketball court. I want somebody to back down when I tell them, "That was my seat, and I'll excuse you to go find another one." I want to get into a fight (once!) and win.

Okay, no I don't. I'm not a fighter. Let's be friends and try to talk it out over a plate of cheese fries. I really am sorry; you can have the seat. But hell, it would be nice for just one girl to ask me to kill that evil-looking spider in the corner rather than just assuming I'm not macho enough for the task.

So there I stood in the ring that Sunday afternoon in Nicaragua, ready to prove to myself and to every critic I'd come across that I was no wuss after all. I didn't need to fight six bulls or three. I didn't even need to fight two. One. I wanted one pass. I needed one bull to charge, and I needed to square off with him. And then all would be right in my world; I'd never have to do it again. Just one time.

In the ring, Jhonas shook hands with one of his comrades. "I was in prison with this guy!" he yelled at me with a smile. "For being drunk and rowdy!"

I introduced myself and asked for advice. He took my red tablecloth. This second bull was running wild on the other side of the ring. Jhonas's friend tied a rock to each of the bottom corners of my sombra—finding a straw and a strand of plastic bag on the ground to use as string. This would weigh down the bottom and prevent the wind from snatching away my tablecloth and leaving me exposed to the bull.

The other men around us shook their heads and told me I was crazy. Six weekends a year they hosted bullfights, culminating in this final day, and never had a foreigner stepped foot in the ring. They reiterated how dangerous this was.

"One boy broke his leg yesterday," one of them reported.

"And did you see what happened to that drunk guy?" another one asked.

No one had died that season, but later that day, a guy would stagger down the hill to the medical clinic with a bloody, gaping hole in his stomach. These men admired that I wanted to partake in their culture, but this wasn't singing karaoke in Spanish. This wasn't a Wednesday-afternoon soccer game. This was serious, and it struck me that if something happened to me, these Latino gentlemen wouldn't know whom to contact back home. I'd signed up for a basketball league the winter before and had to fill out emergency-contact information, as if all of my teammates and

I would simultaneously find ourselves unconscious and unable to provide the information. But in Nicaragua, I signed nothing. I simply walked across the field with Jhonas and into the ring.

The second bull came and went in a violent fury, while I pressed up against the rails, cowering in the corner. Like a softie. Same with the third. The fourth bull found me hanging from the support of the bleachers, heading in the wrong direction. *I came to this island to relax a little,* I thought, heart tapping much too quickly inside my chest. Six weeks of constant digging under the scalding sun lay ahead of me. *What am I doing? What am I doing taunting an angry and armed bull with a tamale-stained tablecloth when I should be lying in a hammock for a few days?*

Subconsciously, I expected Jhonas to take the sombra, now in his hand, and go first, inspiring me out there. But Jhonas was no hero himself and hung back with me. I watched the brave— or foolish—men dance out in front of the bull. And I hated that I couldn't bring myself to step away from the edge—that I was once again too afraid to step up to the challenge.

By the time the fifth bull burst out and into the ring, I'd had enough of the waiting. Enough of the torment I'd inflicted upon myself.

"Fuck it," I said. *"Dame la sombra."*

I snatched the scarlet tablecloth out of Jhonas's hands and stalked out to the center of the ring. *Take action or go take a nap.*

I can't properly explain the feeling. I was a trembling wreck. This was scary. To say that I've never been struck with so much fear in my life grossly understates the terror of the moment. A thousand things could go wrong, and in that first moment, as I stood six feet from the fuming nostrils of that bull, I was convinced that each one of them would. "Another story to tell," I reasoned, as if "Yeah, y'know, I can't process solid foods anymore because I was gutted by a bull in Nicaragua" is a story worth its price. I imagined myself as the next casualty tossed under the bleachers. My heart raced, blood pumped furiously through each vein and vessel in my body. My breathing came ragged and short, but I was somehow able to steady my feet and hands.

I remembered that I didn't know my way around with a bull. *These guys see bulls every day*, I thought. My naïveté led me into the ring, but I wasn't sure what to count on to get me out.

A man in a white tank top in the first row to the right shot both of his arms in the air in violent thrusts, screaming.

And then my mind cleared; I focused. I'd been thinking about Ivana, that gorgeous Slovak girl, ever since I left Honduras—and though she would be in my thoughts for the balance of my time in Nicaragua, she slipped out of my mind that moment. I stood on the free-throw line at the end of the game. I was performing onstage for a boisterous audience. I was meeting with executives to make a monumental sale.

I was in the ring with the bull. And that's all that mattered. Laser focus.

But he turned away. I tried to sneak back around to his left, but he made three or four passes at another torero before they lassoed him and dragged him back to the corral.

Sixty seconds passed.

My nerves still tense, muscles coiling painfully in my calves and thighs, readying me for what lay ahead. The next bull, a dirty brown beast, pounded the earth as he burst in, just as furious as the former. I steadied myself.

"Closer!" Jhonas yelled, and the gallery standing around him echoed his advice. *"Más cerca! Más cerca!"*

Closer? I thought. *Closer? You sure? Really? Hm. Closer.*

But they were right; and I edged closer. The bull's rolling black eyes met mine, and he let out a deep guttural snort. I thought my heart might shatter my sternum. At last, he charged. His powerful hindquarters propelled him toward me—fifteen hundred pounds of deadly muscle. Every nerve in my body thrummed, quivered. I made a quick move to my right and waved my sombra over his face as he ducked to strike my leg. He bolted past, leaving me unscathed. My first pass. Wow. The sensation was indescribable. The vulnerability. The rush of pure relief and surging adrenaline that followed.

The crowd was getting into it now, too. "Ooooohhh!" they shouted, pumping their fists in the air. The foreigner was going to give it a go after all. *Silly bull*, I thought. *Bring it on, compadre. You don't want none of this.* But he did.

The announcer shouted: "Hey! Hey! Hey! Watch out! He's dangerous! Watch out!" The brown bull stalked to the corner and looked around, confused. He turned to his left and came back at me. He pounded toward me as I stood cavalier. I didn't move in time—his bony head slammed into my side, pinning me against the wooden barricade of the arena. Flailing panic swept through me but didn't paralyze me. I swiped down with my right hand, battering his head, while dashing two quick steps to my left to free myself.

"While dashing two quick steps to my left to free myself." I'm about as quick as paint dripping down the side of a bucket.

The crowd gasped, screamed. "Ayyyy!" They started laughing and pointing. The professionals may manage to escape injury, but odds are against the rookie, and this added an element of arousal. The crowd wanted blood, too. This bull's head was hard and solid, though his horns had been shaved to rounded tips. He charged forward to the right and hit me again. His massive head struck my thigh hard, an impact that would have knocked me off my feet if I hadn't been trapped against the boards. Nevertheless, the blow left a lingering black-blue bruise on my thigh for a week.

The cowboys lassoed him, dragged him away kicking and fighting.

Now I was ready. He was a good practice bull, the one without fully spiked horns, but the next fella didn't have nubs. He was white, slender in the relative sense, and quicker than the practice bull. His horns curved up to sharp daggerlike points, as strong as a boar's tusk. One swipe would pierce the skin, at which point he would drive his horn up and into his victim. He wouldn't pull out right away; he would swing his head to the left and right and unwrap the stomach or leg or chest of whomever thought it would be a good idea to go for a ride on his horns.

This was the bull I'd been waiting to face. I wanted to say to Jhonas: "Here we go. Now, if I die, go to La Ceiba in Honduras. Find a Slovak girl named Ivana. Tell her that I *am* brave. That I am man."

But there was no time for conversation. Guys around me roared with advice in Spanish, but even my English wasn't firing on all cylinders. The bull, gliding lighter on his hooves than the others, dodged at the two other matadors in the ring, and then he came to me. He ducked his head, and I lowered my sombra, my red tablecloth. He lowered his head, horns nearly scraping the ground. I lowered my sombra still more, until the bottom half wrinkled against the rutted dirt. He let up, turned back to this left, posturing while he picked his next target. He paused. And then moved back to his right, toward me.

A foot away now, time slipped down a few gears into slow motion. People always say this, but I swear that's how it feels. Your mind recalls the details in slow, fragmented flashes, frames set down one after another much too slowly.

This white demon of a bull lowered his head again and came at me. I lured him in with my cloth, snapping it back and forth. A quick, taunting yelp—more noise than words—slipped from my lips. And there he stood, two—not three—inches away from me, horns poking into the redness of my cloth. I floated on my toes. I fixed my gaze on this gargantuan animal. I lowered my sombra back down at him. He jolted up. A quick, short move to his right, driving into my sombra.

I stood unharmed as he turned back to his left.

They lassoed the beast. I breathed a sigh of relief. I'd had enough. I sucked in another deep breath. And another in an attempt to calm the staccato race of my heart. I strode toward Jhonas, completely satisfied—nay, *high* from the rush of standing face-to-face with a bull.

The music played all the way through, that horrendous, tuneless music, and the announcer, the hype man, kept right on going without pause: "Hey! He's got a sombra! The foreigner! He's visiting from the United States! Straight from California, ladies and gentlemen! From the United States! From California! He's got a sombra! Representing the United States! Hey! Hey! Watch out, gentlemen! This bull is dangerous!"

Of course I remember few of these outside details. I've learned the balance from an amateur video I got from an American spectator who found me afterward. When I was in the ring, I was just doing whatever I could not to get gored or go to the bathroom in my shorts. I was more or less oblivious of my surroundings. But watching the video now, I can see the anger in the bull's dilated pupils; I can see the snot slinging from his nose; I can see the focus in my movements; and I can sense the adrenaline flushing through my central nervous system.

What a rush! No feeling like it. I could have kept going for ten more bulls, thirty, fifty, a hundred, but at what point is it enough? At what point have I "been there, done that?" If I kept going, I was destined to get hurt. Carl Boenish, the father of modern BASE jumping died on a routine jump in Norway. How long until I was ready to come back down to reality, back to normal adventures like skydiving?

Three bulls, that's the answer. I got my fill with three bulls, one with ground-off nubs but a hard skull, and two with heads full of horns. Three bulls, and I'd had enough.

But something went wrong. I was walking back over to Jhonas, a proud, relieved smile plastered on my face, when the bull broke free from the cowboy's ropes. I don't know whether it was an accident or whether the cowboys got tangled and let him go on purpose in order to readjust, but there he was, barreling back at me, straight for my backside. Jhonas screamed out a warning. And I bolted forward, reflexively, without a blink of hesitancy. The bull trailed, lunging for blood and revenge. I reached up into the stands, those rickety wooden stands, grabbed onto the top of the gate, and raised myself up just as the bull arrived to try to slash my ass down the middle. I lifted myself high into the air, braced my right foot on the gate, and swept my left foot over the bull's horns. Three inches, that's what I see in the video. Three more inches, and I'd have been fitted for a colostomy pouch. Another two inches after that, and my friends back in Honduras would thereafter refer to me as *Adán sin Bola*. One lady yelped with fear above the others. Everyone hollered and clapped and pointed. This is what they came for; some displayed their throats as they cocked back to laugh. Twenty seconds later, the woman standing next to the cameraman declared, earnestly, "He's lucky."

And she was right. I was lucky.

Outside we sat down for drinks (where I scored extra points with the waitress for bringing my own tablecloth). I had to go to the bathroom—the exposed outhouse—and the German kid at the table told me to watch my head, that, for whatever reason, there was barbed wire hanging over the entrance. When I came back to the table, blood was rolling down my forehead. They laughed and pulled out their cameras.

Stephen Peele, the American sitting across the table from me, shook his head. "So, you step into the ring with the bulls, escape injury-free, and you can't go take a piss without gashing your face?"

The next morning, I rented bikes with a Polish couple, Vojtek and Kasha. Despite my stiff muscles and already purple-blue thigh, we rode for a couple of hours around the island, passing road workers and pedestrian traffic. Every five minutes, someone would nod at me and say, *"Oye, torero!"* They'd smile.

A half kilometer from our arrival back into town, we passed by three cowboys on horseback. They were leading the bulls back to their farms. The first two bulls came and went. The third, a white one, glared out of the corner of his right eye, crossed the street and charged at me. Kasha and I, riding together up front, jumped off our bikes and into the ditch. I lost my right sandal. I literally jumped out of my sandal.

The cowboy regained his grip on the rope, and the bull fell back in line, headed for home. We continued down the road amid playful chuckles. "He recognizes you from yesterday," Kasha surmised. "I've got to watch the company I keep around bulls."

Yeah, far from legendary status. But you can bet that every party I go to from now on, every gala, charity event, every social affair actually, I will find a way to work bullfighting into conversation. I'll be that guy in the corner, napkin in hand, demonstrating the proper way to make a pass at this vicious animal, likely forgetting the more humbling scenes from my bullfighting career.

"Ah, shit! No way! You climbed Mount Mitchell? Nice. Very cool, man. Sounds like fun. Hey, have you ever fought a bull?"

"You went where for your honeymoon? Ah, a Caribbean cruise? Very nice. You know a country that borders the Caribbean? Nicaragua. And do you know what I did the last time I was in Nicaragua? I fought bulls."

"Finance, you say? Cool, man. Oh, the stock market? That's kind of like the commodities market, right? Futures in corn and tobacco and whatnot? And livestock? Yeah, livestock, like cattle. Oh hey, that reminds me of my bullfighting days back in Nicaragua."

"You like chicken-salad sandwiches? Well, I like to fight bulls."

A Traveling Companion

D id I get lonely on this journey? Sure I did, just as you might whenever you saunter off from home by yourself for any extended amount of time. Excitement fought with anxiety about being in Central America and, at times, I found myself uneasily curious about what would happen next; there were nights I lay in bed alone wishing for just one hour at a table with Korey to barter stories over a plate of Bojangles' fried chicken.

"Oh, boohoo," you say. "Lonely? Is poor Adam gonna cry about not being able to see his friends and family for a little while as he gallivants around the world meeting great people and piling up the best experiences of his life?" Fair question, but over a thousand miles from home, a realization struck me—being away from family and friends was going to be trickier than I originally thought. I work well alone, but I also dig a charming companion.

I connected to home, though, with a book or a movie or by clicking through pictures of yesteryear on my notebook computer. Sometimes I would just go to Subway, and it would be enough, buying a club sandwich at just about the same price that I would pay in North Carolina. Other times, I e-mailed my brother and Pops and Ma and Korey and Tony and Matt and made sure we were still on for dinner and drinks and paintball when I returned to the States.

Holidays, believe it or not, were easy to deal with. Before I left, my friends back home gave me a bagful of gag gifts—toilet paper and Imodium A-D for all of the street food I was bound to sample; a pet boulder and a bag full of used snorkel gear to fill every last bit of excess space in my pack; and *Sixth Grade Writing Skills*, a resource for my journal.

My mom, though, as mothers will do, saw my departure as no laughing matter. She spent the month leading up to my departure preparing my going-away gift. *Holidays on the Move* she called it as she handed me the stack of handcrafted cards and pictures for each of the big days I would miss. Flashy commands on the outside of each envelope reminded me not to open them until their designated dates. Long hours—days and late nights—she had committed to this endeavor, and the significant additional weight made me smile just about every time I heaved my pack onto my shoulders. My birthday, Christmas, the New Year, July Fourth. On Halloween, I opened the corresponding card and smiled down at her swirly handwriting: "Happy treats and happy times! Did you remember to pack your superhero outfit?"

Sometimes, my present location didn't celebrate a particular holiday. Thanksgiving means nothing in Honduras, a country where they are quick to celebrate any occasion at all. But on November 24, I found a quiet moment to sit down on my bunk alone. I thought for a moment of my family gathered around the table, exchanging stories about what they were thankful for before they dug into the feast laid out before them. My stomach rumbled at the imaginary smell of turkey and Ma's overstuffed twice-baked potatoes. Blinking, I eased the envelope open. It momentarily transported me back to North Carolina: "This is the trip of a lifetime!" she wrote. "Enjoy it! I'm thankful for *you*!"

The other holidays that aren't even officially recognized in the States—just another excuse to pile into a bar with friends—she included anyway. On Saint Patrick's Day: "Here's good luck coming your way!"

And she always added a quote or an idea that had absolutely nothing to do with that particular holiday at all. On Easter: "To the world, you may be one person, but to one person (me!), you are the world."

In each card, she often questioned where I was and where I was headed: "Okay, so, where are you gonna go now? It's getting colder here, y'know. Maybe it'll snow. You're probably hot where you are, huh?"

On Valentine's Day, she asked how many pretty ladies I had romanced so far. She reminded me that time was ticking. "I can't wait until my grandbabies come along, and we get to do all of this all over again."

And pictures filled each envelope, eight or ten or twelve or fifteen snapshots of me celebrating that particular holiday with the people who had made me happy since childhood. Dressed as a scarecrow on Halloween, posing with my brother, the clown; my pops dragging the Christmas tree he'd just chopped down; Ma laughing as she held me, all swaddled in a white cloth on my literal birthday; roasting a pig with the Leggetts and the Litowskys and Mike Stewart and all my other friends; at bat in a baseball game; fishing off a bridge; baking brownies; fireworks, speeches, and dinner parties.

She left out her divorce from my father and her ill-advised gifts ("Sweatpants? Again? Really, Ma? I'm seventeen years old! You people are the reason I can't get a girlfriend") and fights with my brother and reminders of all of the birthdays I'd spent in after-school detention. She never mentioned the time I air-balled a layup in a game at Merrimack or the time, at age fifteen, I bloated our home phone bill with a sex-talk hotline. But she did include a picture of me dressed as a cheerleader for a powder-puff football game at Southeast Raleigh High School—complete with scarlet blush, blue eye shadow, a skirt, and a full-bosomed pair of breasts. (Travel tip: this isn't the kind of photo you want in your pack when crossing foreign borders.)

Some days on this journey were tough, but mostly, one activity or another kept me too engaged to let the isolation bother me. On holidays, though, the days when I pined for steaks on a grill with longtime friends or board games with my family, I was well cared for by a woman cooking dinner thousands of miles away. She told me she loved me, she missed me, she was excited for what a great trip I was having, and that she was looking forward to hearing all of my stories upon my return.

And that was sufficient incentive to keep me grounded in the present.

Parasites

I don't necessarily collaborate well as part of a team. Nothing personal, I just never think we'll be able to work in partnership for the greater good of the organization. Here we are with one common goal—perhaps, if we can agree on that—and here we are with all these distinct personalities trying to mesh together to reach that goal.

Steph is high-strung, Lucy is tranquil; Chrissy likes meetings to be relaxed and social, but Manuel wants to get down to business and save the storytelling for later; Mike is happy all the time, and Pete is sad; Andrew is always late, and Suze always has to leave early for one reason or the other; Dave may be the boss, but he *will* stop talking to me like that; Pauline refuses to volunteer for anything; Jenn is organized, Stacey is cluttered; Armond rarely speaks, and Cindy won't shut the hell up; Jimmy wastes all that talent on apathy; Larry picks his nose; Lindsey has a bad attitude because no one will listen to her suggestions; and Murph? Murph, a guy I'm meant to trust on the basketball court, is sleeping with my girlfriend—well, she's not technically my girlfriend, she's my ex-girlfriend, but we're still trying to work things out, and it's been going really well lately, and Murph knows this—and, yeah, it's not officially cheating, but that's still kind of fucked up that my own teammate would sleep with her, to say nothing of her culpability in the matter.

Now I ask you: how can Murph and I be expected to work together on a common enterprise, to win games and championships, when every time I look across the locker room at him, I picture him inside of my girl? More than that, I'm distracted by thoughts of what I'm doing so wrong that she needs to find comfort in the arms of another guy. *This is all my fault, isn't it?*

And this is before each of our individual ideas is fully introduced. You want to go one way, Orville wants to go another way, and I want to go another. Even if your idea is better than mine, which it probably is, I'm still going to be resentful of the fact that we didn't at least get to try mine out. I ain't no sweetheart myself, after all. Blame launches, fingers point, and then the real drama begins.

Besides, people are generally unreliable anyway. If you ask Roy to pull his weight and buy a bag of bananas for the kids on Thursday, you're probably going to find yourself having to leave fifteen minutes early on Thursday morning so you can stop by the store yourself.

This is how it was for me in Honduras. Nobody was sleeping with my girl, but the disparity of personalities dampened our attempts at being optimally productive. Laura wanted to do a science project on Thursday, and when we vetoed her proposal— just that one simple proposal—she checked out for the rest of the hour we spent planning. Kelsie chimed in *only* to voice dissonance. Mariana never prepared for a meeting, didn't have thirty minutes during the week to brainstorm ideas for activities. Shreva did, though, but all her ideas involved having the little nestlings draw pictures in their journals for hours at a time.

And Martin? Every day with the kids in Honduras, from nine to four, Martin sat off to the side—rarely in the circle—as the rest of us volunteers danced and skipped rope and constructed bracelets out of beads and yarn and reviewed common English phrases and studied geography with the children. We'd be fighting to retain attention through story time, and Martin would be just sitting there. We'd be lining them up to go to the bathroom, and Martin would be just sitting there. We'd be cutting and pasting; Martin, sitting there. We'd be playing kickball, and, well, he loved to play kickball. But everything else? Sitting there; no energy, no enthusiasm; rarely speaking, never leading an exercise. We had parties and tearful good-byes for Jennifer and Kerryn, but not one kid wondered about Martin the day after his flight took off for home. *What are you doing here?* I wanted to ask him. *Why would you waste your time here, quite literally getting in our way, when it's evident that you don't even like children?* But I let him be, as I already knew the answer: he was halfheartedly following his girlfriend around the world until she got tired of helping the hindered.

This is Honduras, people! Look at these kids! They are hopelessly, eternally stuck in a life of poverty! We can put our egos and our petty disagreements and our languid attitudes aside for a couple months or longer and try to do something about it. Let's focus our energy on making a positive impact on these kids who have almost exactly nothing. Right? Right? They have nothing! Come on!

But I never yelled or got angry. I took it in stride. I was at peace with joining a team in Honduras, and my ire could only get in the way of the cheerful energy I hoped to convey to the children. Anyhow, there were plenty of extraordinary people volunteering with Honduras Child Alliance, too, and I sought to feed off their liveliness. Great people doing great things. Those children loved Ivana and her relentlessly chipper demeanor; Jennifer hung out with her kids long after-hours, while the rest of us stumbled home exhausted; Emily donated enough money to build bathrooms for six families, and Jim went about assembling the crew to build them; Jürgen, at forty-five, had quit his job in Germany to spend a year volunteering with those who could only fantasize about his cushy life back home; Fabienne from Switzerland and Anna from Belgium worked into the night preparing snacks for the kids for the next day; various people added shifts to their evening schedule to teach English to adults in the El Porvenir community; and Carly, our hardy forewoman, worked long hours and into the weekend to organize all of us into as straight a line as possible.

Volunteers' motives vary, and abroad, out of earshot and eyeshot of moms and dads and friends, true motivations are unearthed and exaggerated. Some do-gooders sincerely want to make a proper impact and others are just delaying adulthood, using these last moments to booze and find a fine-looking Honduran to bang. Just as I quickly learned to bypass Martin and Kelsie and Mariana, I was inspired by Carly and Jim and Jürgen.

So, yeah, even though my greatest memories were born on the basketball court growing up, I've never worked well as part of a team, and this dynamic persisted when I had volunteered in Honduras. I recognize this as a flaw, but I have other, more pressing flaws to doctor first. Really, though, I'm on the fence regarding the power of teamwork anyway. Studies conflict about whether more work can be accomplished together or individually, and to me, it's to each his or her own. Teamwork, when efficient, forces people to put their own selfishness aside, because other people are counting on them. Trusting other people and sacrificing for others is a beautiful and courageous thing and can often produce amazing results.

Yet some teams—the dysfunctional ones—take every chance they get to socialize and recess for smoke breaks every half hour and deflect accountability when shit hits the fan. Every chance to half-ass the ropes course during the team-building retreat to the mountains. And to generally be as inefficient as possible back in the cubicle. Many people join up only so they can gain the satisfaction of being a part of something—to belong—and many team members merely hang with the group anyway, obtaining nourishment and hoping for some ultimate gain or advantage.

So just as five heads can—and should—be better than one, so, too, has plenty been accomplished by individuals sitting alone at their workbenches, and I—more often than not—associate myself with that camp. Value can bloom from the sovereign mind, too.

Maybe I work better by myself because I'm not that guy who makes friends wherever he goes. "Hi, how are ya? I'm Adam

Shepard. Pleased to meet ya. Great party, eh? Beautiful spread of cheeses. Right, so, what do you do for a living . . . ? Oh, wow, dental hygienist? I'm not supposed to be meeting you for another four months. Ha. Ha. Ha." I'm basically graceless and lack charisma. I get by in social settings, but even then, I'm that guy who stands by laughing awkwardly for a half hour, just barely allowed in the circle, munching on his fourth plate of chicken fingers after he's already divvied up his one good bullfighting story and inquired whether termites will be served.

All of this, though, meant that when I sought my next— and final (for this trip)—volunteer opportunity in Nicaragua, I needed to step away from collaboration. Either I was going to work completely on my own (not a realistic scenario in the world of volunteering) or I needed a clear-cut directive: I'll wait here while you guys pool your ingenuity over there in the corner and then tell me what to do. Tell me what to do, and then I'm going to bow my head and go do it.

I wanted a water project. I wanted to dig a trench and lay down some pipes and a pump. The water in Central America looks clean, but it's filthy—loaded with parasites—and families use it to wash and cook and quench thirst. I knew digging a trench would be hard work, but it was the only possibility that I could think of that would require simple instructions, nominal mental capacity, and no input on my part. "Start digging here," they'd say. "Three feet deep, two feet wide, and stop when you get over there," and they'd point to some vague spot, knowing I wouldn't make it that far before they came back to give me further instructions. This was an ideal scenario.

But I didn't get any responses to my e-mails. Well, I did, nine actually, but they were all snubs, in the vein of, "We don't accept foreigners to work on our water projects; we rely on natives to do all of the work," or "We work only with groups of five or more that want to come together."

What! You work only with groups! I want to come dig a trench for six weeks! I want to help! All I need is a shovel! I'll sleep in a tent and pay for my own food! What are you talking about, you accept only groups of five or more? Come on! Is there no Ditches Without Borders?

I sent twenty-two emails to twenty-two organizations in Nicaragua, and I thought that would be way too many, that I'd have my pick of opportunities. I was straightforward and polite:

Hi, Mr./Mrs. [Last Name],

I am writing to you from Honduras with another month to go on my volunteer program (with Honduras Child Alliance). I came across your site about the work you do in Latin America, and I really want to know how I can lend a hand on a water project in Nicaragua. I would like to dig a ditch for six weeks if you can find a place for me.

Do you have a water project I can latch on to starting around January-ish? I'm pretty simple: I can live with a family or anywhere else you want to put me, and I can prepare my own food. (I can cover all my own expenses and pay any administrative fees as well.) . . . I'm just looking for a shovel and a spot to dig (and I'm happy to buy my own shovel).

Thank you! And cheers to the work you are doing . . .

Adam

Zero positive replies. Zero!

Volunteering is big business, and if you're going at it solo, finding any affordable opportunity to lend your hand isn't easy. But this wasn't a new concept for me. I tried to volunteer in Guatemala, but the admission process was twelve weeks. Twelve weeks! I paid them twenty-five dollars to take fifteen minutes to look over my application and maybe call a reference or two, and they said they needed twelve weeks of consideration.

And Cross-Cultural Solutions? Here's an organization that is doing great things around the world in a variety of different capacities: childhood development, education of at-risk youth, elderly care, the empowerment of women. Housing is in abundant supply in the States, but with Cross-Cultural Solutions, maybe I could work abroad to help a family that would otherwise be living in an exposed wooden shanty, or assist with the building of an orphanage. And do you know it would cost me $2,988 to volunteer with them for a couple weeks? $2,988! For a couple weeks! A night in a Guatemalan hostel costs seven dollars, but you can quickly negotiate that down to six, five if you're staying for an extended period. A homestay with a family is even cheaper (and better for cultural immersion). But $2,988! And that's in the bargain-priced "off-peak volunteering season," after I'd have already scared up the additional funds to pay for my own round-trip airfare, visas, immunizations, Internet, laundry, and postcards home. Cross-Cultural Solutions would cover my housing and meals, though, and for $2,988, there had better be a veritable cornucopia of breakfast foods strewn upon the fluffy Egyptian bedcovers as soon as my alarm clock went off. *I'll have a Western omelet, please, and French toast, coffee cake, loaded hash browns, and four buttermilk pancakes with blueberries and whipped cream. Oh, and you know those little wieners that you usually see just at cocktail parties? I'll take a bowl of those, too, thanks; I know they're not typically served for breakfast, but while I'm working hard out there building orphanages, tutoring at-risk youth, caring for the elderly, and signing my savings account over to you, I'd like to indulge a little. And give me a bell, too, please, because when I've decided that I'd like to take a bite, for $2,988, Miss Guatemala better be standing directly outside my door in her lacy nightgown ready to feed it to me by hand.*

But $2,988! Really? Lunch in Guatemala usually cost me three dollars for a plate, never more than four, and I'm a big eater. Cooking for yourself costs much less.

Since when was volunteering limited to the affluent?

And don't get me started on the salaries of the directors of these "nonprofit" organizations. I don't hate Cross-Cultural

Solutions, nor do I hate any other major nonprofit organization—
many are doing great things around the world—but if you want
to buy a pretty house and drive a sleek BMW, shouldn't you be
working for Google or Nike instead?

I wrote to Cross-Cultural Solutions asking whether I could
just show up and be put to work on a crew building a house
for a needy family in Guatemala. I'd be happy to cover all my
own expenses; just give me a place and a time, and I'll show
up ready to work. I'll bring my own hammer, I explained.
The program advisor/corporate relations specialist simply
wrote back that their fees are in place so as not to burden the
community with the support of volunteers and that with my
financial constraints, Cross-Cultural Solutions wasn't going to
be a good fit for me.

It's not just Cross-Cultural Solutions. Finding an affordable
place abroad to offer your services gratis isn't easy. Expenses
add up: administrative costs, salaries for employees,
application fees, predeparture-handbook printing fees, office-
maintenance fees, website hosting fees, and a little cash for
the annual staff retreat into the mountains to hold hands on
the ropes course. I get it. But in reality, whenever a dollar goes
to charity, not only do I not know how much of that dollar will
actually go to help someone, I can pretty much bet the next
dollar in my pocket that however much of my first dollar makes
it through to the poor, starving children of Africa won't be used
the way I'd like it to be used. Worse, I don't know whether my
donation will be received by the beneficiary with a greedy
hand or a little fortitude.

Honorable organizations are still out there, though; you
just have to do a little legwork, and I was fortunate to have
found Honduras Child Alliance. It was a great fit for me: a small
organization, refusing to get any bigger, keeping a tight leash on
how they spend their money. If I had a problem or a question, I
walked three minutes around the corner in El Porvenir to Charlie's
house to talk to him about it, or I e-mailed Eve back in Pennsylvania,
and she would usually e-mail me back before I logged off. You can

see right on their website *exactly* what Honduras Child Alliance is doing to help, and if you want to come from the United States to visit your sponsored child and take him or her twelve kilometers into the big city to eat at Pizza Hut for the first time in his or her life, well, by George, hop on a flight, good buddy, and come on down to shiny town. Let's order a round of cheesy bread for the table and brownie sundaes for dessert. The Honduras Child Alliance directors aren't bringing home for-profit salaries, and *every* supply is used and then reused and then reused, and then, when it's worn down to the nub, it's donated to a destitute yet industrious family who can find a new function for it altogether.

Finding another Honduras Child Alliance ("Send us your application, and we'll be in contact within two days") appeared overly ambitious. Twenty-two emails sent to twenty-two clean-water organizations in Nicaragua, and I got nothing better than one confounded guy who couldn't process my motives: "You want to dig?" he wrote to me. "That's it? Just dig a trench? In Nicaragua? I don't understand." Mostly, though, I was ignored as crazy or quixotic. Even the Rotary Club (each of their local affiliates in Nicaragua and Costa Rica and then the Central American branch as a whole), which I *know* is working on water projects all over the world, didn't get back to me.

Was I pissed? Yeah, I was pissed. How would you feel if you went to a bar, beamed flirtatious vibes at twenty-two people individually throughout the night, bought them each a round of their drink of choice, *separately,* and then they each ended up turning to you and saying, "Sorry, but . . . uh . . . you're really just not my type"? You'd be pissed, too. We've all been rejected, sure, but twenty-two times in rapid-fire succession? I just wanted a shovel. *I'll take care of everything else, folks, just hand me a shovel and point to a spot where I can start digging.* Instead, just because I didn't fit into the little bubble of an organization (twenty-two organizations!), I couldn't find an outlet for six weeks of sweat. Couldn't even get a first date to chat for a little while over dinner.

But then, just as your keys are always in the last place you look, my twenty-third e-mail kindled a positive response. Opportunity—and Jesus—beckoned.

Digging Forward

Jim Palmer, a sturdy man with a rim of hair surrounding an otherwise bare head, is a born and bred Texan and one of four brothers. His closest brother, John, got into drugs as he worked through high school, and it gradually got worse.

"He wasn't a bum, always asking for money," Jim told me at breakfast one morning. "More of a con man, though, always coming up with excuses and deceiving his way out of every situation. He didn't care who he hurt, nor did he care about the effects of what he was doing.

"This was dreadful for me to watch, especially because he and I were always tight."

After high school, John spent two years in the Navy before faking incurable seasickness and being medically discharged. When he turned twenty, police busted him for possession of marijuana. While waiting to beat the rap, John ran low on dough and caught up with some old friends. Together they made a run to Tijuana. The group bought a little cocaine to distribute for a week's worth of spending money as he awaited his time in front of the judge. Back over the border in San Diego, the driver of the car ran a stop sign, and the police carted everyone off in handcuffs, cited for possession with intent to sell.

"So, the parole officer calls my dad back in Texas. Says he's got his son. 'Now, sir,' the officer says. 'I understand you're a minister, and I'm a Christian man myself, so if you will come out to get him, I can speak with the judge, and, because he's twenty and a minor in the state of California, I'm fairly certain we'll be able release him into your custody.'"

Jim's father faced the most difficult decision of his life. He cared deeply for his son, but John hadn't responded to any other punishment or penalty. Jim said to me: "'If I don't come get him, what will happen?' my father asked, and the parole officer basically said that he would be sentenced to two years in federal boot camp, probably serve about a year if he acted right.

"So, my father says to the guy, 'I'm not going to come out to California. This will be good for 'im. He ought to learn the consequences of his actions.'"

After being convicted, John served nine months before being paroled on good behavior. He had meanwhile grown very close to both Jim and their father through a daily exchange of letters.

"So he came back to Marshall, [Texas], started getting in phenomenal shape at the gym, met a wonderful young lady, and held a steady job. He started studying forestry. Wanted to be a forest ranger. Man, he loved the out of doors. The fast life was a distant memory, and we were all proud of him and what he now had the potential to accomplish."

And then, he was diagnosed with cancer. Rhabdomyosarcoma. This highly malignant neoplasm, in its rarest form, has few survivors, even now. Twenty-six years ago, even as an otherwise healthy young man, John was told he wouldn't last a year.

"This was devastating, you see," Jim told me. He leaned back, sighed. His blue eyes were heavy and a little bloodshot. "After this incredible reformation, I now had to watch him go through all the chemo and radiation and surgeries. Of course he is one hundred percent positively convinced that he is going to beat this cancer, but as time passed, reality sunk in. He went from a strapping two hundred pounds to ninety-eight pounds after nine months of treatment. He lost all his hair. Lost all his teeth. He was wilting, knew he was dying. I was living over twelve hundred miles away in Phoenix, and my father calls me and solemnly tells me that I need to come home to see my brother. At the time, I was directing an inner city community center which ministered to Hispanic and black street kids and gangs. I tell my father that I've got a few things to finish up, that I can be there by the weekend. 'Jimmy,' my dad says. 'He may not make it to the weekend.'

"So I get in the car. I drove twenty-four hours straight through from Phoenix to Marshall with my wife, and I sat at my brother's bedside for three days. And those were just about the most amazing moments of my life. John was cycling in and out of consciousness—twenty minutes awake, twenty minutes asleep.

Whenever he was awake, we relived every fort we ever built, every fish we'd caught, every girl we'd dated, every touchdown we'd been part of, and every dream we'd ever had."

Jim paused and took a sip of coffee. He let his gaze rove out the window and over the two palm trees in front of his house, but then he turned back to me.

"As I was leaving, he said, 'Jim, I don't know why God has cut my life short, but I believe God is going to give you a long life. Don't waste one minute doing anything but what God wants you to do.'"

Jim left on Saturday morning to head back home, knowing this was the last time he would see his brother alive. On the way home, he pulled over on the side of the road, climbed out of the car, and spoke to God. Kneeling in the ditch with the wind from passing cars tugging at him, he said, "All right, God. Here I am. What do you want me to do?"

Those last days with John and then that night on the side of the highway directed Jim to the seminary and then ultimately to spend twenty-eight years in Central America.

John died two days later, on Monday, and Jim and his wife, Viola, flew back for the funeral, a celebration of John's life.

Since then, they've served the people of Honduras and Nicaragua as Baptist missionaries in various capacities, from education to road construction to installing water pumps. Jim will probably still be making trips to Central America long into retirement. "The infrastructure is weak here, see," he told me over that morning cup of coffee, "but there can be simple changes: a smoother road out to a rural village opens up the ability to bring goods to market in town; a new school could mean a more solid education and better opportunities for underprivileged children, perhaps even the chance to one day go to college in Tegucigalpa or Managua; and you already know that clean water is an issue."

A month before, he'd been the lone affirmative respondent to the extra few e-mails I didn't originally think I'd have to send. He wrote:

Adam,

Just received your e-mail.

To answer your main question, yes, we always have a place for people to serve.

We work with the Miskito people, an indigenous group who live on the Atlantic coast of Honduras and Nicaragua. We assist the Miskito believers in building churches, training leaders, and developing agricultural and water projects.

Loyd Miguel is our Mission coordinator. He will be in Mexico and the United States for Christmas, returning to Puerto Cabezas, Nicaragua, around January 15. We have a mission compound and a large network of churches scattered across the jungle where we help dig clean water wells.

Let's work on details and seek the Lord's direction with this project.

Jim

I'm not a religious guy, but I know to take an opportunity when it's the only one on the table. I emailed Jim back, a message spiced with an annoying amount of exclamation points, saying that I would be in Puerto Cabezas on January 16, ready to meet him and Loyd and move forward as they saw fit.

Sparse brown and green spots of grass and anorexic pine trees speckle the Nicaraguan countryside. Villages are scattered around the region, and each member of a community often relies on his or her neighbors for support.

The water problems in Central America are beyond comprehension. Back home, when I get thirsty, I turn on the faucet, I hold a cup under it, I fill it up, and I drink without fear of cholera or cramps or diarrhea. Then, after dinner, I go to the bathroom, I flush toilet paper down the commode, and it flows off to never-never land to be processed.

But in Central America, the first warning people give you is to not drink the water. The water they drink from the faucet is not actually potable, nor do they have the septic system to process toilet paper. So after dinner, you have to wipe, crumple, and place the tissue in that trash can by your right leg.

Back in El Porvenir, when the town's water supply ran low, they simply shut it off, without warning, for twenty-four hours. The governments of these Central American countries sometimes provide deworming pills for their citizens; other times missionaries will come through with boxes of medication. But by and large, people are left to deal with the gut-churning effects of drinking tainted water. Half of the Miskito population is situated along the Coco River, and the other half is spread along tributaries, always near a source to wash dirty laundry on a rock or draw water for cooking. But few people, if any, have access to safe drinking water.

So I dug. Jim and Loyd and Pastor Gener, the foreman of each construction project, handed me a shovel and directed me to a bare patch of earth that looked no different from any other patch around me. "Start digging here," Pastor Gener directed. "Two feet deep, one foot wide, and stop when you get over there." He pointed to some vague spot of land, knowing I wouldn't make it that far before he came back to give me further instructions.

I thought a lot about Ivana those days outside, baking in the sun. Driving in that spade again and again, I thought about how she was back in Honduras, still running around with those children. About how much fun I'd had with her—cooking dinner, chatting on the beach, dancing. I wiped sweat streaming off my brow before it could trickle into my eyes, and I thought about how the gods of love had handed me opportunity on a silver platter early that one Sunday morning after a night of dancing at the club, and how I had replied, "No, thanks. I'm not in the business of impressing women. I'll stick to clumsiness." About how she'd given me more chances.

I e-mailed her. And she e-mailed back. We spoke on Skype as often as possible. I said, "I miss ya, kid!"

Most days in Nicaragua, Pastor Gener and the other workers and I listened to the radio as we dug. They had few local stations, and those stations were *very* local and generally religious. They were both a source of entertainment and a means of relaying information. One guy ran everything. He'd say in a soft, monotone voice, as if on a classical radio station back in the States, "All right. That sure was a good song. God is good. And up next, we have Alejandra Barteña from the Dia de Gracia Baptist Church. Welcome, Alejandra."

Alejandra's voice would scream over the airwaves in Spanish or the native Miskito for a half hour about Jesus. A half hour, straight. I mean absolutely hollering, crying to the heavens; she'd pour herself into it, burn calories: "I'M TELLING YOU THAT JESUS IS THE ANSWER! WE ALL SUFFER FOR HIM! YOU CAN GO TO CHURCH ALL YOU WANT ON SUNDAYS, BUT IF YOUR DAILY EXISTENCE IS NOT IN THE NAME OF JESUS, THEN YOUR PRIORITIES ARE NOT IN ORDER! AMEN! I SAY, I TELL YOU, AMEN! JESUS! JESUS IS THE ANSWER! AMEN!" You can hear her stop every ten minutes or so to take a sip of water—purified, I presume. But mostly, there's screaming.

Then, the director would return, again in his monotone. "All right. That was Alejandra Barteña from the Dia de Gracia Baptist Church. Thank you, Alejandra. Now we will play a few songs. But first, Tagoberto Gabayo, your mother wants to wish you a very happy thirteenth birthday. Also, Manuel Dinario, someone has turned in your driver's license, and I have it right here in my hand, so come on down to the station whenever you get a moment to retrieve it." And then he'd play some songs.

We worked on many projects during the six weeks I spent down in Puerto Cabezas. My time in Nicaragua kept me as busy and productive as I've ever been in my life. We measured, dug, and poured the foundation for a battered-women's shelter. I learned how to drive on both sides of the road as we traveled seventeen hours round-trip by truck, bucking down a pothole-riddled dirt road straight out of the nineteenth-century American West into Puerto Lempira, Honduras. There we operated on an ailing tractor and sawmill at another Baptist Mission. In a remote village, I sat outside a hovel of a schoolhouse and constructed balloon animals to keep children pacified as they waited in line to see one of the missionary doctors. I rode two hours upriver to another remote village with a group of optometrists to distribute eyeglasses to the elderly, people who'd suffered from foggy vision for years. (You've never seen so many smiling faces in one place.)

But mostly, we dug. No machines, no heavy equipment, and no Ivana next to me to cheer me on. We worked in two-man groups—one dude hefted a pick to loosen the soil, the other followed behind with a shovel to heave the soil out. I've never popped so much ibuprofen so fast or finished so many days so filthy as I did during those days in Nicaragua. My lower back throbbed on both ends of a night's rest, and mud and concrete caked on my boots. I've worked harder twice—negotiating sofas through front doors as a mover in Charleston and then mustering cattle in Australia—but I've rarely felt as satisfied at the end of a day's labor. I knew I offered a teeny-weeny, though perhaps soon-forgotten, role in a family's ability to drink clean water and in a woman's opportunity to be housed away from her abusive husband. It was great.

Installing a water pump is a tricky endeavor.

First, I was surprised to learn that a very significant percentage of wells drilled worldwide in the last twenty years are no longer functioning. Lacking both spare parts and the knowledge needed for pump maintenance, primitive villages struggle to operate shiny new technology. One lost washer or bolt usually kills a pump that supplied a whole village, taking with it all hope of drinking cool, clean water again. Billions of dollars of investment over the years amount now to scrap metal.

Also, many of those wells and pumps were dug and built for the entire village, which means that lines of accountability can be gray. "Community wells are a horrible idea out here in northeastern Nicaragua," Jim Palmer said to me. "Getting people to work together is not easy. What belongs to everyone belongs to no one. Back home, we have a civil government that the Miskito people don't have. Out here, there isn't a reliable, centralized system of order. Back home, if someone throws garbage over my fence, I'm going to call the law. In Puerto Cabezas, if someone throws garbage over your fence, you're going to walk over with your machete and chat with him about it. And this also affects how we install our pumps."

Jim learned this over his twenty-eight years in Central America. Now, his crew does two things differently: one, they install a simple rope-and-washer pump—the most basic level of technology. A child can operate it. Construction, though arduous, comes with simple instructions: dig a big hole; construct a concrete enclosure; run PVC from the bottom to the top; top it off with a wheelie-thing that pulls water to the surface.

The only thing left to do is grab the handle, spin it clockwise, and fill your bucket.

"I've heard other groups, enthusiastic groups, tell stories about their indestructible water systems. Built by NASA. State-of-the-art. Steel construction. Then they get out to these rural areas, and they're always destroyed. When we come swooping in with our brilliant Western ways, it's critical that we also work with the current local culture." A solar-powered water pumping system sounds great on paper but is useless if it's difficult to manage.

Second, Jim Palmer's crew doesn't build a pump for an entire village. They build it for one family. This is an artful process, and a vital one, as it demands ownership and accountability. "Digging the well is easy," Jim said. (It is not.) "Finding a way to maintain it is tough, and we've seen great success with all the people from a village or neighborhood coming to that one family for water. The family runs it, and we work hard to select a family that we know will run it efficiently. So there's never any question who should be in charge, and we never have to worry about a community well being destroyed or vandalized or neglected when the appointed operator doesn't feel like walking to the center of the village to open it up."

Finally, you have to find workers capable of putting forth the effort to get the job done efficiently. The blue-collar Nicaraguan workers I worked alongside for six weeks were the same as anywhere else in the world. I met just as many sloths as I did hard workers. René always had his shovel working, but Marcel kept wandering off to take a leak in the trees or carve some trinket out of wood. Once, he found a dead bird and spent the balance of the morning plucking its feathers and chopping off its extremities so he could fry the meat for lunch.

I couldn't blame him. They were each—regardless of experience or work ethic—earning a hundred córdobas a day. A hundred córdobas a *day*. That's 58.3 percent of the current *hourly* minimum wage in the United States. Regardless of experience or age. In the States, even if you somehow manage to fall into a job that actually pays minimum wage, you're quickly given opportunities for raises as the months pass.

This was wild to me. The problems that exist in developing nations make the problems in the United States look simple and easily manageable. And now, here were strong and able Nicaraguans working very hard for rock-bottom pay. I couldn't believe it. I couldn't understand the idea of such grueling work for such little money. Still, it was important for me to see these things, to witness them personally. Travel is like that, providing an escape from our reality and into the real world.

I asked Ricardo, one of the guys digging alongside me, about this—about this idea that digging could be it for him, forever.

"Something will come up," he surmised. He picked another patch of dirt loose, and I grunted as I shoveled it out. The intensity of our work disrupted our calm surroundings next to the river— lush trees, still air, an occasional peeping bird—but he stopped, bracing his pick against the ground and leaning on it for a moment. He mopped sweat off his forehead and looked to the sky in contemplation. "Yeah, something will come up. It always does."

"Why don't you sneak into the United States like so many others? In just one hour, you could easily make twice what you make here in a day."

He hesitated, citing his family in Nicaragua, but said that he had connections in Texas and this was a realistic possibility for a six- or twelve-month stint.

"Or five years," I said. A layer of mud covered my shirt, quickly caking under the sizzle of the sun. I smelled ripe. I consistently shoveled out half the amount of dirt that everyone else did. But even if I couldn't be taken seriously as a shoveler, I could have a good plan. "In five years, you can save enough to buy your family a house, for cash, here in Puerto Cabezas. You can come back with the funds to start your own business. You'll be forty-one and never have to pick up a shovel again in your life except to hand it to your son."

This was a wild idea, I know, but it was one with initiative. Many Nicaraguans skip the border to Costa Rica to work illegally, and virtually the same immigration issues exist along that border as the border separating Mexico from California, Texas, New Mexico, and Arizona. Maybe Ricardo, hints of gray already appearing in his hair, had never been taught that initiative or even the ability to see the bigger picture, to dream. Maybe he was content with his life, although the dark expression on his face as he slung dirt showed otherwise. Maybe—and this is a very scary thought—he figured that hustling up a hundred cords a day with a shovel in his hand was as good as he was meant to do. Ever.

El Chavo, in contrast, didn't want to hear about what he was "meant" to do, and he wasn't falling into the glittery opportunities of the drug trade. I never learned his name—I don't think anybody did since we all just called him "the Boy"— but I learned plenty about him in the weeks I worked across the trench from him.

"I got my backpack last night," he announced to me one day. His already huge ears seemed to perk up a size when he got excited.

I slapped him on the back and offered a giant smile. I was proud of this minor achievement, a major achievement in his world. "Good. What's left?"

"Notebook, pencil, and a pen." He had already made his biggest purchase, the required uniform of blue pants and a white shirt.

"And then?"

"Saturday, payday, I will have the two hundred córdobas to pay for my matriculation." He could go to the second-rate public school for free, or by showing a little financial initiative, he could earn a much more respectable diploma from a private school set up, again, by the Baptist Mission.

Now, let's pause a moment for consideration. I'm standing next to a fifteen-year-old kid who is spending his school vacation months working in the most blue-collar setting there is just so he can save up to pay for a backpack and school supplies. And his own tuition! At age fifteen, I spent my days on the basketball court and my nights chasing girls around the neighborhood on my bicycle. Any money I saved from cutting grass on the weekends went directly into my basketball-shoe fund or to my Ice Cream for the Ladies fund. I'll drop El Chavo's daily pay out of my pocket and won't spend more than ninety seconds looking for it, yet here he is taking every cent he makes—at fifteen years old—and investing it in his education.

I don't know where that comes from in the ambition-killing Nicaraguan environment. Who taught El Chavo to be a go-getter like that? His mom? I met her for ten minutes—she was the lady to know if you wanted fresh-caught lobster tails—and that is a possibility. A mentor? The church? Who's to say? Maybe he was just born with what the next kid wasn't. Me? I grow up in those surroundings and my third priority *might* be my education, right after my relentless pursuit of illegal employment over the border and trekking backpacks full of cocaine to a safe house in Honduras.

Cocaine. The drug trade runs rampant on the Caribbean coast of Nicaragua. All of Central America provides a corridor to run cocaine from Colombia to the United States, but Honduras and Nicaragua are positioned at the halfway mark. A small plane cannot make it all the way from Colombia to the States and must refuel. Boats, the same, and port towns in Honduras and Nicaragua—with minimal funding to staff personnel for the military, coast guard, or police force—are powerless, vulnerable gateways to the north. There are boats on the water, and there are submarines under it.

Cocaine is killing the economy in Honduras and Nicaragua in more ways than you'd think. First, there is the obvious income gap that comes when guys zoom into town with trunks full of cash. (Or barrels: twice I heard an unsubstantiated story of a dealer who didn't have anywhere to hide four barrels loaded with twenties, so he buried them in his backyard. When he went to dig them up, worms had eaten all his loot.)

Then, these drug traffickers open up "legitimate" businesses—a hotel, a little restaurant on the water, a grocery store in the center plaza—so they can clean their dirty drug money. What they do, though, is set their prices at near cost (since they don't need to make a profit), and mom-and-pop operations, trying to run legitimate businesses, are undercut until they fail.

Now, here's the kicker, a factor that shows how the drug trade affects the everyday life of Honduran and Nicaraguan men. Regular dudes—your neighbor, your brother, your uncle—go down to the shore for a couple hours on a day off or after an honest day's work. They stand around and down a couple of beers. They shoot the bull with other neighbors and brothers and uncles, the whole time keeping an eye on the waves crashing to shore. What are they watching for? A brick of cocaine. The *narcos* running major weight up the coast by boat or submarine will dump everything at the sight of approaching federal agents. Lost bricks of cocaine, at some point or another, wash ashore, often on the shores of Nicaragua or Honduras. Anybody standing on the beach can snatch it up, hurry into town, and sell it to the right guy for a bagful of cash, all before dinner.

Locals claim you can hear the ocean if you hold a kilo up to your ear.

And these are regular guys! These aren't drug traffickers. This is that dude who sells you fish in the morning. The man who delivers your gas tank on Saturdays. That gent you wave to when you scamper off to school. These are masons and ditch diggers and guys selling ice cream from the cooler off the front of their bicycles. Your uncle. The drug trade has turned regular guys into dealers. I couldn't believe it until I passed by the beach myself and Kaveeta, the organizer of the missions groups at Verbo Church, pointed these guys out, groups of three or four settled in cliques within their marked territory. In Puerto Lempira, Oscar told me about a guy who was penniless and drunk three months before. "Adam," he said, "within a week, he built a house with cash, and he just broke ground on a new gas station."

Mostly, though, the drug trade puts a moratorium on ambition. Why put in an honest-day's work in the first place? Why strain every muscle in your body under a glaring sun for a pittance that will barely keep you afloat? Tired, wide eyes peer down the street at that sleek two-story house built by that known *narcotraficante* who never seems to be working much. I'd like his lifestyle. Why risk it, you ask? Fair question, one I'd think about twice as an American. But in Nicaragua, consider the options.

School is important, but upon graduation, there is little guarantee of finding a job in a specific field. Plenty of guys with college diplomas return home to drive taxis.

Starting a business is a possibility, but with so many regulations, it's extremely difficult to rival the already established competition. In the United States, if you want to start a business, you need a hundred bucks and a dream. It might take two days to complete the proper paperwork and print some full-color business cards—maybe a little longer if you require specific licensing and decide to sit through *all* of Suze Orman's audio books—but in Nicaragua, there can be many months of red tape to work through, and even then, starting a business requires a deep purse and connections.

And if a business is profitable? All eyes shift in that direction. Jason Puracal, a former Peace Corps volunteer living in Nicaragua, was sentenced to twenty-two years in prison for drug trafficking. Prosecutors concluded, upon noting his successful company and fat bank account, that he must be dealing drugs. Despite having literally no evidence, they managed to convict Puracal. The government released him only after many appeals, pressure from the United Nations, and two years of his life spent in a ramshackle Nicaraguan prison.

Working is a possibility, but doing what? Slinging dirt out of trenches for a hundred cords a day? Opening a corner shop to sell snacks and sodas to passersby? Moving to Guatemala to harvest corn on the mountainside?

Lobster divers in Nicaragua make good money, but those guys, not even certified to scuba dive in the first place, are making ten to fourteen back-to-back twenty-five-minute dives to 125 to 150 feet per day (per day!). For fifteen to eighteen days at a stretch. The PADI dive planner says you shouldn't dive to more than eighty-two feet for twenty-three minutes without spending time at the surface to decompress; the suggested surface time for *one* dive by a professionally-trained diver at the depths swum by a Nicaraguan lobsterman is twenty-four hours; never mind the suggested safety stops on ascension. Decompression sickness paralyzes these guys all the time.

Mining is the only other lucrative blue-collar occupation, but it's not entirely healthy. Tremors send faulty tunnels crashing down on top of teams of miners, burying them alive. Even if you escape being crushed or buried, breathing in that coal dust day after day guarantees you an early exit by fifty-five or so, thanks to a nasty killer called black lung disease.

Most guys just go to work building houses or roads under the relentless baking sun for a hundred cords a day. *No, gracias.*

So let's think about this: I've got a chance—a chance—to run this backpack of cocaine through the mountains into Honduras over two days for five hundred dollars? And if I get caught, I can bribe the police or the judge in Honduras or the warden of the prison in Nicaragua for my release? Hm. *Eight dollars a day working in the scorching field, times sixty days, minus lunch money, plus my baby would love one of those Rachael Ray ten-piece cookware sets with nonstick surfaces for easy cleanup . . . Where's that backpack, you say?* Guys are "escaping" all of the time from prison in Nicaragua. Halfway through my stay, one Colombian trafficker bribed the warden to have his guards take him to the hospital where the Colombian bribed the doctor—get this—to write a little note to the judge that he was in a coma and he would be for the rest of his life. *Poof!* He disappeared back to South America while all parties continued to investigate his health.

My life in Puerto Cabezas was mundane. Everything. Work and play, both. Though tasty, even the food lacks imagination and is on a flat cycle: rice and beans and chicken with a side of plantain chips; rice and beans and fried turtle with a side of plantain chips; *nacatamales*; enchiladas. Repeat.

And there is very little personal initiative. Nicaraguans aren't lazy or indolent, necessarily, but children learn not to dream for the future, that it's better to merely scratch along day-by-day. This culture lives very much for this moment right now, with little regard for how an investment of time or saved money can improve one's lifestyle in the longer term. And forget change. "Weed Eaters could revolutionize this place," one American guy offered as an idea for replacing those haggard young men bent over whacking machetes at the ground, but reality opposed him—there was no one around to service these machines. "Surely," he reasoned, confused, "one person in this town of fifty thousand could learn. Hell, they keep these retired American school buses running for so many years passed their expiration. Why not a Weed Eater?"

But hope enters the picture, inch by inch. A few people challenge the standard criteria of this middling existence. In the face of appealing yet illicit decisions, El Chavo was making a more sensible one. I heard ambition in conversations with him and Polo and other people who wanted to make honest, prosperous livings. Loyd's brother played with the idea of opening a small—just two or three employees—fish-processing facility. René was going to school for forestry engineering and wanted to get his doctorate. Aaron had the mechanical capabilities to open his own garage.

I worked side by side with these men, listened to their dreams and their struggles. And as many struggles as they faced, these men were proof that hope does exist in this tiny, worn-out country. With a decreasingly corrupt government under President Daniel Ortega, an increasingly self-sustaining lifestyle, and a slowly strengthening infrastructure—the paved road from Managua to Puerto Cabezas is underway and the second floor of the new school is almost complete—the seemingly perpetual fight against both the *narcos* and passivity will wage on.

Brief Encounters

It was Sunday in Nicaragua, eleven-thirty, just after church let out. Evelyn, the cook at the Baptist Mission where I lived, had Sundays off, so meals weren't served then. I hadn't eaten since the plate of fried turtle and rice she prepared at six o'clock the evening before, so any advertisement promoting nourishment found me an easy target.

Leaving my temporary home at the mission, I wandered into town. Delicious scents drew me this way and that. Someone had scrawled HAY NACATAMALES on a poster at the first food stand in the small but crowded market. Like every other food stand, this one was squat and sturdy and lacked paint or decoration. Rusty nails held grainy, uneven boards together—a sign offering food topped the whole rough picture off, and behind it all stood a lady.

"Hay nacatamales?" I inquired.

She looked at the poster, smiled, and said that was all she had. I ordered two, one beef and one chicken. Nacatamales, the Nicaraguan version of a tamale, are succulent blends of rice and cornmeal dough, stuffed with your meat of choice, wrapped in banana leaves, and steamed or boiled. For a dollar, you'll get change, and one is enough to fill you up if you get it from that lady on the main drag down the street from Verbo Church (on the right, just before you get to the Pepsi distributor).

"Y un tenedor?" I asked.

She shook her head. *"No. Lo siento, pero no lo tengo."*

"Y una servilleta?"

"No. Lo siento." She didn't have a fork or a napkin. She offered only nacatamales and a 7 Up and that's about it, but I didn't care. I wandered half a block down the street to the concrete slab in front of the *Sala de Belleza*. There were six or eight housing units around back. This wouldn't be the first time I would sit on some strangers' front grounds eating with my hands, nor the last. I trimmed off the string and peeled open the banana leaves. I set the steaming leaves on the three-foot concrete wall and started stuffing my face. Strolling by on foot or bicycle, passersby twisted their heads to stare. Everyone. Curious where I went wrong in planning this meal, they couldn't help but stare at a gringo eating a Nicaraguan treasure in such a manner. No one pointed, but two separate pairs of girls swiveled their heads back around, laughing, after they passed. One teenage boy stopped to question how I could possibly eat all of that food in one sitting, and then he appealed for a bite.

A young woman stepped out through the front gate and stopped. A thin black blouse draped over her torso and jeans.

"Necesitas un tenedor?" she offered, her eyes flickering from my face to the nacatamales and back again.

I really didn't need a fork now, not with my hands already covered in warm dough, but I recognized that it would be rude to turn down her hospitality. "Okay, *gracias*," I said.

"Y una servilleta?"

A napkin I did need. She returned inside and came out with both. She extended them toward me, then stopped. Her head tilted to the side as she invited me inside to sit down. Didn't know me from a guy on the news wanted for kidnapping, but she loaded my lunch onto a chipped white plate and invited me to sit down at her dining room table. For fifteen minutes we chatted; she practiced her English, and I practiced my Spanish.

Her name was Marginee Callejas. "What are you doing here?" she wondered, since white people don't pass through Puerto Cabezas often. When they do, they certainly don't spend their time eating nacatamales on the street by the handful. "Yes, volunteer, but why Puerto Cabezas?"

She sat at the table with me now, leaning forward in her chair. The window to the street was open; a faint breeze slipped in and tugged at the ends of her dark hair. Outside, two dogs barked and snarled. I told the young woman my story. How I came to arrive in Nicaragua. How I sang karaoke. How much I enjoyed being in Honduras. How I met a girl, and I hoped to meet back up with her. How I fought bulls.

It is freeing, the nature of a one-time conversation.

She told me her story. She was a doctor working two blocks away at the public medical clinic. "And one day, I go to the United States," she announced confidently, "to visit my cousins in Miami." Despite being young for her career, at twenty-four, her maturity defied her age. Braces laced her teeth, and kids called her Doctor Callejas. She had her life planned out. To the United States it was.

With a proud note in her voice and a slightly upturned chin, she told me about her family in a distant village. Her father died six years prior, and her mom had assumed both parenting roles for her two brothers. Marginee was going to visit them for twenty days beginning on Tuesday. She said she was passionate about music. She said she was human and therefore as imperfect as everyone else. She said she didn't like animal abuse.

We talked, as always, about the drug trade and the dangerous spots to avoid. "Do not swim at the sea," she warned, "but there are places you go on the river."

"Really?" I asked. "On that river right outside of town?"

"Yes," she answered. "But this is not very clean. Maybe you do not go swimming."

I couldn't finish both nacatamales, just as the boy outside had predicted. I barely finished one despite how hopelessly hungry I was. She fed the leftovers to a couple of loitering stray dogs. She led me to the sink, where I washed my hands. She rinsed my plate and my fork. She took care of my little bag of trash.

She mentioned she had to go meet some friends. I had a far walk ahead of me to get to the supermarket.

"So, bye," I said.

"Bye," she said with a grin.

We hugged.

"Thanks."

"You are welcome."

I loaded my backpack onto my right shoulder and walked off toward the center of town.

I'm an optimist, sure, but not an eternal and unrealistic one. I know there is evil in this world; indeed, I've met plenty of awful people in my life. It's different on the road, though, as the venomous side of existence rarely surfaces. Travelers are generally excited to chat, cordial at a minimum. Natives love to meet foreigners, and they often listen attentively to stories of life back home. Even the mean ones tolerate, with a slight smile, the smell and unkempt nature and mouthy behavior of the backpacker because, well, the backpacker's money is just as good as everyone else's. It doesn't serve them to have a toxic attitude.

Mostly I turn away from the things I cannot change. Instead, I focus on what I can contribute to, even if its effect is pocket-size. The junior paupers of Honduras? I can work with a vacation activities program. Parasites in the water? I can help put in a rope-and-washer pump. Perpetually lazy or hostile people or the seemingly endless drug trade among Colombia, Central America, and the United States? Not much for me to offer in assistance.

So I acknowledge the evil in passing but don't permit it to destruct my otherwise positive temperament. Then I pause to cherish the instances that I get to spend with wonderful people—an hour, a day, a month, a year. Travel teaches us to open ourselves up and allow total strangers into our lives. I sat with the delightful Marginee Callejas for fifteen minutes in Puerto Cabezas, Nicaragua, and I walked out of her house and onto a mucky street knowing that I'd never see her again in my life.

Exit Stage Left

It wasn't hard for me to leave home on day one; I knew I'd be back. "See ya in a year, guys. Later." There was a party, and everyone was cheerful. Pops gave me a hug and a kiss on the cheek. Even my mom didn't cry.

It was tougher to leave Antigua and El Porvenir and Puerto Cabezas. I may never return to Guatemala to see Beatríz again. Or Javier and Luis and Carlos and Esther in Honduras. Or Marginee Callejas and Loyd Miguel and Jim Palmer in Nicaragua. I'm excited about the next destination, sure, but I didn't want to leave just yet. I wanted this moment to freeze in time.

But it didn't. Life moves. The next destination beckons. Hairlines recede, senses fade, and metabolisms slow. We glide from one site to the next, in anticipation of those meetings with the Marginees of the world, as momentary as they might be, and ultimately, we're just left with a file of photographs, a smile, and a "Man, those were some good times. Now, where to next?"

Flora Herrera

There is one woman I can't stop thinking about.

Flora Herrera is from Kisaliya, a little village seven kilometers outside of the larger village of Waspán, Nicaragua. I met her as we finished up our final water project during my last week in Central America.

At age twenty-five, Flora met a guy. They got serious; they got married; they brought a shy and beautiful daughter into the world. A few days after Flora turned twenty-eight, they started building a house together. When Flora discovered that her husband was bedding another woman nearby, she cast him out of her home and out of her life. Male fidelity is rare in the macho culture of Nicaragua, although it is even rarer for a woman to throw out her unfaithful partner. Men may be the chiefs in Nicaragua—running the house, bringing home the shekels, and coming and going as they please—but Flora would have rather fended for herself than endure a fractured relationship.

So at twenty-eight, a year younger than I was when I started my one-year whirl around the world, Flora set out to finish constructing her house on her own. Financially broke yet determined, she collected boards and nails one by one and went to work. I've seen a picture. Flora was a striking woman then, with a contagious, warm disposition. I imagine the sun on her shoulders as she perches atop a ladder, hammer in her gentle hand, pounding nails with precision.

Then a board fell. It struck her from behind and broke her back. There were no hospitals nearby, and they couldn't do anything for her at the local clinic in Waspán. Traveling by bus to a hospital twenty hours away was expensive yet ultimately manageable, but in her poor condition, she wasn't yet up to the task. As I mentioned before, potholes, broad and deep, riddle the dirt highways of Nicaragua. So her brother, a good man, she told me, carried her three excruciating blocks to his house, and put her to bed until she recovered enough to endure the grueling trip to the hospital.

Her back never healed, though, and Flora Herrera has lain in that bed for sixteen years. Sixteen years. Sixteen years on that same thin, foam pad in that one-room shack. Her old and ragged driver's license dates her at forty-four years old, and she looks eighty-four. Her eyes are enlarged and protruding from their sockets. Her jawline is bony; her shoulders come to a point; wiry arms hang limp at her sides. She is disappearing, a skeleton wrapped in skin. When I tell you that I've seen a ghost, her name is Flora Herrera. She eats a spoonful of rice on rare occasions, but she's committed herself by and large to a liquid diet because she's ashamed of the messy bedpan that her daughter would have to clean up. She owns no books, no TV, no radio. Can't afford them. That dream house of hers, that dream of the twenty-eight-year-old Flora, is a dream long extinguished; her days drag by in a wooden hut, fourteen-by-sixteen feet, with four posters on the wall.

Problem has heaped upon problem, leaving Flora gradually weaker. Her hands are coiled and her feet are gnarled. None of them function. Her eating habits have given rise to painful ulcers in her stomach. Being forced to lie in the same position all day, every day, has birthed further problems in her crippled back and legs. Her speech, though you can sense the passion, slurs. Her jaw has atrophied, and when she speaks too long, her mouth falls open and won't close without the aid of someone else's hand to hold it in place. She can't lift her cheeks to smile. And when I reached down to hug her delicate frame, she couldn't raise her arms to hug me back.

So there she lies in her bed at forty-four years old, staring at her posters on the wall and waiting for the end. All because of a board that broke her back. Her wheelchair busted long ago, so now it doesn't matter whether Flora is a sunrise or a sunset kind of person because she hasn't seen either in many years.

I imagine the sun on her shoulders as she perches atop a ladder, hammer in her gentle hand, pounding nails with precision.

A year after her accident, Flora's brother got into a fistfight with another guy over some petty disagreement, and the police shot them both dead. After that, during the early years of Flora's malady, neighbors checked in on Flora, but they trickled out of the picture as her condition worsened. Now, Flora's daughter, struggling to make ends meet with a family of her own, watches after her mother.

My meeting with Flora, her daughter, and her granddaughter came as a surprise. I was in Kisaliya with Pastor Gener, the mason who directed the water project. One night, after we were done forming the concrete for the cap of the well, we bathed in the river. He turned to me and said there was a woman whom we needed to go visit and pray with. "Cool," I replied. Flora lay horizontal when we arrived, but her daughter gathered two pillows and propped her at a forty-five-degree angle to face us.

Flora's indomitable spirit amazed me. This woman was on death's doorstep, but she, for whatever reason, just wasn't ready to go. She talked with all of the vigor she could rally about her life, how it used to be and what had happened to her. She asked me to tell her a story, and Pastor Gener translated into Miskito, her native language. I told her how I had spent a dollar on Valentine's Day to buy Ivana two *pastelitos*, those beefy minicalzones in Honduras, while Ivana had likewise spent the previous two months secretly learning how to play the guitar so she could surprise me with a song. "You have a few things to learn about impressing a woman," Flora offered, and we all laughed.

And when it came time to pray, she looked to Pastor Gener and asked him whether he could pray for Sergio, her young neighbor who had a minor ailment of his own.

Tears filled her eyes as we prepared to leave; she looked up at me with a heartbreaking light in her eyes. It felt as if she wanted to reach out, wanted to grab my hand. "I don't get visitors," she said to us. "You don't know what it means to me that you two came here." With an earnest look, she made Pastor Gener promise that when he returned, he would bring a copy of the picture of all of us together.

I can't stop thinking about her. I see her tired, sunken face as I sit in the sand, watching the sun rise over a rippling ocean horizon. Her name whispers through my mind when I see a young woman at work atop a ladder, laughing and full of life and energy.

People ask me why I took this trip, and now I know why. This trip is for me, indeed, and all of the good times I am destined to have. This trip is for my seventy-year-old self, sure, but this trip is also for the Flora Herreras of this world, people imprisoned by their circumstances, who will never be able to take a trip like mine.

She can't, but I can, and I will.

I can't say for certain which places I will one day revisit. I have loved various spots along this journey, but I'm always excited to spend my time uncovering another rock, writing another chapter. One thing I can assure you, though: one day soon, before it's too late, I will return to Kisaliya, that rural village outside of Waspán, where a bowl of unsalted white rice is a full meal. I will sit cross-legged beside Flora in her wooden hut, and I will tell her the stories of my trip. I'll tell her about bullfighting and mustering and volunteering with those children in Honduras—the sweet ones and the bratty ones alike. I will show her pictures of scuba diving and bungee jumping and sailing. We'll debate Nicaragua's policies on tourist visas.

And then I will pick her up, carry her gently outside, and place her in a padded chair. Together, Flora Herrera and I are going to watch the sun set.

Over Here to the Right

After I wrote my first book four years ago, ABC called and asked me to do an interview on *20/20*. I sat across from John Stossel as he fired off a series of questions about living among the homeless and working from the bottom up to achieve the American Dream.

"So, Adam," he asked. "After this unique experience you've had, my question is this: Which education do you value more? Your college education or the education you received on the streets?"

In an effort not to upset anyone back at my college, I rendered some diplomatic answer about the value of both educations. "You know, John," I responded, "it's really not fair to value one over the other. They're both important." But when the camera stopped rolling, I confided that I could survive without my college education. In such a fast-paced, winner-take-all world, however, I wasn't so sure how I could manage without the street sense I'd accumulated along the way.

Fast-forward. My days of digging had finished. I was in Managua, Nicaragua, having just flown an hour from Puerto Cabezas. The next day I was heading to Costa Rica for two days and then on to New Zealand.

But first I had to get to Granada for a very important rendezvous. With Ivana. Somehow, inexplicably, my scrappy pursuit had worked. The doing of the dishes, the handwritten notes, the late-night talks and long walks, the early-morning bike rides, the emails, the Skyping. I enjoyed every minute with this girl, and she had finally said, "Okay, I would like to go with you." If all went as planned, I would meet Ivana in Granada and we would travel together, happily ever after, to Costa Rica and then to New Zealand. I hoped all would go as planned.

Outside the Managua airport, I approached the first taxi. Two hundred córdobas. *He can suck a fat one.* Another driver approached me, and I offered a hundred. Always investigate your price with the first guy and negotiate with the second. Street smarts.

"To go to Tica Bus?" the second taxi driver asked me, our entire conversation in Spanish.

"Yes. I know it's on the other side, but that is what I paid to get from that side before."

He raised his bushy eyebrows at me, hesitant and skeptical, but it looked as if he needed the business. "Okay," he said.

He led me to his cab, around farmers and families and businessmen and tourists clutching their belongings. He already had one passenger sitting directly behind him. The driver tossed my bags in the vacant seat in the back, and I sat in front. We all started chatting. The guy in the back remarked that he'd just arrived from Puerto Cabezas, as well, and I told him how much I enjoyed his hometown. He asked whether I took any photos.

"Yeah, a few," I said passively. I was thinking about Ivana. "The pier. I liked the pier very much." *I can't wait to see her. I should get flowers. Maybe bring her some food. No. Just flowers.*

"Can we see them?"

"My camera is buried in my pack," I lied. "It would take too long to dig it out."

They assured me that they had time, that they'd love to see my photos.

"No. Maybe later." I brought a polite smile to my face and glanced out the front window, waiting for the driver to take the hint and start driving.

"We have time," the driver insisted. "We would love to see your photos. Get your camera. I am sure you have some great photos."

"No. Maybe later." Their adamant pursuit of my pictures started to make me a feel a bit awkward.

A tense silence hung in the air for thirty seconds. Peppy tunes filtered out of a radio set in the dashboard.

"What about your computer?" the driver asked. "Do you have a computer with your pictures?"

"No. No computer." What was going on? Was this guy playing a game with me?

"Hey," said the guy in the backseat, thick mustache twitching with the word. He raised his eyebrows and perked the glasses set on the bridge of his nose. "I am in town from Port just so I can buy a motor for my boat. I have to change two thousand dollars into córdobas. Do you mind if we stop to do that?"

I hesitated, glancing at my watch. "Really, I've got to get to my hostel." *Get to the hostel, drop my stuff off, go meet Ivana. Is she as excited as I am? She must be! She could've said no, but she said yes. She must be excited.*

"No problem," he replied but continued his argument. "It will just take three minutes. Three minutes out of your way. And I will pay your taxi fare."

Well, I'll tell you what: that man had me at, "I will pay your taxi fare."

So we pulled up to the curb down the street from the place to change money. The driver told me that I should get out—the lady at the exchange didn't like gringos—and they would be right back to pick me up. "You can leave your bags in the car," the driver told me. "We'll be back in a minute."

Right. This guy had me mixed up with some green and gullible American tourist. I climbed out at the corner and grabbed both of my bags. They circled the block.

"Closed," they said, the passenger smacking his forehead like he was so dumb for forgetting. "The money place is closed on Sundays."

Right.

So I reentered the taxi to finish the route to my hostel near the Tica Bus station.

"Yeah, closed on Sundays."

"No good," I said, attempting courtesy. I really wasn't paying attention. *What if she doesn't show up in Granada? That could happen. My goodness, what if she changed her mind?*

The driver cast a sideways glance at me as he pulled away from the curb. "How long are you in town? I can give you a tour of the city."

"No, thank you." I wished he would stop talking so much.

"Do you need to stop and get money? We can stop if you would like. I know where to get the best rates." He glanced away to honk at a guy crossing the street slowly in front of us.

"No." *Okay, calm down. Of course she's coming. No worries.*

The driver showed me his Nicaraguan driver's license and asked whether we had the same one in the States.

"No, pretty different," I observed. *But what if the spark isn't there? What if it's different when it's just the two of us? What if our relationship starts to wither under the harsh and constant light of traveling by ourselves?*

I reached to the backseat for my bag, fished out my wallet. Trying to match their tone, I excitedly showed them my license, complete with an explanation about what the little plastic card would allow me to do. "Class C. I can drive cars and small trucks, but I can't drive a motorcycle or a big truck." Excitedly, I tell you. Mostly, I was really impressed with the fluidity of my Spanish at that point, and I was showing off. Pride before the fall.

I put my wallet—my wallet with the $216 in Nicaraguan bills brimming from its seams—back into my pack. I tossed my pack in the backseat next to the passenger and turned back around. My pops enjoyed that. I can't remember exactly what he said when I related that part of the story to him, but it was something about, "Jesus Christ, honey. If you had your checkbook with you, would you have written the sons 'a bitches a check, too?"

Then, the regular questions.

"Where else have you visited while you've been in Central America?"

"Oh, really? That sounds like fun. Do you think you'll come back to do it again?"

"Where are you headed next?"

The driver pointed off to the right to show me some houses that Daniel Ortega, the president of Nicaragua, had given to the poor.

"He just gave them houses?" I asked leaning toward the window to catch a better view of the concrete-block walls and small windows that made up said houses. *Okay. What's my first move when I see her? Go straight in for the kiss? Stick with a hug at the start? Should I be goofy and shake her hand?*

"Yes. Just gave houses to the people."

"They don't have to do anything for them?"

"No, nothing."

Up to that point, I hadn't paid any attention to the driver's incessant chatter. But now I found myself interested. I wanted to know more about Ortega's generosity. I turned to face the driver again. "But if they are just given something like that, how can they appreciate it? If they don't have to earn it or pay for it, where is the incentive for them to go out and work?"

The driver pointed off to the right again and ranted for thirty seconds about how some have their own little businesses—"right over there, in that corner, see?"—while others maintain jobs with the city. The recipients of these houses were asked to paint them in their spare time. Indeed, fresh coats of paint, mostly white, but a few pale greens or grays, covered each one of those houses. I had just read in the *New York Times*—not forty-eight hours prior—that the mayor of Nogales, Mexico, had initiated a program supplying free paint to anyone in his town wishing to spruce up their home.

All this made sense. The red flags—how the driver had approached me at the airport, the questions about my camera and my computer, the whole two-thousand-dollar story, the way he reached back to tuck in my bag next to his other passenger, his enthusiasm to share random vignettes—didn't surface until my second rum and Coke that night.

I was curious, even a little upset, about Ortega just giving these houses away. "For nothing?" I asked again. And the driver was thrilled to answer my questions. But it was all a ruse, of course. I was getting robbed, and I didn't discover the truth until six minutes later when I stepped out of their cab: while I was pondering houses and paint and social systems, the backseat passenger fingered the zipper, reached into my pack, and snagged my wallet. I had been watching his right hand during the whole ride, but while I spent so much time peering out the window and listening to the driver babble on about Ortega's almsgiving, the mustachioed gentleman in the backseat was digging into my pack.

Street smarts.

The backseat driver had offered to pay my fare, so there was no need for me to pull out my wallet. He got me. *They* got me. Those boys had spotted me as soon as I exited the terminal. Indeed, they'd known they were going to rob my sweet gringo ass a week earlier while I was still 484 kilometers away capping that last water well.

In Puerto Cabezas, the night before, Loyd's brother, Franklin, had cooked an amazing meal for my departure. He sent me off with a bagful of johnnycakes.

I specifically recall thinking that afternoon in that cab in Managua, as the driver gave me a guided tour of his fair city, while he and his partner were ripping me off, *Man, I love Nicaragua. These people are great.*

At the same time, the two gentlemen in the cab must have been thinking, *Man, I love Americans. These people are a bunch of schmucks.*

It could have been much worse, though I'll spare you the silver-lining spiel. Yeah, I prefer the okeydoke to a knife in the gut, but the fact is that I returned from volunteering in Puerto Cabezas, landed in Managua, and was promptly relieved of my ATM card, my driver's license, and my entire bankroll. That sucks.

I called my bank, cancelled my ATM card, and used the emergency credit card hidden in my pack to draw enough cash to float me. I called my pops, who spent a full five minutes laughing at me.

After that, I crammed into a one-hour shuttle from Managua to Granada. Ivana wasn't there. I waited. She didn't show. I walked up and down every tourist-riddled street in town, scanning the crowds. I inquired at five hostels. I couldn't find her. As I sat with an outside view at O'Shea's on Calle La Calzada, I said to the waiter, "If you spot the girl in this picture, I will give you fifteen dollars."

But she never showed. I walked back to the dorm room. I was confused. Dispirited. She said she'd be there. *She* was *excited. I know she was. What happened? Did I misread this entire scenario? Is she just late? Border crossings can be a nightmare in Central America, so maybe she just got held up.*

I went to bed. I woke up the next morning. I ran. I showered. I stuffed my pack. I checked out of my hostel. I walked the mile to the bus station.

And there, in a chair across the station in Granada, with her back to me, sat the most beautiful girl I've ever seen. I walked up behind her. I touched her shoulder. She turned. And her face, with the warmest smile you could ever imagine, betrayed my same level of excitement. All my doubts had been silly.

We kissed. We filled out forms. And we walked hand in hand toward the bus, ready to travel to the other side of the world.

NEW ZEALAND

A Traveling Companion, Part Deux

Ah, yes. The Girl.

It's all about The Girl, really. If I'd wanted to get laid, I would have stayed home. The women in the States are as beautiful as any in the world. I don't need to hop on a plane to find a bar to terrorize, and if promiscuity motivated me during this trip, I could easily be blinded to amazing hikes and volunteering and the Copán Ruins and bullfighting.

For me, the excitement and challenge of the late-night liquored-up pursuit has slowly waned. Besides, I've never really been a let's-go-out-and-meet-some-chicks kind of guy. My dating life is pretty plain: boy goes out; boy meets girl; boy woos girl; girl is unimpressed, but sends boy off with a polite rejection; boy retreats to evaluate what he can do better next time. Many are fascinated by my lack of game back home—I'm an average-looking guy, I go to the gym, and I have enough fun experiences and stories to get me through the first ten minutes or so of a date. But after that, the process of courtship grows unsteady for me. And sadly, my clumsiness with women translates into many languages across the globe. My game is weak. I'm the Chicago Cubs of dating.

I'd certainly never committed to remaining celibate for this year, or for that matter, for any stretch of my life longer than game day in college. Gandhi can have that, and besides, celibacy is just asking for messy nocturnal emissions. Why would I want to purposefully prohibit myself from enjoying one of life's greatest pleasures?

No need to force it, though; staking out a piece of neutral territory on the subject seemed about right, at least for a while. When I left North Carolina, I never intended to seek out women, and I likewise never planned to avoid them. I never really thought about it. I just wanted to climb a few ruins and volunteer for a little while.

"Loosen up a little, Shep!" my friends back home said, patting me on the back as we gathered at Tony's house. *You only live once, yada, yada, yada.* "You're traveling. You're visiting wondrous places. You're going to meet beautiful women from all over the world. Go out and get some." Before I left, one of my friends set the over/under at me sleeping with six women. Citing the contrast of my lack of game and my appeal as a foreigner, four guys took the over ("I'll take the *way* over," Korey said. Tony added, "Even you can't strike out every night"), and one person, Scott, took the *way* under. Colin informed me that I wasn't that good looking, but said I could still count on "raking in the booty" when I got to Europe. Five lunches at Bojangles' were set to be exchanged, one way or another.

Me? Of course I cherish the warmth of a woman's body pressed up against mine under the covers. But I'm over being in bed with a woman for the sake of getting off. Gone is the bestial thrill of the chase. Why hunt for sex when I know we're going to have to bother with the strained conversation afterward and then this business about, "Why isn't she returning any of my phone calls?" While I'm certainly not refined, I'm at least beyond the superficiality. It's irresponsible to be loose, sure, but more than that, it's empty. It's missing something. *Who is this girl?* We strip, we have at it, and then we retreat, covering our shallow decision with some pathetic justification. Then we immediately direct our attention back to the reality of our lives—work, our grocery lists, gas prices, our low self-esteem, etc.

So I designated my return to the States—after my year spent traveling and experiencing the world—as a time to resume a more authentic search. In the meantime, I wouldn't worry one way or the other about meeting members of the opposite gender.

This, of course, eased a lot of tension from my life, but also presented occasional bouts of anxiety. Sometimes, when I haven't relieved myself for five or six days in a row, I have this recurring dream. My seventh-grade English teacher, Ms. Reynolds, peeks her head around the corner into the kitchen—it's usually the kitchen, although I've seen her twice or so in the living room. A purple low-cut V-neck sweater drapes over her curved form, and a pair of dark jeans hugs her hips. She reaches toward me, and I slide my right hand behind her neck. For a moment, we both hesitate. I look into her eyes and she into mine. Then I pull her toward me, my fingers easing gentle pressure against the back of her neck, feeling how soft her skin is there and how her dark hair falls over my hands. Our lips meet—gentle, tentative at first. My left hand stretches to her lower back. She smiles. We don't speak a word.

Everything speeds up, as if I'd asked permission with that first kiss. As if she'd given it with her smile and banished all doubt of where this was headed. My lips still enveloping hers, I begin to tug at her clothes, a hasty effort to remove them. She grabs my forearm to slow me down, pulling back just a little to meet my gaze. Her expression reassures me that this will be worth having a little patience. We leave our socks on most of the time; can't be bothered to take them off.

She wraps her arms around my neck and jumps to hug my waist with her legs. I lift her and set her on the cool marble countertop. She asks something lame and cliché but forgivable, like, "Are you ready to give it all you got, big boy?" And then the fun starts. She on the counter. Me on the counter. Both of us on the counter. We move frequently, assuming new positions.

But I never finish. These sessions can go for hours, days—who can equate real time to a dream world?—but I never get to the end. Skipping from first-person to third-person throughout, I can look across the room to see sweat dripping off the tips of my hair and then look down to see it gliding along my exposed chest, arms, and abdomen. Every muscle straining, I work hard to ensure that both parties are satisfied here. But I never finish. She shudders with pleasure, over and over throughout the evening, but I'm lost. I give myself a pep talk. I create new scenes in my mind—Ms. Reynolds and I in her car in the school parking lot during lunch break; Ms. Reynolds assigning me to after-school detention with a wink that says it's a front for something more fun. I tell myself to relax and just be in the moment. But I never finish. Time passes—a lot of very satisfying yet very confusing time—and then, abruptly, the dream shifts to a new backdrop, one where I am bewildered and she's just around the corner there, tidying up my room. "If you put things away as you go," she says, "you won't ever have to perform such extensive cleaning."

And me, with no climax.

Ms. Reynolds would be in her early fifties by now, but when she makes appearances in the night, she's always the same thirty-five years old from when she stood in front of the class, teaching us proper grammar or how to dissect classic literature. I haven't seen her since I left middle school, and I don't understand why my mind raises her as the subject of these late-night fixations. She was good looking, sure—shoulder-length, wavy brown hair and eyes so blue they seemed concurrently to sink into her head and reach out to grab you—but anyone qualified to wear a skirt could have starred in my daytime fantasies at age thirteen. Now that my hormones have tamed, I have a narrower focus on my preferences. I'm much more meticulous with my selection process; yet there she's remained: Ms. Reynolds peeking her head into the kitchen.

This is all bittersweet. Most of me wishes she would stay away and let me sort out my own sex life, or she would at least wear something besides that same purple V-neck sweater. But then sometimes I'm glad she remains: the ideas that Ms. Reynolds comes up with in her twisted, graphic imagination sure beat other dreams I've experienced. I'm talking about some dirty moves, replete with accompanying dirty talk and the oddest toys. I've even had to shoot down a bizarre suggestion or two of hers.

Convinced that the Ms. Reynolds dream would be the extent of my love life this trip, I didn't really spend any time worrying about any lack of real physical companionship.

Then Ivana came out of nowhere, a situation without explanation. Traveling, it's not difficult to find attractive people. Stunning. Dazzling. My goodness there are some gorgeous people on the streets of this world, and Ivana could have been just another one along the way. I met her on the dance floor, failed to defend our fort from an apparently phantom intruder, and figured, "Well, there goes that."

But I kept on to win her over. My time in Honduras with Ivana was tick-ticking away, and I knew I'd probably never see her again. Unless we had concrete plans. This was alien territory for both of us, sure, but while we were here, I reasoned, shouldn't we just go ahead and make a move or bust?

We made arrangements, bought flights, created sample itineraries and lists of must-sees and must-dos. In the meantime, she entertained me with her mispronunciations.

"Do you think we could go to *Thighland*?" she had asked back in Honduras. "I've always wanted to go to *Thighland*."

"Yes," I said, choking back a smile and refraining from correcting her. "We can go to Thighland." For two weeks, she pronounced it with that soft *th* until someone else heard her and set her straight. "Thailand, Thighland," I said. "I reckon it really could go either way."

One day she asked me whether an adult could get kidnapped. "Yes," I noted, "but we call it adult-napping. It's disrespectful in my country to say that an adult got kidnapped."

And a week later, I cut her off mid-sentence. "*Deepers*," I said. "The word you wanted there was *deepers*."

"Really? Not *diapers*? I thought babies wore *diapers*."

"No, no. *Deepers*," I said, somehow managing a deadpan look. "They wear *deepers*. You're spelling it right, but it's one of those tricky pronunciations we were talking about earlier."

"*Deepers*," she said, repeating the word so it would stick. "Okay, *deepers. Deepers.* Got it."

I entertained myself in this manner just as Ivana entertained herself by laughing with her mom in Slovak on video calls. They giggled repeatedly about my mustache or my shaggy hair or my growing stomach. Right in front of me. Lots of chunky, foreign words. Lots of pointing and laughing.

Something clicked. "This is different," she had declared to me as we curled up on the couch to watch a movie back in Honduras, and she was right. As we were walking around El Porvenir, everything seemed to flow so easily. There was no tension between us, and we resolved all disputes in a composed manner. Rather than letting a problem fester and then letting it all out in one big explosion of emotion, she'd say, "It bothers me when you . . ." and I'd say, "Okay, I won't do that anymore," and she'd say, "Okay, cool. Let's go get some *pastelitos*." I've dated some good girls in my life, but I've never known a relationship like that.

This *was* different. I felt it as much as she did.

She looked out for me in Honduras. She always showed up at my door with a smile and something in her hand for me. A banana, a corkscrew, wineglasses, a pan for frying when ours wasn't big enough, matches, ideas for a program to do with the children. One day, I had a swollen toe. Very swollen, and I don't know how it had happened. Two times in a year, my toe mysteriously swelled, as if something had bitten me in the night or an infection had germinated from within. Ivana told me to wrap a tomato around it. "Cut the tomato in half, dig a little bit out, and then wrap it around your toe." I may have given her a look like she was crazy. I mean, a tomato? I wanted to make guacamole; here enters Doctor Ragu. "Put a bag around your foot so the tomato juice doesn't drip on your bed in the night. Try to keep it elevated."

The next morning the toe was back to regular size. And I wasn't even using a prescription tomato.

This girl shines bright, and as I detoured through Nicaragua for two months to participate in numerous manly ventures to offset the mortal I'd been in Honduras, I was as excited as I'd ever been in my life to get going to New Zealand.

In a Spotless Land

New Zealand is a wonderland. Just as glorious as your parents told you it was when you were a kid. Green hills roll; mountaintops cut into morning's first light; emerald lakes glisten.

But it's too immaculate. No blemishes; no calluses; neither scrape nor scar. Quite perfect and complete, really. Idyllic. Geography's supermodel. And every day falls into the same cycle:

1. Hop on a tour bus crammed with other tourists and all their bulky luggage and chattering voices;
2. Drive through amazing landscapes that make you wish you were off the steamy bus so you could take a breath of the fresh air drifting off that nearby mountain;
3. Arrive at destination;
4. Get off tour bus;
5. Skydive or soak in hot springs or hike on a glacier or partake in some other scenic activity;
6. Get back on tour bus with same group of tourists;
7. Drive through more amazing landscapes toward the next destination.

Everything is so regimented. I have a picture of Ivana and me before we hopped on a daytime cruise. In this picture you can see two brown paper lunch bags, each marked with a little note from the tour company that says, THIS LUNCH BELONGS TO: _____.

In town, it's always, "Over here to the right, ladies and gentlemen, you'll see a bunch of well-accessorized rich people. And over here to the left . . . a bunch of well-accessorized rich people." Make sure the batteries in your camera are charged: out of town, it's infinite sheep and exquisite backdrops.

New Zealand isn't real life. It's a fairy-tale, except there's no evil in the good-versus-evil scenario. I need glimpses of reality to keep me in touch, to help me appreciate the beauty of these lush landscapes, to keep them from feeling like a movie set. Just drive me through the 'hood one time. Please. One indication of the real world. Show me a gritty defect, harmless even, a benign brown mole on the skin of this fine country. Show me a street or two of the downtrodden, whose tired bloodshot eyes follow you as you pass by. Give me a guy with a tomato wrapped around his toe. Okay, I'll settle for a shady-looking dude with a baggy jacket and a scowl. A mean person, mad at something? Maybe you could introduce me to someone—just one person—to be short with me when I'm asking for directions to the cinema. No? Everybody is *so* jolly *all* the time in New Zealand. It's like stepping into a country full of peppy golden retrievers. It's always "Cheers!" and "No worries, mate!" and "Sweet as!" and "Enjoy the show!"

Oh, go blow yourself with all of your eternal elation and gourmet dishes at waterfront restaurants.

Central America? Gritty. I might get invited over for dinner or I might be squeezed by vicious glances to cross to the other side of the street as I stroll to the market. Nobody knows. I wake up with no idea what might happen. I could find myself hanging on to the top of a chicken bus on Ometepe Island or leaping from a thirty-foot platform into the blue waters of Lake Atitlán. *Let's visit a women's craft cooperative in the village of San Antonio in the morning and leave time to roast marshmallows at the summit of Volcán Pacaya in the afternoon.* In Central America, I took chances, tested the edge, and came out the other side satisfied that I cleared my own little path rather than waking up with everything set up for me. Faced a little uncertainty. Figured some things out on my own. In Guatemala or Honduras or Nicaragua, as soon as I stepped wide of the Gringo Trail, I was different, unique, an anomaly among a group of natives. Even *on* the Gringo Trail, my skin color and gawkiness outed me so clearly as a sightseer, but at least I had an identity. On my own. In New Zealand? Nobody looked twice my way.

If you neglect to go to the bathroom before hiking in New Zealand, you can pretty much count on toilets positioned at the beginning of the trail, end of the trail, and along the trail itself. If you neglect to go to the bathroom before hiking in Central America, you can pretty much count on taking a shit in the woods.

In Wellington I watched a guy throw his chewed wad of gum to the edge of a sidewalk, just short of the grass and thus in the path of passing pedestrians. I quickly grew bitter. *What kind of lazy upbringing*, I thought facetiously, *led that young man to behave in such a reckless manner. Is there still hope for his future?*

Everybody is a sweetheart. The plane ride to New Zealand opens a portal to a new world. These people aren't human.

Feeling rebellious, Ivana and I stepped off the bus and hitchhiked from Rotorua to Taupo, and dammit if Richard Adams, some random dude, didn't pick us up in his white truck, give us a tour of his hometown, take us to his shop to show us where his team of engineers builds geothermal machinery, and stop short of inviting us to stay at his house only because we had already arranged accommodation.

Come on.

We overnighted at Lake Wanaka, where I had a chance to catch up on a little writing over a glass of wine. Well, that glass of wine turned into a bottle, and that bottle turned into, "Hey, let's go out and get a drink." You know how it is.

Guests and regulars in New Zealand pubs rave about this game called Killer Pool. Each player gets three lives, and each time you miss a shot, you lose a life. Last man standing wins a bar tab.

I, obliterated and staggering slightly, bowed out after three ungraceful shots, one of which didn't make it to within six inches of any pocket. So, I settled on my barstool to the side of the table. One of the remaining players stood directly in front of me, sizing up an easy gimme shot. Drunk as I was, I poked him in the ass. Like a jerk. One pointer finger for each cheek. A little *he-he* moment for the crowd. He missed the shot and turned to me. Broad shouldered and with fists big enough to do damage, he just smiled off the awkward moment. Back in Raleigh, I would have gotten slugged in the nose, and I would have deserved it, but this fellow smiled and shrugged it off.

I felt bad about it, so I careened up to the bar to order him a beer. And one for me, too. You know how it is. I walked up to him, handed him the beer, and slapped him on the shoulder, proclaiming, "Cheers, mate. Sorry 'bout that shot, mate. No worries, mate. Enjoy the beer, mate." Problem was that he was standing on the other side of the pool room and I had delivered the beer to some random dude. Like a jerk. *I mean, sober up, Shep. Jesus.*

But dig this: the guy I poked ended up the last man standing out of the twenty-five or so players. And don't you know that, instead of pointing and laughing, he waved me over into his group of four to share the bar tab he'd won?

Come on.

One afternoon, I embarked on a search for a couple of ripe avocados, essential to completing Ivana's and my dinner plates. The lady at the fruit and veggies shop near my hostel had only hard ones, but of course she—without my urging—referred me to her competition. "Have you been to Romano's yet?" she asked. "Two blocks down that way, turn right, half a block on your right. They probably have your avocados."

Come on.

One of Ivana's teeth had been bleeding lightly at the gumline for several weeks, and she feared it could worsen or apply pressure to her other teeth. We were heading to the Australian outback next to work on a remote million-acre cattle station for two months; if she had a serious tooth issue, she needed to fix it pronto. So we stopped in at Advanced Dental Care in Nelson for a consultation.

"We're booked for the next three weeks," the receptionist explained with a sympathetic grimace. "Booked solid."

We had three more days in Nelson, and it was our last stop of two days or more.

"But hold on," she said. "Let me go speak to Dr. Quin." It was late morning, minutes shy of lunchtime, and Dr. Gerry Quin, one of four dentists at this office, had just performed an emergency procedure. He was on his way home to read. As she passed, the receptionist smiled and mentioned that "He's one of ten doctors in the world chosen to study [some long, scientific word that you and I can never hope to pronounce] in Boston. He's very busy."

Well, would you believe it—that dude stepped out, introduced himself to Ivana, ushered her back to the chair for a checkup on her tooth, and ensured her that nothing was seriously wrong? "I'm certain you can wait until you return home in July to see your own dentist," he said, smiling and patting her arm. "You'll be fine until then."

And he didn't charge Ivana a nickel! "Enjoy the rest of your time in New Zealand," his receptionist piped merrily. She gave Ivana a sample pack of pain medicine and offered to write a prescription for more. "For your tooth or in case you get kicked by a cow in Australia," she said.

I mean, come on, man. Who are these "people?"

I'm not asking you to rob me, but I know there has to be somebody out there who wants to tell me I'm so ugly it looks as if I've cycled through a dryer full of rocks. A cross word? An evil glare? Nothing? No matter our scrupulous search, we couldn't get away from smiling faces for a single, momentary dose of a daring situation.

What I'm trying to tell you is that traveling in New Zealand is incredible. They're backwards about which side of the road to drive and how to write the date—is it March 5 or May 3?—but they got everything else exactly right. I can't recall all the seven deadly sins, but I'm pretty sure Ivana and I committed each of the pleasure-seeking ones while in New Zealand. We swam in natural hot pools; hiked Tongariro, the "greatest one-day walk in the world" (and it was); Rollerbladed along the Auckland waterfront; and watched the sun set at Wanaka. We went hang gliding. We rolled down a seven-hundred-foot-long hill inside a gigantic inflated ball. We ate fish and chips as a warm sun kissed our skin on Tahunanui Beach. In Dunedin we sprinted up Baldwin, the world's steepest street (and when we got halfway up, Ivana looked over at me and said, "This street sure is steep.") We cruised Milford Sound, toured Abel Tasman, learned all we could about the history of the Māori, and fed sheep out of the palms of our hands. We skipped rocks at Lake Tekapo, Ivana making my tosses look silly. We cheered with seventy-five Japanese tourists as two of their comrades bungee jumped from a bridge in Queenstown, and I tell you that I'm rarely as entertained as I was that sunny afternoon. In two and a half days, I went to Fergburger four times, only one of them during normal mealtime hours. We gorged on meat pies, drank unreasonable amounts of wine, and took naps when we didn't deserve them. We tried, in vain, to spot a kiwi in the wild.

We spent a damned fortune on this hedonism, and I don't regret a dollar.

But on day twenty-three, I started to lose perspective on reality. It wasn't just New Zealand but also being away from the familiarities of home for an extended period of time. My professional prospects were at a standstill, had been, would continue to be. I had no regular workout routine, and I could feel the consequences when I jogged or climbed that steep hill in Dunedin. The conversations I found myself in weren't the same conversations I'd participated in six months before. The people I was meeting, fantastic people indeed, weren't like people I knew. After lunch or a ride on a hang glider, they split, forever. Ma, Pops, Easy, Korey, Surry, Jordan. I wanted to sit in the steam room with Tony and just talk about our day as my muscles relaxed. I wanted a heaping plate of fried chicken and dirty rice and a glass of sweet tea.

The absence, the homesickness, drained me. My energy faded slowly.

Save the first day or two of shock in Guatemala, this was the only time I longed for home. I encountered momentary bursts of depression. Sinister thoughts, disturbing thoughts, began to slip into my mind, along with urges to create a problem in my life, since there weren't any in New Zealand for me to solve. Darkness caught me idle, swept over me like a cloud swelling with rain. Happiness at dawn was genuine and, by late morning, manufactured. *I* was missing. My life lacked depth. In Nicaragua, in Honduras, numerous activities filled my every waking moment— and they were activities that mattered to the people around me. They were important moments of connection as I aided children or dug wells. In New Zealand, I had no purpose other than to make sure my camera was focused and the harness around my waist was taut. There was no pressure, no obligation or responsibility; if I overslept, everything moved along the same path as it would have otherwise. At the end of the day, I had a beautiful picture, but I couldn't grasp its true beauty. The last picture was beautiful and the next one would be, too. They all were. So what was so great about any one of them?

I tried to hide my gloom, and mostly I succeeded. But as the days passed, I started taking everything for granted. I'd saved for this trip, I'd paid for this trip, I'd planned this trip, I'd overcome the doubts about this trip, and then I had the balls to actually get on a plane and embark on this trip. But all those ideas knotted together and sat dead in the corner while I was in New Zealand. I forgot where I came from, forgot what it took to get there.

Here I had a wonderful young woman with me in a wonderful place, and I started getting snappy over trivial things. She wanted to go grab sandwiches for dinner, and I got an attitude. Like a prick.

Everything was perfect, but so much perfection day after day made me uncomfortable. Even perfection can become monotonous.

I needed to get away, just for a day. So I went fishing. For backpackers, fishing off the coast isn't advertised in any bus guide. It's more difficult to arrange. You have to do a little legwork. I wanted this badly, not only to get away from the tedium of vibrant normalcy that New Zealand offers, but also because "fish off the coast of New Zealand" was the only New Zealand item from my list of 142 good times. I received three polite rejections in other towns, but then I called up Moeraki Fishing Charters and told Callum, the skipper, "I've been here twenty-three days, man. My time is running out to have the opportunity to do this. Tell me you have a spot on your boat."

"When do you want to go?"

"Next Saturday."

He paused a moment. I heard the sound of paper crinkling and imagined him flipping through a planner, pages covered in appointments scrawled in blue ink. Then he replied slowly, as if still mulling over the paper. "I have a fishing club going out next Saturday, but let me ask my wife if we can get you in there."

The skipper, ostensibly the man in charge, then asked his wife if I could go. She said yes.

I hitchhiked the seventy-six kilometers from Dunedin to Moeraki, stayed over Friday night, and met the fishing club at the dock at 7 A.M. We rode the fishing boat an hour out to sea, bouncing over light waves, and dropped our lines.

There were some nibbles on our lines but nothing coming up. We sat in the gently rocking boat, staring down and out across the glittering water. Breathed in the fresh salty air. Waited.

Steering from the center of the boat, Callum moved us to another spot.

No luck.

Another spot.

No luck.

Another and another and another. By eleven o'clock, we'd caught one bin full of blue cod and the less coveted sea perch. The crew from the day before had caught five bins by noon. They'd drifted at one point for two hours straight; by comparison, my group hadn't been at any one spot longer than ten or twelve minutes.

I sat near the front of the boat, holding my rod loosely in my hands. My gaze swept over the sea around us, the calm waters devoid of boats, save for our own. I inhaled deeply. Before long, we all shed our jackets as the sun warmed the air around us. The salty aroma of the ocean filled our nostrils; the soothing slap of waves buffeted the boat's hull.

Staring earnestly at two screens in the wheelhouse, Callum couldn't believe that his navigational tools could be leading him to the wrong hotspots. Fish were biting—as one could see from sudden and erratic yanks of our poles—but we pulled few of them up to the surface on our hooks. Eighty mollymawks, a cousin of the albatross with a wingspan reaching eight feet, surrounded our boat and pecked at our bait. John caught an octopus, a mess of bulbous, deep purple arms; the old man next to me caught a little shark.

So at eleven-thirty, Callum stopped the boat and grabbed his own rod. He U-turned out of the wheelhouse and onto the deck, starboard side. He dropped his line and waited for it to feed out to the bottom, about thirty-three meters. He reeled in once to lock in his hooks just off the ocean floor. He waited maybe twenty seconds. He yanked up once. I leaned over the edge, curious to see whether he could do what we hadn't yet managed. He paused another ten seconds. He yanked up again, his stocky arms flexing. He started reeling in his line with a sort of illogical enthusiasm. Moments later he pulled in two of the four biggest blue cod that we, as a boat, caught all day. Ten of us men, grown men with beards and farts and graphic language and at least some knowledge of the sea, caught the other two throughout the duration of the entire day.

Callum, a faint smirk painted on his chapped lips, dropped his fish in the second bin and went back into the wheelhouse to light a cigarette. He looked around with a single raised eyebrow but didn't say a word. "There are fish down there to be caught," he wanted us to know. "I'm directing you rookies to the right place. You namby-pambies just need to start pulling 'em in."

Committed to catching our quota, we arrived back to shore by late afternoon rather than by lunchtime as the website advertised. Filleted, our catch as a boat measured forty kilos of blue cod and sea perch, which meant each man walked away with four. I estimated that I caught two-and-a-half of those and then realized that I was that guy on the team who doesn't pull his weight.

I hitchhiked an hour-plus back to Dunedin to meet up with Ivana. She smiled, brushed a kiss on my cheek, and peered into the bag in my hand. A playful smirk washed over her face as she said, "Don't even lie to me and tell me that you caught all that fish."

She hooked her arm with mine, and we walked to the store to buy a couple of bottles of sauvignon blanc. Ivana fried up the fish and prepared some scrumptious mini–potato cakes. Put this girl in any kitchen, with any ingredients. Give her some leftover ham, a couple eggs, some all-purpose seasoning, some soy sauce, two ripe bananas, an old rusty pan, some duct tape, and a match, and she is going to come back at you with the tastiest soufflé you've ever known. That night we sat for dinner with the college students we were couchsurfing with in Dunedin: Dave, Tyler, Dan, Jeremy, and Evan. Ivana put her hand on my thigh. I smiled. Everyone was in good spirits, seven of us around the table in that tiny kitchen. We raised our glasses. The guys congratulated me on my expedition at sea and complimented Ivana on the best dish they'd had in a year.

Sense Draws Dollars

New Zealand is bloody expensive and dripping with wealth. I don't know the specific facts on income in New Zealand relative to the rest of the world, but I do know that somebody forgot to welcome the people on that island—North and South alike—to join everyone else in the world's current financial crisis. The median weekly rent for a three-bedroom house in Auckland is 19.047 percent more expensive than it was this time a year ago, at which point it was more expensive than the year before that. A bar in New Zealand was offering Long Island Iced Tea (U.S. $3.50 in Central America) on special . . . for U.S. $16.34! That's crazy. I figured that couldn't be the right price, or else it must be a pitcher's worth of the lethal brew, so I tested it out: I ordered one, and sure enough, that bastard at the bar handed me the cocktail on the rocks and invited me to deal him the full sixteen and change. Ain't nothin' "special" about that.

In many places, it's necessary to spend to have fun, and New Zealand is one of these places. But on my trip, I also knew to remain wise. Everybody we traveled with knew that Hobbiton and the movie set where they filmed *The Lord of the Rings* trilogy are tourist traps, way overpriced, but in Queenstown, one shan't skip out on the Milford Sound cruise just because he or she is pinching pennies.

Auckland reminded me of Boston, except a little cleaner, more modern, and without the seedy side. The buildings are glossy and reflective, windows freshly cleaned without streaks. Distinguished people rush about in business suits, sunsets drip from the sky at the waterfront, minimal buggage. The harbor teems with yachts, and locals pack into corner wine bars from happy hour into the evening.

Even the destitute are of a sophisticated ilk, a relief from the street hustlers of my first five months of travel. Our first night in Auckland, Ivana and I wandered down Queen Street, and—true story—we passed a guy cradling a cello, playing symphonies for spare change. A cello. He must have had a hundred and fifty dollars in coins strewn in his case.

I watched him as we passed, an idea sparking in my head. I had thus far kept my gambling problem under strict supervision—declining offers to join local poker games and avoiding strategically placed casinos—but I needed to scratch my swelling competitive itch.

"We could go play pool," I suggested to Ivana.

She pulled her gaze away from a happy couple walking with their children. "Pool? Billiards?"

"Yes, pool, billiards."

We were walking away from the city and approaching the waterfront.

Ivana's slim shoulders raised and dropped in a shrug. "Okay."

"But let's bet something." It was hard to keep the excitement from my voice.

"Okay. Massages?" she asked.

I grinned. "I like where your head's at, babe, but I'm good for a massage win or lose."

"Right. I *will* remind you that you said that."

"Here's what I was thinking. We'll play two out of three, and the loser has to go downtown and play the harmonica on the street for a half hour."

We neared the waterfront at this point, the faint sound of waves lapping against a barnacle serenading us. "The harmonica?" Ivana asked. "You can't play the harmonica."

"Exactly. You can't either."

"I don't understand."

We gathered around the pool table at our hostel. The room was mostly empty. I laughed as Ivana continued to invent Slovak rules. I beat her two out of three, despite a variety of silly errors. Don't call it a hustle—I'm not a shark—but I may or may not have underestimated a little on how many times I'd played before. She went upstairs to download harmonica tips for beginners, but I told her I would give her a month, until we got to Christchurch, our final destination, to practice.

Well, that plan fell through. For one, she only found forty-five minutes to practice during the month, and she spent those forty-five minutes developing bad habits that made her sound even worse. Two, Christchurch was a broken town, literally, still reeling from a series of devastating earthquakes—one of them among the strongest ever recorded in an urban area—in the eighteen months prior to our arrival. Any tall buildings that hadn't already fallen were condemned and in the process of being demolished. The earthquake the year before our arrival killed 185 people from twenty different countries. Everyone lost so much; it would have been classless for me to demand that we perform our mockery in that city.

So we waited until our flight landed in Melbourne. She found a set of stairs on the busy corner of Elizabeth and La Trobe and made good on the bet, puffing a half hour's worth of unmelodic tunes for the masses.

Now, I want you to picture this girl: this bashful, innocent Slovak girl, sitting on a concrete step among hundreds of passing pedestrians in a foreign land, with a baseball cap full of change set in front of her crossed legs. She hesitated at first. She smiled sweetly. Her head ducked to face the ground so no one could see her flushed face. She breathed lightly, whispered discords barely reaching my ears. Every now and then she peered out from behind the sunny blonde hair covering her face to see whether anyone was watching. At that point, she hadn't blown into a harmonica more than sixty minutes in her life, and the sum of her knowledge consisted of a Google search for "harmonica for beginners."

And then, inspiration struck.

She must have thought something along the lines of, *Screw it, let's seize the day, bitches*, because she upped the tempo. She raised her head to face the crowd at the corner waiting to cross the street—men in pin-striped suits, a few weary travelers in safari outfits. Evening had begun to set around us, and the streetlights washed her with fluorescent light. She made eye contact with those waiting to cross the street, if only for a moment at a time. She tried to string notes together to make a tune. And she couldn't. She was awful, a sad contrast to her dulcet singing voice, and she knew it. But she played on with confidence, blowing grating notes out of that little piece of metal. At her best, she sounded like a slowly unfolding ironing board, and at her worst, a finback whale trapped in a Norwegian gill net. Ladies gazed and smirked; businessmen wrinkled their brows in confusion. This was new to Ivana, being the center of attention, but she bought into it completely. Abashed, just this side of horrified, her face glowed red.

Per our agreement, this continued for half an hour, but more fun, I was up to my own antics, our preset deal having been that she had to act as if she didn't know me. She couldn't stop playing for a half hour, no matter what I did. We had only two rules: I couldn't touch her, and I couldn't take my pants off.

I strode by every couple or three minutes, tossed in a few coins, and made requests with the straightest face I could muster.

"Play some 'Amazing Grace,' please.

"'Piano Man?'"

Of course, she knew exactly zero songs. She tried "Hey Jude" ten times in a row. I struck an annoyed pose and raised my voice. "Ugh, you just played that one! And why do you keep playing in G minor? How 'bout a little F flat?" How 'bout I had no idea what I was saying, and her nerves couldn't keep her from laughing while she was playing. Every time she laughed, wheezing notes bubbled out of the harmonica in quick, breathy bursts.

I stood there, staring. This was so bad, the only explanation to the public was that she had been hired to keep pigeons away.

I followed all of this with an interpretive dance, my hands and feet flailing in a mix between a rain-dance and an Irish jig. The way Ivana fought hard not to smile filled me up on the inside. After that, I tossed a twenty into her hat and pulled out change.

"This is brutal. But getting better." I walked away. I came back with a note scrawled in blue ink on a wrinkled piece of paper and set it next to her for the crowd to read: THE QUICKER I RAISE MONEY FOR DINNER, THE QUICKER YOU DON'T HAVE TO HEAR THIS HARMONICA ANYMORE.

She played and played, zipping nonsensically up and down that harmonica. As her prescribed time drew to its end, I calmly took the instrument from her, set it against my lips, and started violently blowing and sucking in and out of it as if I had just come to the surface after three minutes underwater. A full sixty seconds I did this, and a full sixty seconds Ivana looked down at her shoes. Outside the two of us, nobody was amused.

Ivana faced a trying task that night, and I was surprised—nay proud—that she'd gone through with settling her debt. She'd braved the streets of Melbourne to raise exactly zero dollars and zero cents. The only thing left to do was to celebrate over sushi.

AUSTRALIA

Off the Block

What were our parents doing when they were our age?
I have pieces of my father's earlier life in my mind—
frog gigging and playing baseball and intramural sports as a
youngster, dropping out of law school in favor of business school,
fighting in Vietnam, cowboying in Wyoming, skiing in Colorado—
but what was he *really* doing? I'm sure he smoked tons of pot in
Vietnam; I'm sure he enjoyed a drink or two in his twenties. He's
a handsome man, so I'm sure there were women.

Pops is my hero, the one and only, and I would be proud
to one day become the man he is today. He is ethical and he is
passionate and he is disciplined and he is well-read and he is
humble and he is as fun to spend time with as anyone I've ever
met. When I was a teenager, he turned away longer hours and
bigger dollars at work so he could meet me at the gym to shoot
hoops after school.

Now, here I am as a young man, at a moment he once was.
As time passes, I will travel. I will play in kickball leagues. I will
work out at the gym. I will read as often as possible. I will eat
tasty food. I will invest my money wisely. I will start businesses,
successes and failures. I will watch the game with the fellas.
I will meet great people and see wondrous places and hold
ancient artifacts.

But, above all that, if I can be a father and a family man like
him, my life will be complete.

Chance Encounters, Chance Adventures

I t's interesting to me: the past circumstances that have led to us being here in our present positions. At a dinner table; the college we've chosen to attend; where we take a vacation; the books we read.

If I hadn't finished watching the news and had instead left ten minutes earlier, would I be caught in this much traffic?

If I hadn't gone to Rachel's Cinco de Mayo party and met Richard, whom would I have ended up marrying?

Hypotheticals like these may be absurd, but they're fascinating nonetheless. *How did I get here? And how could my actions in this moment affect the next?*

Twenty years ago, Robin and Lyle Mills, at fifty years old apiece and with four grown boys, traded in their sheep farm in Western Australia for partnership in a floundering cattle station. They wanted a change of scenery, maybe, but also, cattle represented the most potential for profit in the livestock market. At fifty, they were risking their entire life savings, but with the children grown, they had room to chance.

A cattle station is a way of life just as much as it is a long-term business investment. Here they were on this lonely, wide-open land, and they worked hard every day but Sunday. They could either love the long, sweaty hours or they could move to the city to sit in an office or wait tables.

"At this point, we are asset rich, but cash poor," Lyle told me. "We take a cruise once a year, but we sacrifice almost every other luxury for increased equity in the station. We put the money toward fencing or new equipment."

And this is why they've now successfully built a highly efficient and extremely productive large-scale cattle breeding and fattening operation. Other stations grind, but Warrawagine Station, a place that has changed owners a number of times over the last hundred years, now runs better than ever. The Mills family—parents, children, and grandchildren—have staked their lives and their livelihoods on managing twenty-five thousand feral cattle a year on a million-acre station in the outback. They raise and repair windmills, dig wells, string and mend fences, upgrade machinery, and then the muster begins.

"It's a challenge, but it's a very fun and rewarding challenge," Robin told me. "We care about making money, but just as much, we care about the well-being of these cattle."

And I agree. If the USDA flew to Western Australia to investigate Warrawagine, they would end up leaving with a journal full of notes on how animals should be handled.

Shortly after the Mills' speculative purchase twenty years ago, Surry Roberts, a retired physician from Raleigh, North Carolina, signed up for a camel trek across the desert.

"I got tricked into going," he told me. "Warwick Deacock, the owner of AusVenture, sent me a telegram saying that my friend Cliff Ball, an Aussie who I had traveled with to the Himalayas a number of times, was signing up for a camel trek across Western Australia. Three weeks later, I got another telegram from Warwick saying that Cliff had already sent in his money and that I better hurry up or I would miss out on the trip.

"Well, I sent in my money, and when I landed in Perth to meet up for this expedition, I mentioned to Cliff that it wasn't very considerate that he had failed to mention anything about the trip directly to me. He said, 'What do you mean? I received a telegram from Warwick saying that you were signing up for the camel trek and I had better hurry up and send in my money!'"

Over the course of thirty-one days, they traversed five hundred miles of scrubby flat land, following the historic course of Colonel Peter Warburton, who made a daring crossing through the Gibson and Great Sandy Deserts 120 years earlier.

"We periodically crossed hundred-foot sand dunes, and one day it went to one hundred and twelve degrees, hotter than we expected," Surry said. "Four nights later, the milk froze in cartons."

One town they passed by, Marble Bar, holds the world record for 160 consecutive days above a hundred degrees.

"But we were all up for this adventure, and we were much better supplied than Warburton would have been over a century before." The nights were brilliant: "You could almost read small type under the glowing night sky of the Southern Cross." Colonel Warburton's great-grandson, Ridge Warburton, accompanied the group on their trek, as well, and by night, the crew took turns reading from his great-grandfather's journal.

A little over halfway through the journey to the coast, short on food and looking for a place to camp, Surry's camel train came upon the newly purchased Warrawagine station. Robin and Lyle put steaks on the grill and a beer in each person's hand. They served ice cream. Everyone stayed up late by the river, one-upping the last story told.

Some thirty-five years before that night, freshman orientation was beginning at UNC. Dubbed Camp New Hope, the orientation lasted five days. All the freshman shared a few cabins, and it was in one of those cabins that future doctor/camel pilot Surry Roberts met my father. They rushed different fraternities in the fall but saw a lot of each other that year. Pops subsequently dropped out to join the army for a couple years but reconnected with Surry upon his return. They later met on the intramural football field, law school versus med school, and then didn't see each other until three years later in the chow line at Fort Bragg. Surry was a doctor with the 82nd Airborne Division, and Pops was a civilian at the Special Warfare School. They randomly connected again in Pleiku, Vietnam, at the PX, a trading post on the Army base: Surry was working as a physician with the 5th Special Forces at the Montagnard Hospital, and Pops, a district senior advisor, was in town for supplies. They visited each other on the weekends and have been close friends ever since.

Surry attended Freshman Camp as a young man and got tricked into mounting a camel as an old one. I told him I was looking to get gone for a year. "I've got just the spot for you to hang your hat for a few months," he said to me. "You can't go around the world without getting on a motorbike to muster a herd of cattle. Let me make a call."

I struggled to hide my skepticism. Australia wants to kill you. Lingering in that place is like walking around with a permanent BITE ME sign taped to your back. Great white shark attacks aren't uncommon there. The box jellyfish is one of the most lethal animals in the world. No one has developed an antidote for the bite of a blue-ringed octopus, which simply paralyzes all functions until its victim suffocates. Saltwater crocodiles can grow up to eighteen feet long and are well camouflaged by their bumpy, muddy-green skin. Three hundred people drown per year in Australia. Twenty die from horse-riding accidents. Many people climb Uluru, and most of them make it back down without tumbling off the side to their doom. There are aggressive spiders and bees that can cause anaphylactic shock and snails with harpoonlike teeth. You can't piss against a tree without the fear of a dingo sneaking up to gnaw a chunk out of your Achilles. Of the top ten most venomous snakes in the world, ten of them are found in Australia.

"Plus," I told Surry, "I've never ridden a motorbike. And I don't understand how it can have anything to do with gathering cattle."

"Perfect," Surry offered, preparing to craft an e-mail to Lyle and Robin. "All the more reason to go."

On a Roll

There's good luck, and there's bad luck. There are happy moments, and there are gloomy moments. There are fun jobs, and there are unenviable jobs. And some days, every one of these wraps into one big adventure.

Robin tasked Ivana; Stixy, the head jackaroo at Warrawagine; and me with mending the fence running through the river crossing. Every year during the three-month wet season, muddied water rushes down these rivers and wipes out the barbed-wire fences. Every year, they're put back up, and every year, the rushing water, packed with a hefty dose of woodland debris, bowls through the fence again.

Fencing sucks. Let's agree on that. Mending or laying it down fresh—it doesn't matter; it sucks. You ride along the boundary in a dusty old truck, one arm hanging out the window and the wind playing with your hair as your gaze skims the fence. A hundred meters, three hundred meters, five hundred meters! And then you spot that snapped line. You curse the world. You get out, you find each end, and you ply loops. You prick your hand on a barb and curse yourself for not wearing gloves. You pull your gloves on and snap off a length of wire from the back of your pickup truck. You maneuver around a pile of dried cow dung and into the thorny spinifex grass. Its barbs prick through your pants and into your legs. Curse the spinifex. You fumble to drag each end of the barbed wire back together. The sun ignites the back of your neck and your exposed arms. You grab the strainer, attach it to each end, and pull the snapped line as tight as possible with your pliers. Dust and sweat marble your neck; two flies have been buzzing around your face since daybreak. You loop your new wire into one end, cinch it tight. You scratch your arm on a barb, curse the wire for being a little bitch. Tighten the strainer with quivering muscles. This is the eighth patch you've mended, and it isn't even noon. You step into a double shot of wet cow dung. You tie off the second loop, *slowly* undo the strainer so nothing snaps, wipe away the sweat, and take a swig of water. Sometimes you get lucky and only have to straighten a post and sledge it into the ground or drag tree branches off a fallen bit of fence, but you spend most of your time fumbling and straining and pulling and pricking. And then, as my father did during his days as a cowboy out in Wyoming, you're standing on an anthill, and you don't realize it until the bastards have climbed knee-high and started nipping your skin.

Fencing sucks.

But then you take pause. The flies momentarily find other prey; a breeze floats through and cools the sweat on your face, your arms, your neck; grasshoppers buzz; leaves rustle; the breeze stops; everything is still; you drink in that steaming sun with your eyes pressed closed. It is a fantastically hot day in Western Australia. A beautifully hot day. You resign to the heat and sweat and dust and sunburn, and take a moment to admire the Jabirus, the parakeets, the hawks, an eagle with an eight-foot wingspan, the kangaroos, the donkeys, the emus, the little lizards poking their heads up to watch your activities, the endless termite mounds. The vast emptiness. "Over there?" I asked Ivana three times a week during our time in Australia. "Do you see any people or houses over there?" The void is full of life. Ivana and I were fencing that Tuesday, six days before the start of the mustering season, and I realized that as much as fencing sucks, doing it in the outback of Australia has its perks.

We needed more spools of barbed wire, so Stixy elected Ivana to take the ninety-minute round-trip to the homestead to pick it up.

"Three rolls oughta be *aw-rot*," he said. Stixy is a true outback Australian, complete with crusty boots and a dusty ten-gallon hat. Tall and gangly, he walks and talks with purpose. His work shirts are often missing the two breast pockets since he has to rip them off when he forgets to bring toilet paper from the homestead. When we met him, he'd worked four mustering seasons at Warrawagine, and you can count on him being out there in the future if you ever decide to stop by. "And grab an extra *strainah*, if you don't mind," he added.

He and I drove star pickets into the ground. I envied Ivana's air-conditioned reprieve from the heat but was proud that Stixy was confident she could navigate her way through twenty kilometers of the outback's rutted roads and actually come back to our end with the necessary supplies. Ivana is beautiful and brilliant and witty and compassionate, but she's not tough. She often overnurses minor injuries—a knee bumped getting into the car, a pounding hangover—and she veiled herself in the beige curtain covering the corner window when Jimmy brought in a baby python—a foot long—that was neither venomous nor threatened to bite. She is dependable, no doubt, but driving through emptiness to load up a few rolls of barbed wire isn't easy.

So Stixy and I walked along the dry, rocky riverbed, carrying hefty sledgehammers and slamming metal star pickets into the ground. Stixy was always pretty patient with me. He said, "You can always try it like this if you'd like," rather than, "My God, you sure are the stupidest cocksucker I ever met."

An hour passed.

I glanced at the horizon. Ivana was due back from the homestead.

Two hours. My gaze kept wandering back in the direction she should have been coming from, squinting in an attempt to see a white pickup truck where there was none.

Two and a half.

Following a lengthy search for cell reception, phone raised to the sky, Stixy called Robin back at the office.

"Have you seen Ivana? I told her to come see you at the office when she got to the homestead. We need supplies."

Robin hadn't seen her, but he responded that he was going for a ride, so he would look for her. Stixy disconnected as I chewed my lip and a mouthful of concerns.

Another hour passed. Out of star pickets, we crossed the river and radioed the homestead. No word. The horizon sat empty as it had for hours. *This is not good.* If something had gone wrong, if she'd run out of fuel or popped a tire, why hadn't she used the two-way radio to call for help?

A message rang through on Stixy's phone: *Call the homestead immediately.* He stalked back and forth until he found reception. On speakerphone, I heard the conversation:

"Ivana's okay. She rolled the truck a few times on the S-bend, wasn't wearing her seat belt. She's got a few scratches on her lower back and a bruised elbow. But she's okay."

I asked to speak with her. A two-hour roadside wait had dried her tears, but she greatly exaggerated the events of her morning. "What's that?" I asked. "Three rolls? Maybe four . . . ? And a gash on your lower back? How's your elbow . . . ? You think you tore something?" After looking at the crash site, three or four rolls was quickly reduced to one, no more than two, and later analysis of Ivana's injuries downgraded *gashes* to *scratches and mere bruises*.

Eighty percent of the way home, she'd taken the S-bend—now landmarked as "Ivana's S-bend"—too fast. She swerved a trifle this way to avoid a group of startled, scuttling birds. The back of the truck fishtailed, and—perhaps confused by driving on the other side of the vehicle—she overcorrected. She swerved again. And then again, this time losing control. Her side tires dug into the shrubby clay as the top kept going. The opposite side of the truck lifted off the ground and tumbled over the upper half. Homegirl wide-eyed the grass, upside down, about an inch and a half away, in sheer horror. Her head hit the roof. The driver's side window and the windshield shattered. Everything from the back of the truck—wrenches and wires and sledgehammers and pliers and chains and star pickets and droppers and water jugs and lunch boxes and toilet paper and cans of Pepsi Max—scattered, sprayed this way and that in a series of clattering thumps. The vehicle made a full rotation and bounced to an upright stop.

I know three other people who have been in single car accidents, all the result of intoxication. One died instantly. The second won't ever stand up on his own again. The third walked away from the scene. (Actually, he ran away and hid out at a friend's house until he sobered up.) Ivana was lucky. Toyota makes a quality Land Cruiser, and that's the *only* reason she was able to walk away from the accident. It's the same Toyota pickup truck that they use to drive on those pothole-riddled roads in Nicaragua. You can't find it in the States. Robin has run the gamut of vehicles from around the world and won't purchase any other work vehicle than these Toyota Land Cruiser pickup trucks. They last longer than any other make or model, despite the bumps and bruises they accumulate every day, and they're easy to maintain. If Ivana had been in any other vehicle, everyone predicted broken arms, legs, or both—or worse.

Robin arrived on the scene with his daughter-in-law Lynda, and Ivana let go, tears leaking down her cheeks as she rested her head on Lynda's shoulder. She was broken, emotionally more than anything, and she was sorry for all the damage.

"You're alive," Robin said.

"It's not about the car," Lynda offered. "It's about you. We've got insurance. A car can be replaced. A sweet girl like you cannot."

Excessively sugary, maybe, but that's how it was. *Is.* When life's little bumps get in the way, it's nice to have people around to help you dust off.

That night Ivana didn't want to leave our room to show her face at the cookhouse for dinner. I sat with her a while on the bed. With some coaxing, I managed to lead her across the lawn to go eat.

Ivana stepped inside, head tucked down and face bright red. I led her to the table and grabbed a plate for her meal. Most were already eating, clinking their knives and forks against their plates. The few words spoken dealt with business—what we'd accomplished that day, what we hoped to finish by tomorrow. For the first five minutes, nobody so much as mentioned the accident.

Then, breaking a silence, Stixy said, "So, blondie. You know we're still waiting for those supplies."

Ivana sat to my left. She smiled nervously and flushed. Bandages covered her left arm. And for the first time, I saw a little cut on her chin—red with the skin raised around it. She smiled awkwardly and cleared her throat: "At least I had the courtesy to land it upright on its wheels."

Everyone laughed.

I laughed, too, but I was blinking back tears. Something about that little cut made the event much more real for me. Ivana exaggerates pain, but this could have been a disaster. She could have broken something. She could be in a wheelchair. She could have been killed. *Wow, right?* She had only a few bandages, a bruise here and there, but she could have been killed. I slipped my arm around her and rubbed gentle circles into her neck. Now I was the one staring at my plate, hoping none of those real men noticed me blinking.

"Well, that was mighty nice of you, Eve," Davo said with a smile. He always called her Eve. "Quite considerate, I say."

"Listen to you, Davo," said Lynda. "Don't pick on her just because you can't get the loader started."

The conversation drifted off to talk of how, despite Davo's skill at fixing anything mechanical, he just couldn't figure out the problem with the loader. And everything was just fine.

A Native Tale

What do you call an Aborigine falling off a cliff in a minivan?
A waste. You could fit plenty more in the back.

What is the difference between an Aborigine and a park bench?
A park bench can support a family.

We were in Melbourne, being hosted by friends of friends for a long weekend. On a train ride to attend a party celebrating the end of the term and a brief respite before exams, each person attempted to outmatch the last joke told.

"Why do Aborigines smell so bad?" Remmy asked.
No answer.
"So blind people can hate them, too."
Laughter.

They crowded in and lowered their voices, but I still couldn't believe how casually these jokes flew from one to the other in the circle.

I also had questions to ask. Why are Australia's Aborigines dispatched so far from modern society's gate? Why the racial barrier? Why such hatred?

Not everyone in Australia shares the hateful attitudes I observed, of course. At Warrawagine Station, the Mills family was very friendly with many Aborigines: Robin employed Aborigines; Scott invited Aborigines to hunt; everyone spoke fondly of Aborigines when the topic of segregation arose at dinner.

Even among polite company, though, there existed a very clear separation between the natives and everyone else, and while uncommon, open racism seemed to be accepted. I was appalled by the jokes told by the mix of guys and girls hosting us in Melbourne. I have been to some remote nooks of the States, but even there, I've never heard such filthy language used to describe another race. I was surprised and confused. Mostly, I was disappointed.

At the house we went to for the end-of-semester party, there was a swastika carved into a wooden bench on the back porch. Another swastika was painted on a huge empty water jug sitting on a shelf in the kitchen. A swastika, just hanging out on the water bottle; just hanging out on the shelf. People walked by it as if it was totally unremarkable, normal. *Yeah, you know. A swastika. A water jug. That's what we drink out of when we're thirsty. You ready for another burger?*

Post–World War II, who could imagine seeing multiple swastikas in someone's home?

Swastikas may be an extreme occurrence, but a clear divide still strangles Australia. A black man comes into the bar to pick up a case of Export and the crowd around him falls instinctively silent; he pays; he leaves; conversation picks up again. Another couple natives sit off in the shade of a dark corner while the whites laugh and joke by the bar.

The biggest riddle, however, is why Australia's native people have struggled to fit into society while the Māori, New Zealand's native people, just over that sea there, have not only fused into society but thrived in it, becoming not only accepted and respected but represented so prominently along the tourist trail. Both indigenous groups—each with dark skin and eccentric rituals—were minding their own business when the British arrived. For years, there were gatherings and intermixing and trading, but then the British whipped out their weapons and started bullying. And now, here we are with two completely different fates bestowed upon the natives of these two countries. Why? Years after colonization, why is one group the butt of jokes over lunch, in those few times they're even remembered, while the other group is, despite persistent social problems of their own, now an important part of its country's national identity?

Australia was colonized by criminals and prostitutes. The first settlers were British explorers who found the island ripe for unloading the overflow of prisoners glutting jail cells back home. After their sentences ended, most prisoners stayed in the new land. Indigenous peoples were already there, of course, having—over the course of tens of thousands of years—established the longest surviving artistic, musical, and spiritual traditions on the planet. Their art was some of the oldest and finest—and most intricately crafted—in the world. They developed exceptional musical instruments. They had a rich and fascinating oral tradition. Their culture was strong.

Initial relations between the two groups were civil—trading for food, water, and clothes—but as the settler population swelled, conflict over land and resources flared up. Aborigines rebelled, a futile pursuit considering the primitive Aboriginal weaponry in the face of the Brits' firepower. Aborigines knew their environment well, but their forces were sparse and divided, and they couldn't offer worthy resistance in such a vast landscape. There were occasional skirmishes and battles in the open, but mostly British ranches and settlements slowly pushed Aborigines onto more and more marginal tracts of land. Over time, gold and agriculture brought prosperity to the British colonies, while the Aborigines were dismissed or pushed out of the way. Reports home by early settlers said that the land was unoccupied; Aborigines were originally dubbed "flora and fauna" by nonindigenous inhabitants.

Traditional Aboriginal society is nomadic. Sharing is a major component of the hunter-gatherer lifestyle. They followed food across the land, settled down for a spell when it was available, and moved along when it wasn't. When British occupation restricted their movement, many Aborigines died of starvation. Others were beaten and enslaved. Many contracted diseases from the newcomers. Alcohol was introduced, inviting symptoms of the social sickness that continue even today. Hundreds of thousands of lives were lost. Now there are almost no natives left. Tasmania, an island off the southern coast of Australia, saw a genuine genocide. The Aboriginal culture began to dissolve.

In 1869, the government of Australia thought assimilation might be a right fancy idea to save the "naturally" dying Aboriginal people. Government officials began to take Aboriginal children from their families. The children were given to white families to be raised as white children, or they were put in orphanages to be raised the white way, to adapt to white society. As many as one hundred thousand children were stolen during the one hundred years between 1870 and 1970. 1970!

Was this child thievery the result of a desire to wipe out the population in a "clean" way? Or was it guilt? Or genuine fear for the children? No one knows for sure the exact motivation, though historians are quick to offer theories. These thefts preserved the Aborigines, they say; these thefts prevented a race from self-destruction; these thefts protected the Aborigines; these thefts gave them a shot at a better life.

Except they clearly didn't.

New Zealand is a different story. When Dutch explorer Abel Tasman sailed up the West Coast, he met with a group of natives unlike any other on the planet. The Māori had domesticated plants and animals for their personal use. They were accomplished fisherman and seamen and skilled artisans, and they'd developed their own fast-paced sports. Their advanced societal structure based on social standing (*mana*) and reciprocity (*utu*) meant that conflicts, though endemic, were also resolvable.

Māori also rapidly gained a reputation as skilled warriors. Hulky, tough fellas they were. An early encounter with Tasman's crew resulted in the naming of Murderers Bay, after a skirmish between his crew and the locals led to several Dutch casualties. Tasman's crew didn't stay ashore for too long because they were being killed and eaten by the Māori. *Killed and eaten.* The Māori didn't possess modern weapons, yet they managed to combat intruders. Kill and eat them. A common trophy was the severed head of the enemy. While it can be argued that Europeans sought peace with the people they encountered in these new lands, the fact persists that they were attempting to take over the land. In Australia, it was easy. In New Zealand, though, the Māori fought back.

Years gave way to colonization. Sealers and whalers came to New Zealand, setting up small bases around the coast. Missionaries were next, moving in on Māori communities. The major wave was British settlers sailing to New Zealand, lured by the promises of private settlement charter companies. The Treaty of Waitangi was signed, ostensibly uniting both sides, and for more than a decade, there was relative peace. However, as the number of British settlers increased, the Māori found themselves increasingly dispossessed of their own land. Eventually, an uneasy, tumultuous coexistence gave way to open warfare. However, the Māori turned out to be highly capable of defending their land, certainly more so than the Aborigines in Australia.

Much of the Māori success came down to advantages in organization and tactics. While intertribal conflict still occurred, with Māori fighting both for and against the British settlers, several prominent Northern tribes unified against intruders in the 1850s under a newly created Māori king. Facing the prospect of conquest, the Māori leveraged their knowledge of local conditions to undermine British military superiority, developing trench warfare and enticing the troops into areas where they could be ambushed and wiped out.

Once, during a British-Māori battle just north of Wellington, a group of Māori held up a white flag, walked to the middle of the field, and spoke directly with the British officers. "Could you lend us some bullets?" they asked. "We've run out." They wanted to continue the fracas, which they said was great fun.

The Māori were effective warriors, and they defended their land against conquest for far longer than expected. They won tactical victories, and this earned them the grudging respect of many Pākehā, nonnative New Zealanders, making it much harder to simply marginalize and forget them. It created traditions of strength and independence, which were important for holding communities together in the dark times.

And the Māori were accommodating. They traded for the guns and potatoes and neat trinkets that the British had brought with them from home, offering land, food, labor, and their own knowledge of agriculture in return. They had a social organization that the settlers could relate to. The Treaty of Waitangi, signed in 1840 and thereafter forgotten, was given new prominence in the 1960s and '70s as Māori culture underwent what would become known as the Māori Renaissance. The Māori have managed to create a place for themselves among the white men. They have been adaptable, and they are very much a part of daily life in New Zealand. There are powerful Māori politicians and social leaders who work to shape a positive discourse around race relations in New Zealand. More than a billion dollars have been given in historical redress. Most Māori are educated at the same schools everybody else's kids are educated, and all children, Māori or not, are exposed to the Māori language during their education. Everyone eats together and shops together. Many sites and towns are named in Māori. Māori is one of the two official spoken languages of New Zealand, and it's custom to sing New Zealand's national anthem in both Māori and English. *Kia ora*, a traditional Māori greeting meaning "be well" is a regular phrase in New Zealand English. There are television stations entirely in the Māori language—no subtitles. A traditional Māori war dance is performed before rugby games.

It's fascinating. Though racial intolerance is certain to exist on some level in every country, New Zealand included, I never heard one cross word spoken about the Māori.

The tourist trail is loaded with opportunities to dip into Māori history. Bus drivers offered tidbits at random, not to sound cultured or relevant, but because they are proud. "*Aotearoa* means 'Land of the Long White Cloud,'" Soap, our driver, informed us over the sound system during one of the first few days of our adventure through New Zealand. "When the Māori first navigated here by canoe from Polynesia, there was a huge white cloud covering the entire North Island. So there ya go. Today, *Aotearoa* is one of many common Māori terms blended into our vocabulary."

Conversely, racism in Australia today has taken a different form than I've seen in any of my travels, and equality in Australia remains a fantasy. Some nonindigenous Australians point fingers and call names, while others are ashamed of the way Aborigines are treated. No one knows how to bridge the gap. The Aboriginal life expectancy lags behind that of the white man by twenty years; they go to the hospital three times as much; statistics for things like incarceration, suicide, and mortality are two to twenty times as bad as those of the nonindigenous; Aborigines still don't own much of the land originally taken from them.

It's unfortunate that colonials never recognized Aboriginal achievements: it's not your everyday person who can simply walk along and know which plants to eat and which to avoid. Australia is a beautiful but brutal land, and to navigate it the way the Aborigines have is impressive. Ivana and I went camping for one night along the riverbank at Warrawagine Station, and—as serene as our adventure was—we wondered how we could ever make it one more night in the Australian outback. The sun was hot, the mosquitoes were relentless, and it took an old magazine for kindling and a lighter to start the fire at dusk. I caught a three-kilo catfish and managed to scrape out two-and-a-half bites of meat after cleaning it. Ivana cast her line into a tree, and midway through the night, she left her sleeping bag to finish her slumber in the truck. "The potential for me to get bitten is simply too high," she declared. We would have both gone hungry at breakfast if Pete, the cook back at the station, hadn't loaded his famous meatballs into a Tupperware container. "Just in case the fish aren't biting," he'd said. That morning at breakfast under a tree, I said to Ivana: "Can you imagine having to survive out here without these meatballs?" And she added: "Or Tupperware?"

Wonderful artistic creations and adaptation to the land, though, were not enough for the Aborigines to ward off conquest. The Aborigines simply consumed as needed and walked north or south or east or west when food became sparse. Their lifestyle couldn't be expected to embrace a sophisticated form of trade. Woggabaliri, the sport of the Wiradjuri people of New South Wales, was a cooperative game without any element of competition. The Aboriginal way of life just doesn't seem to show any signs of winners and losers.

Responding to European settlement, therefore, was a challenging experience for the Aborigines, while, on the other hand, the Māori way of life has always been adapting and advancing and was much more compatible with the society of their invaders. Mutual dependence, as an example, has always been an important means of association for the Māori, so having already established trading patterns among themselves, shifting to trade with the Europeans—for muskets, for instance, which changed warfare both with the Brits and among themselves— was an easy and logical transition.

Even when many Māori saw settlers snatch their land from them, they were culturally better equipped to handle the transition. When urban centers began to spring up, the poor among the Māori were pulled into more populated and resource-laden areas of New Zealand, rather than pushed farther and farther into the outback where there was little opportunity, as the Aborigines were. Both groups struggled to maintain their identity, but while the Māori came into town and blended there, the Aborigines fell victim to the white man's vices and kept mostly to the barren outback.

Today, while the Māori are present in everyday life, I never really saw many Aborigines. Once, I passed by an indigenous family at the grocery store, and I saw three aboriginal gentlemen across the room at a pub in Marble Bar, but that was it. I saw zero among four hundred or so college students in Melbourne. They have remained with their own kind. The white man's efforts to help have been largely rejected or poorly received. Aborigines, now predominantly welfare dependent and detached, are dismissed as lazy, ungrateful drunks. Some Aboriginal children go to school and some do not. "Generous" tracts of land have been offered by the government but denied on the grounds that it's still not enough. It will never be enough, many say. One governmental program gave houses to many Aboriginal families, but most of those houses—rarely maintained and now dilapidated—were used only for storage or to accommodate an excessive number of people in substandard conditions.

One Aboriginal leader, Lowitja O'Donoghue, has said that the government has spoiled and patronized Aborigines and that "the time has come for white people to get out of remote communities." The government has failed to deliver efficient welfare, and the Aborigines have failed in their receipt of it.

So the government of Australia is offering to help, but is it a half-assed effort?

The Aborigines say they want help, but are they pulling their own weight?

Where must we place the balance of a government helping its people and those people helping themselves?

This entire dynamic irks me, and worse, I recognize that mutually agreeable solutions are a fantasy. I remain just as stumped as people who are far, far more intelligent than I am. I know the government of Australia wants to champion its underclass and offer equality; I know that Aborigines don't want to be poor and uneducated and afflicted with diabetes at alarming rates.

Beneath all these problems rests the undercurrent of racism. Racism is a vicious circle. People hear stories of drunkenness and child abuse and believe them. The mainstream then casually condemns them as a drunk, abusive race of people. This condemnation begins to define these people, so they start to play the role of the victim, thinking that's all they can do. They drink; their children play in the streets rather than going to school; they stop caring for their houses. They start to have liver problems; their children can't get jobs because they're uneducated; their houses become basically unlivable. So they drink.

So how is this cycle meant to end? If the plight of the modern indigenous Australian can be traced back to the destruction of the social norms that reinforced positive behavior, should they now be expected to adjust their thinking? Shouldn't we all—the world over—be held to the same standard of forward movement rather than expecting that everything will always be as it always was? If manufacturing jobs were here last week but gone today, should you and I cry about it and complain to politicians that we want those jobs back or should we educate ourselves for the next wave of employment?

Imagine that you're a young Aborigine. Your parents had no jobs, and their parents had no jobs, and you did poorly at school because you had no support at home. Now, how are you meant to derive the motivation to compete in this modern capitalist society?

Likewise, once you near adulthood, and you've witnessed success, shouldn't you be expected to make your own effort at achieving it rather than playing the victim and looking for handouts?

Maybe the cycle won't end, ever. Maybe government will always place a limit on its aid to its citizens, since it's been proven that unlimited aid doesn't solve these kinds of problems anyway. And maybe certain slothful members of every racial group will always exist to drag that group down, no matter the level of support they receive and no matter how much success other members of that group have enjoyed. Maybe the cycle isn't designed to end.

Really, both sides are ignorant: most whites don't know a single native, and they draw conclusions from the propaganda they see on TV or hear from their friends. This is laughable; you can't expect understanding if you don't know each other.

When a culture is so broken and has spent so many years oppressed and resisting change, perhaps the end result will always be a self-perpetuating cycle of dependency and despondency.

Why do I care about all of this? I'm not Australian; I know Aborigines only via a glance across the grocery store or pub, and I've seen authentic Māori only in brochures. In answer, I say that these are the kinds of questions, and this is the kind of curiosity, that spark when traveling. I sing karaoke, I visit a monolithic castle, I eat salami and sip wine out of the bottle next to a picturesque river, I climb a mountain, I go fishing off the coast, and I muster a mob. And then I take a moment to relate my present circumstances to my life back home. In the United States, we have the same lower class–upper class social dynamic they have in Australia and we're baffled by the same questions about how to narrow the gap. Hundreds of years ago, the same European conquest happening elsewhere in the world was happening in my home country. Colonizers met natives and traded with them; there were feasts, and there was story time by the fire; life was good; then, a new generation of Americans emerged, busting out their muskets and pushing the natives onto reservations to create their own autonomous life in the corner over there. A theft of children happened to the Cherokee of North Carolina as it did to the Aborigines of Australia.

Today in the States, some tribes have prospered; many Native Americans have stepped off the reservation to go to universities and find work and blend into the rest of the country; but others still have a low quality of life and struggle to find their own cultural identity. What leads to such different outcomes? How does one succeed among persecution while another fails?

These questions only beget more, but above all, I'm wondering this: Am *I* just as guilty as those I judge of preserving weak relations among races? I walked into that house for that party in Melbourne and saw two swastikas. Despite my repulsion, I remained silent. I should have said something. Anything. Maybe I should have stood atop a wooden chair to deliver a lecture or maybe I should have cleansed that house of its swastikas. At the very least, I could have raised a few questions. I wrote home that it "bothered me" and that "this was disgusting," yet in the moment, I stood idle and did nothing. Now in that house, hate persists.

And on the train? Those awful jokes? I should have told those guys what I really thought about their sick humor. Tragedy is a mere news bulletin until witnessed. I witnessed it. And, like a coward, I turned the other way. You might say it's not my place, but my goodness, it is!

So, here we are. Land was stolen. Children were stolen. Livelihoods were stolen. The days of yore were ugly and shameful, an embarrassment and black mark on the history of Australia.

Now how do we light a fire of hope under the seats of a race of people whose culture of achievement is relatively stagnant and so different from the Anglo-Protestant industrialists who conquered them? And most important for tomorrow, how do we get a younger generation—on both sides of the aisle here—excited about the culture of a native group that, historically, has been so incredibly oppressed and so resistant to discipline? What can Aborigines do to garner more respect from the white man, and why won't the white man stretch a little further to extend that respect?

How do we bridge the divide?

Bare Significance

Working on a million-acre cattle station—with one homestead in the middle for twenty or so people—lends perspective.

First, there is the open land, the immense vacancy of human life. Within a hundred meters in any direction, only the tweeting chatter of birds or the brush of dry grass can be heard. Sharp hills—not mountains—poke into the horizon, and the sun casts the most intricate tangles of shadow between trees. Weekday musters are insane and chaotic, but on the weekend, the lazy-flowing river behind the homestead sets a tempo as serene as anywhere I've ever been.

More important for me, though, my early experiences in Australia proved to me how incredibly unskilled I really am. In this arena, one must own a wide breadth of skills or he or she will perish. Our homestead was positioned a hundred kilometers or more from another human and hours from the nearest town. Mail came in by plane. For firewood, we felled a tree, and if a new roof was needed, we grabbed a ladder and a hammer.

If your car breaks down in Raleigh, North Carolina, you call AAA; if your car breaks down in the outback of Western Australia, you grab a can of Emu Export Lager and a ratchet set, pop the hood, and start fiddling.

Ben Mills is twenty-one, and he can do a hundred things I can't. He's a mechanic, a welder, and a builder. He drives a tractor-trailer rig, a Bobcat, a Ditch Witch, a loader, and any other piece of construction equipment with wheels. He painted the helicopter. The one that he flies for the mustering season. Ben feeds the cattle in the yard, a job that would take me twenty-plus minutes, in less than four, and he can raise a fence faster than a washed-up actor can accept an invitation from *Dancing With the Stars*. He came just short of a career as a professional motocross racer, and he can roll a micky—a young wild bull—from his bike. Confident as he is knowledgeable, he makes deals with the buyers coming in from Port Hedland and Broome. He uses words like *indiscriminately* and *subvert* in normal conversation. He reports the riveting stories of his life with fancy phraseology like "I grabbed four gears straightaway" to describe a speedy escape from a scene. He can put a round in the hump of a camel from three hundred meters away, and when he goes fishing, he comes home with dinner for the whole family. When something breaks, I leave it ("It still works, you just need a third hand in the mix to hold that lever in place"), while Ben takes it apart, hooks a quick sip of his beer, and puts the unit back together again.

I'm pretty sure that when the prime minister of Australia presses the red panic button, Ben's cell phone rings.

Me? I'm proud to know Ben. I listen and watch carefully, happy to learn from him and guys like him. But it stings a little to realize how little I bring to the table on the ranch. Standing next to him, I sometimes felt pretty worthless. Back home I have a degree in business, even if eight of my neighbors do, as well. Colleagues ask me questions, and whether they take action or not, they at least nod and say, "Yeah, I see what you're saying. That's interesting." I work, and my work carries at least *some* weight. I get occasional handshakes and e-mails after jobs well done. You may have me in darts and foosball, but I've got you in H-O-R-S-E and rummy, and, win or lose, I can take you the distance in tennis.

I matter a little back home.

But Australia brought me back down to Earth. Life at Warrawagine was humbling. I truly believe that the cattle operation would have run smoother if Ivana and I hadn't shown up for those two months. I struggle to recall anything positive coming from our hands while employed in Australia, save a couple of extra-shiny toilets, some mended fences, and Ivana's luscious apple pie—a dessert that can give even the grouchiest twit a half chub. Other than that, we just broke shit and stood idly by, feeling useless as we waited for instructions. I remember one day, while traveling in the rumbling buggy behind a mob of cattle as dust swirled into our eyes, I turned to Ivana and remarked, "Literally, if we were not here right now, if we just disappeared—*poof!*—I don't think anyone would say anything until they saw our empty placemats at the dinner table."

Imagine that. Imagine showing up with fifty levels of enthusiasm yet being so perfectly useless that when your superior looks at you, his first immediate thought is, "What easy job can I give you so that you won't be in our way?"

High Stakes Revisited

I love a good game of rock-paper-scissors. Name me a place, any place where rock-paper-scissors isn't fun. Car trips, waiting at the bus terminal, at dinner, at brunch, before homework, after homework. During a commercial, before you mow the lawn, or between sets at the gym. Always a good time to play.

And it's a useful game, too. My turn to buy lunch? Your turn to buy lunch? Who knows? Rock-paper-scissors knows.

You want me to investigate the guy outside your window? Palms up!

Rarely does rock-paper-scissors get ugly, losses never critical. "Aw, shucks. Okay, you can have shotgun." But that shouldn't detract from the utility of this great game, either. Rock-paper-scissors (or *shoushiling* during the Chinese Han Dynasty and *piedra, papel, o tijera* in Central America), no matter your location in the world, can resolve your conflict.

Follow me now to the dusty cattle yards of Warrawagine Station in Western Australia. Two days before, we mustered a sizeable mob of seven or eight hundred cattle; we drafted bulls, steers, heifers, and cows into holding pens or paddocks. Now we were down to a hundred calves, milling about and lowing after their older companions. They all needed to be tagged and either spayed or elastrated (a tidy procedure where a little rubber band is wrapped over a young male's scrotum, cutting blood flow to his testicles and giving them the opportunity to safely fall off on their own in a couple weeks' time).

Calves don't know pressure. They've spent their young lives wandering about with Mommy, never having been channeled or pushed into this pen or that. Calves have never been called into the yards, and thus they don't understand that when you're tapping them on the head or pulling their ears or twisting their tails or standing behind them, yelling and waving your arms, you want them to go through that opening not a half a meter in front of their faces. They kick, they buck, and they turn to bunt their snotty muzzles and bony heads against your legs. Calves have dealt far more damage to my body than their bulkier parents ever have. Drafting calves is a disaster, so much so that Ben— Ben the Hero, Ben who has an answer for everything—said with a slight shrug, "Just do whatever you can" when asked how we were supposed to get these cud-chewing demons through the gates.

Then came a sturdy little bull calf, a micky, who wanted nothing to do with having his jewels removed. He dug his hooves into the dirt and stood in the raceway, a narrow channel formed of five-foot-high metal gates leading from the larger pen to the smaller one, for three minutes—two minutes and fifty seconds longer than the average rebel—while we tried everything to get him moving. I loved him. He was the bull I would be. *Screw you guys. You want me to move, you best go get a crane.* The other calves were rambunctious and obstinate, but they were also a bit witless—uncertain how to escape the shouting banshees we'd become. This fella, though, he'd figured it out: cattle that sit motionless, calf or fully grown, lazy or defiant, stop up the whole system indefinitely. Imagine if every cow just plopped down during the muster, simply refused to go anywhere; you can bet beef wouldn't be among the dinner choices at the next wedding reception you attend.

This guy was bigger than normal, maybe two hundred kilos, so we couldn't just grab him and drag him out as we could the smaller ones. I stood to his right on the steel railway while Jimmy perched on the steel railway to his left. I whistled and smacked the bull's rump and flicked his forehead. I lifted his ear and yelled, "Yeehaw, motherfucker!" Jimmy twisted his tail, up and over and to the side. A twisted tail always gets cattle moving.

"Somebody stick a finger in his ass," Stixy said. All six onlookers laughed. I quickly offered up a *not it*. I yelled into the calf's ear, "Giddy up, partner!"

But Stixy was serious. Standing with his arms folded over his chest, he acted as if he'd seen little bulls like this guy before. "It will work," he said. "I'm telling you." And he was probably right. Finger in my ass, you call my next move.

Jimmy, the youngster of the crew at sixteen years old, raised his forehead and looked across the gates at me. He wasn't keen on this idea, either, though it had to be done. He called for rock-paper-scissors, and as I'd spent so much time championing this game—its honor, its entertainment value, its effectiveness at keeping peace—I couldn't now turn it down during this, the team's most challenging hour.

I glanced around at my audience. Ivana, the peachiest peach in Peachville, was six or seven feet behind me. Jane the Bitch, her face full of malice, stood to the right. Ben had positioned himself off to the left, smiling, his sandy hair dangling just above his eyes and the top two buttons of his shirt undone, so authentic and good-looking you'd think he'd just strolled off the pages of a Louis L'Amour novel and onto the cover of *GQ*.

And me, deflated, in something of a vulnerable position, with no other option. Literally standing atop this micky, I braced him so he couldn't move backward. Jimmy had me similarly braced with a quirk of his eyebrows that dared me to rise to the challenge.

I gave a slight nod, and Jimmy and I shot on four. He threw scissors; I threw paper.

My companions' laughter drowned out the string of curses escaping my lips. I spit on my index finger, stuck it in that little bull's ass, twirled it around slowly and deliberately, and he jolted out of the raceway.

The Muster

Our new employers demoted us just about immediately upon arrival. Tasked with a simple fix in the shop, I broke all three parts of the component. Ivana rolled the pickup truck. Then she jumped at the opportunity to use an electric saw—"I helped build the bathrooms in Honduras!"—and promptly cut a four-inch gash into the picnic table she was bracing the piece of plywood on. I lied and said that I'd ridden a motorbike before, and as I didn't understand how to operate a choke, when Ben instructed me to "please move that red one over there," I labored to get the bike started. Sweat beaded on my forehead. Then, with an audience of Ben, Caitlin, David, Jimmy, and the big boss, Robin, I casually drifted six feet down an embankment. Just slowly rolled down the hill with my hand on the brake while everyone stood by and watched.

Ivana and I are very nice, but they viewed us like kidney stones: wondering when we would go ahead and pass through. Immediately I established my incompetence by not knowing the difference between beef cattle and dairy cattle. "So, when I drink milk," I asked, head cocked to one side, "it comes from a different cow than the ones you have out here?"

Often, a group of guys would assemble and head off in one direction together. "Where are you going?" I'd ask, a hopeful note in my voice.

"The cattle need drafting."

"Y'all need a hand?" I started trotting behind them.

"Naw, we're *aw-rot.*"

And my remarks in social settings didn't earn me any points either. During our lunch break one day at the yards, Ben was discussing the value of well-bred weaners (young cattle who have recently become independent from their moms) on the Indonesian market versus the value of other cattle that a good muster would bring in. I looked up from my sausage roll and replied, "Ha! Ben said *wieners!*"

In most cases, they preferred to be a man short than to have Ivana or me around. On days we weren't out in the paddocks gathering cattle, this meant the lowly chores that no one else wanted fell to us. I became a fencing pro. Ivana, without thinking, in her eagerness to please, did an immaculate job on her first day of cleaning and thenceforth had a scrubber in her hand a couple days a week.

We had been so excited about participating in the muster. It was more than just a longing to play modern cowboy. Over the course of my travels, I'd become fascinated by the cow. In Hinduism, cattle are considered sacred, and for good reason. The cow is a beautiful animal, an animal that stays out of the way, that provides much and asks little, that doesn't bother anyone unless isolated and provoked.

But cows are also very stupid. It's amazing to me how quickly they fall into line along a fence to trot off to—well, who knows where? Little do they know what lies ahead (The beginning of a new civilization on a new planet? Testing a new kind of yummy hay? Vegan ranchers?), yet they're happy to make their way in that direction. Together a mob of cattle represents one extremely mighty unit, with the potential to easily overtake those roughnecks straddling motorbikes behind and to the side; yet there they remain, together, trotting along slowly to their doom, ignorant of their unified power.

Does a smart animal allow itself to be mustered, coerced into a group to be spayed, castrated, dehorned, and sent off to be butchered in some foreign land? I should certainly say not.

Kangaroos? They know better. Consider the great quantity of kangaroos on the million-acre Warrawagine station. Every day, everywhere, you see couples, families, troops of kangaroos poking their heads out of the tall spinifex bushes and around little trees. Their ears perk up, their head jolts right and then left, their noses lifting to the wind. And they are off.

Kangaroo meat is tender and delicious. If you substituted ground kangaroo for ground beef the next time you make meatballs, it would take a snobby palate to disapprove of the change. And it's also healthy. While beef glides straight into my arteries, kangaroo meat boasts high levels of protein and just 2 percent fat. Conjugated linoleic acid, prevalent in kangaroo meat, features anticarcinogenic and antidiabetic properties and has been proven to reduce obesity.

But do you think kangaroos allow themselves to be mustered? *No, ma'am.* You try to muster a kangaroo and he or she is most likely to punch you in the face and then proceed to hop off in one of a number of different directions.

Cattle, though? I've seen an isolated steer on the *opposite* side of a barbed-wire fence actually take a running start so he could jump that fence to join the mob. "Hey, where are you guys going? Can I come, too?"

Mustering cattle in Western Australia is not like the Old West. Motorbikes have replaced the horses of yesterday, along with a single-engine Cessna and off-road buggies and pickup trucks and helicopters chopping through the air. Two-way radios hang on every man's shoulder, silent one moment and blaring the next: "Get down here to the creek! I got two clean skins running loose!" It's exciting, quick-paced work. It's rewarding. The kind of dream job where pleasure matches occupation. Over dinner, these guys actually discuss their day with gusto, often their mouths full of steak; they get paychecks to do what tourists would readily pluck out their MasterCards to join in on.

I came to Australia wanting to hop on a bike. I wanted to buzz across the outback, hot on the heels of six hundred cattle. I mean, how exciting is that, right? *Yeah, so anyway, there I was in*

Australia, keeping this mob in check over on the flats, and my man
in the chopper calls for me to get down to the creek. I grabbed four
gears straightaway so I could help him out with this scrubber who
wouldn't budge.

But it wasn't meant to be. After sliding down the hill in front
of everyone that first day, Scott put me at the helm of a buggy
and Ivana in the passenger seat. A buggy that rocked with seismic
intensity every time you drove off into the bush. A buggy that
sucked in dirt like a magnet. A buggy with no heat for chilly
mornings or AC for hot afternoons. A buggy with no relief from
the wind. A buggy without the excitement of going off sweet
jumps or racing down a flat laneway.

There was one thing, though, about the buggy, an opportunity
to check off item number ninety-three on the *List o' Good Times*:
castrate a wild bull. A buggy spends most of its day on the grated
road along the fence line, slowly driving the mob home and
hollering at the laggards to get their ass in gear.

But then Scott called from the chopper, voice crackling over
the radio. "Adam, you on channel?"

"Yeah."

"Can you see me?"

I kept one hand on the wheel and twisted my head out the
window. He was hovering a half a kilometer a way, windshield
reflecting in the sun. "Yeah, I see you."

"Get back here under my tail!"

"On my way."

The mob was calmly trotting in the proper direction, their
bellies vibrating and heads low. I spun the wheel and headed
toward the chopper. Ivana fumbled to grab the camera to later
prove to my friends that the ensuing events really did happen.

I reached Scott's location out in the bush, and dammit if he
didn't have this little bull running wild under his landing skids.
Cattle, fearful of the powerful *thwak-thwak-thwak* of a helicopter,
run in the opposite direction—and eventually into the rest of the
mob plodding peacefully along the fence line. Still, occasionally
you'll get one that bucks the rules.

I paced up alongside this micky as he sped up. I eased my foot on the gas, keeping time with his unsteady jog. He busted into a full sprint, back hooves hurling dust and grass behind him. I pressed my toes to the floorboard. The buggy's engine roared in protest but kept me by the bull's side. The micky took a slight turn left, and I did, too, as I had my front right fender just off to the left of his backside. Handling cattle is all geometry. In the yards, out in the paddocks, doesn't matter—handling cattle is all about managing angles.

My fender raced inches—inches!—from the brown fuzzy hair on his side. Leaning forward and to the side toward Ivana to get a better assessment of our position, I twisted the steering wheel right, giving his rear quarters a gentle nudge. The back half of his body swerved, jarred from the tap from my right fender, and his legs buckled. He went down in a heap, hind legs rolling over his body. I came to a stop and then inched forward. He lay on the ground, sides heaving, momentarily incapacitated, while I tapped the breaks and then slowly slid the nose of the buggy over the front half of his body to lock him down. His hind legs rested on the outside of the front tires. This had been my opportunity to shine, and, *pop the champagne*, I nailed it.

"Nice work, Adam!" Scott yelled into the radio. He set the helicopter down thirty yards off and exited, knife in hand. I hopped out of the buggy and met him by the micky's heaving side.

Scott handed me the blade. I'm not exaggerating when I tell you that there was a glint in his eye. Oh, how I would have loved for my own father to have been there to witness this. The sound of the chopper blades was the only noise now as I slowly crept around to approach the beast. Scott bent down behind him and raised his back leg, exposing his genitals. I was careful to pierce this bull's sack and remove his bollocks without nicking any vital arteries or veins, which could cause him to slowly and painfully bleed to death. I cut a tiny slit in the left of his scrotum and pushed out his left testicle. He kicked once, but Scott maintained his grip on the bull's leg. I cut a tiny slit in the right side of his scrotum and pushed out his right testicle. His blood speckled my hands, but despite his upset lowing, he was going to be fine. Scott, smiling, gave me a single nod of approval. Nothing else to say. I grabbed a rag from my back pocket to wipe my hands, hopped back in the buggy, reversed it, and let the now-steer rise leisurely on his own. Calmer now, he gathered his bearing and trotted off to join the mob. Ivana, beaming with pride, kissed me on the cheek.

And then my alarm clock woke me from my slumber. *Dammit.*

Instead, in real life, Scott greatly, greatly overestimated my intuition of the what-to-dos and how-to-do-thems of rolling and castrating a bull. He called for me to get on my skates. "Adam! Are you fucking kidding me driving like that! Get your ass over here under my tail!" Scott cursed on the radio once out of every three or four musters and usually at me.

"On my way."

I arrived at the scene, eyes wide and heart racing at the opportunity. I took a generous turn around the left side of the micky, hit the gas hard, and rammed him. He rolled straight through the wire fence, long legs flailing as he flipped into the neighboring paddock. Picture a potato going through a masher and coming out whole on the other side. That poor bastard. He stood up, stunned long enough to snort air out of his nose as if forcing a sneeze, gave me a quick, dark-eyed once-over, and loped off into the other paddock, free to spread his seed until the next year's muster.

Scott said nothing into the radio. He didn't yell or curse. I looked up at him through his windshield. Scott is a courteous man, a gentle man, but I'd just shoved eight hundred dollars into the next paddock. His chopper was loud, buffeting me with waves of wind. Dust swirled. I could see fury in his eyes. But he just pressed his lips together into a thin, white line and said nothing into his mouthpiece; he just glared at me. I glanced at Ivana. She sat with her arms wrapped around herself, eyebrows high on her forehead with a look that said she didn't know whether to weep or break into uncontrollable laughter.

Finally, Scott cut off his stare and turned the chopper back to the other wild cattle.

PHILIPPINES

Manny

Thirty-seven years ago, Ali fought Frazier in the famed Thrilla in Manila. Until I was twenty-two, I thought Manila was somewhere in Africa. In fact, if I sat next to you right now, and I offered you a thousand dollars to name two Filipinos, could you? Probably not. Two Filipinos. Make it ten thousand dollars. Despite all the famous people that this joyful country has produced—Diego Silang, Eddie Romero, Fe del Mundo, Levi Celerio, Carlos Romulo, Lapu-Lapu, Josefa Gabriela Silang—you and I have never heard of any of them.

Rafael Nepomuceno, the six-time world bowling champion?

Benigno Aquino III, the president?

José Rizal, revolutionary, foremost Filipino patriot, and national hero?

Nora Aunor, the internationally acclaimed actress? Huge, she is.

But there is one.

Manny Pacquiao, as I touched down in Manila, had long been regarded as the best pound-for-pound boxer in the world. He is the only boxer—ever—to win a world championship in eight different weight classes. The Boxing Writers Association of America recently named him the Fighter of the Decade.

He and his five siblings grew up in a broken home after his mother discovered that his father was living with another woman. Raised in extreme poverty, Manny was forced to drop out of school at fourteen to help his mother support the family. For a while, he lived on the streets of Manila. There, he started boxing on an amateur level, and the government paid for his room and board.

But where Manny stands now—his status in Filipino lore—is wild. Manny is more than just some kid who worked hard and made it out of the 'hood to run a thousand yards for a Super Bowl contender. This man is an icon. Such an icon, in fact, that he was voted into Congress of the Philippines. Congress. At age thirty-one, with literally zero minutes worth of political experience, *while* still in the prime of his boxing career. This, after he created his own political party, the People's Champ Movement.

He was the first Filipino athlete to show up on a postage stamp. He carried the Filipino flag with pride at the Summer Olympics in Beijing, despite the fact that he wasn't even participating. The Boston Celtics made him an honorary member.

A movie has already been made about his life.

Team Pacquiao, a store at the mall, sells shirts and gloves and DVDs and other memorabilia for the casual or obsessed fan. Stop by to get your own shirt with Manny's profile on the front. No extra charge if it's autographed by the champ.

He throws out first pitches at San Francisco Giants baseball games. He has a doctorate of humanities even though he's never attended college. He's a lieutenant colonel in the Philippine Army. He has starred in numerous Filipino films and recently signed on to play in his first Hollywood feature. He owns real estate all over the world, including a luxurious mansion in Los Angeles. He owns (and plays for) a team in the professional basketball league in his home country.

Manny Pacquiao is so popular that his wife scored her own nationally televised talk show.

He is such an icon that his people cheer with fanatical excitement when assembling to watch him sing karaoke, and he's absolutely one of the top five worst male singers I've ever heard. Seriously. And that includes the barking "Jingle Bells" dog. Go search YouTube for "Manny Pacquiao sings." Atrocious. But people love him, all of him, and if he drops a new album, then just show them the line so they can get their hands on one of the two million copies.

Bleacher Report listed him among the most exciting athletes of all time. *Forbes Magazine* boasted him among their list of the most powerful celebrities in the world. *Time* declared: "He has a myth of origin equal to that of any Greek or Roman hero."

I've told you all of this to tell you one more thing: Manny Pacquiao is outstandingly ordinary looking. Unremarkable in appearance. Consider the dominating presence of the first two or three or five famous athletes that come to your mind right now. Tall and broad shouldered, they have impeccable posture and look incredibly sexy in a tight T-shirt with sweat dripping off their noses. With their success comes confidence, sure, but if Michael Jordan had never picked up a basketball and had instead forged an obscure baseball career, I'd still give him an inquisitive second look when passing him on the street. "Hm. Who's that?"

Manny, though? Even now, when I see him in an interview, the first thing I notice is his underwhelming appearance. What a cutie he is. How I look like more of a professional boxer than he does.

We live in an age of prima donna athletes, who think they are way more important than they actually are, who say things that make them easy to scorn and cheer against. Not only is "Pacman" actually important, the pride of a country, but he carries himself with grace. Max Kellerman, while interviewing Manny, might say, *Champ, your opponent has said that he's going to knock you out, probably by the third round but no later than the fourth, and that you aren't worthy of all of the hype. He says that you're a punk and that you were a good boxer for about fifteen minutes back in your twenties. That your time has passed. That you float like a meat pie and sting like a flea. That he's going to break your face apart and that your once-adoring fans are now going to have to refer to you as Pacenstein. That you look like a canker sore with the mumps. He spits in your general direction. He says—and I'm just reading from the cards here, champ—that you smell like the carpeting in a New Orleans Motel 6 the day after Mardi Gras. When he is hurling the belt over his head after the fight, he's going to point over at your corner and laugh at you. Now, them's fightin' words. What do you have to say to him?*

Manny would just grin and respond, *Ah, he . . . uh . . . he berry good fighter. He train hard. This be good fight. I . . . uh . . . I excited to fight him. He good fighter. It in God's hands now.*

Hasn't lost in seven years, doesn't even remember what it feels like to lose, beating the hell out of everybody who dares to dance in the ring with him, yet if an opponent slings ten different servings of shit his way, Manny would just say, "Ah, he berry good fighter."

Other than the corner across the ring, Manny has no enemies. This is a man who is easy to revere. Manny Pacquiao: legendary yet nondescript. He's short—five-six and some change—just like every other Filipino man. Shaggy, bristly dark hair covers his head, and a scruffy goatee frames his thick lips. He smiles much and says little. He's lean, muscular only when shirtless. He has a considerable entourage, but you certainly wouldn't pick Manny out of that gang as the famous one when they come walking toward you at the mall.

If Manny Pacquiao came up to me at a bar and proclaimed, with that Filipino twist to his tongue, "Excuse me, sir, no disrespect, but I just wanted to come over here and let you know that I think you look like the result of a baboon mating with a lemon tree. And also, again no disrespect, sir, but I will be going home with your girl this evening," my immediate next move would be to pick him up by the seat of his trousers and pile-drive him out the front door. He simply can't be taken seriously in street clothes. He's too adorable.

Yet there he is, all five-six, twenty-million-dollars-or-more-guaranteed-per-fight of him, hailing from a country where many people's dinner tonight will cost about a dollar. He's literally a living legend, knight of the archipelago that is the Philippines, and whilst your friends may think that a Vegas bar is a cool spot to watch him fight, I suspected otherwise.

The heat in Manila scorches, year-round. Sizzling. Australia is hot, but it's that "dry heat" that everyone tells you isn't really so bad. The air in Manila, however, swirls lazily into a miniature cloud over your head and settles on your face and neck and shoulders like a burning, wet towel. Prone to sweat or not, you're going to glisten during the day and then wake up at three in the morning drenched on top of your covers.

And Manila is dirty and dilapidated just like every other busy capital city across the developing world. Ivana and I rode through the city on our first night and felt lousy. The taxi driver—and this really did happen—reached to lock his door at the first red light. Trash litters the streets and clogs up the sewers, people live on sidewalks and along waterways in the city. The walls and foundations of many buildings are already crumbling or cracking. It is Tegucigalpa, Honduras, with cheerier people and an occasional marvel of architecture. A rat crossed my path in the street on night two, but I hesitated to change course at first because I thought it was a kitten.

I said to Aldrich, the manager of the Red Carabao Hostel: "Don't take this the wrong way, but this city scares me a little. Quite filthy, no?"

"Oh, man," he replied. "You should go check out the slums on the north end."

But Ivana and I had only a couple of days in town. We caught up on communication with home. We went shopping and then to a pool party Aldrich was hosting in the chic Malate District by the Manila Bay. On the other side of town, we watched a cockfight, an event as brutal and as captivating as I'd heard.

I bought two tickets to see Manny fight. Ivana asked, "Isn't that the game where they bite each other's ears? I just will not support that."

Watching Pacquiao fight in the Philippines is different than back home, for two reasons. One, you can't bet on the fight. In the States, one of your friends can call up a bookie to lay down a bet, but you can't do this in the Philippines.

"No. No bets," my taxi driver had explained on Saturday night. "No betting on the fight."

"Seriously?" I asked, confused. "This is a betting-man's culture."

He glanced at me in the rearview mirror. "But you can't find anywhere to place a bet. Everybody going for Pacquiao."

"Fair enough. What if I want to bet on Bradley?"

The driver looked at me sternly. "I advise you not to bet against Pacquiao in Manila."

The second reason is that, back home, to watch a fight, you can pay entrance to a bar or you can simply beam the fight, via pay-per-view, onto the big screen at home. In the Philippines, though, your average citizen with a twelve-inch snowy-screen TV and four channels cannot pay to watch the fight on their sagging couch.

So people flock to the cinema. Starting at eight o'clock in the morning, each cinema hosts the fight on every one of their screens. They sell tickets for ten bucks and these theaters fill up until elbows brush elbows.

Ivana and I found our assigned seats fifteen rows back, on the aisle. For the first of the three undercard fights, the theater remained sparsely populated. We bought a bag of popcorn and two waters. A few people trickled in for the second fight, and the theater started to fill up during the third and final undercard, which ended early after a couple illegal blows. By the time the main event hit, the theater was packed. An electricity flowed through the people, a buzzing energy akin to what you feel at the finals of a live sporting event. Murmuring voices babbled throughout the theater, offering predictions. Glancing around, you could see the faces of these people all lit up—not only by the screen casting the flickering white light, but also from the thrill of it. From the excitement. People were pumped.

Nearly every man or woman in the city, senior citizen or child, had packed into a theater somewhere. Boxing is to the Philippines what soccer is to Guatemala—it's the lifeblood of their country, the passion that draws them all together, if only for a few hours. It makes them all equals. Gives them their common ground, no matter their financial status or faith. Corner stands shut down; tricycles stop running. Unlike many American sports, this event offers no excuse for the ladies to assemble for some hassle-free shopping. They're in theaters, too. They yell and scream and cheer just as loudly as their male counterparts. And sometimes a little louder. In an interview six months ago, Joe Tessitore asked, "What motivates you now, Manny?" and Manny answered simply, "I need to be the best I can be so that I can bring honor to my country." It is a well-known fact that the crime rate in Manila drops to zero while Manny is fighting. ("Well," snapped Aaron from Australia, back at the hostel. "He oughtta fight more often.")

Ivana didn't understand it. "This is crazy," she marveled. "These people love this guy. My goodness."

"There's no one like him in American sports," I told her. "We've got sports stars and pop-culture icons and an occasional trustworthy politician, but no one so beloved that they're the spectacle of an entire country." From the Team Pacquiao store at the mall, we each donned shirts displaying Manny's face and autographed by the man himself. Manny-acs we were, but unlike Star Wars fanatics who flock to conventions to help forget they're middle-aged and own lightsabers, we were there to see a fight.

"He's a boxer," she noted, leaning in to be heard over the prefight chatter around us.

"An exceptional boxer," I replied, "dominating the sport on the world stage from a country that most people don't know much about. He's the everyman. He's the identity of this country."

Manny's opponent, Tim Bradley, Jr., was undefeated, 28-0, with twelve knockouts, although this was his first notable fight, his first moment on the big stage. He's serious and stern and focused. He's handsome, with a chiseled chin and a face untarnished despite so many rounds in the ring. He's a vegan, and the muscles rippling through his chest, abdomen, and arms look like they could deflect bullets.

Notably, though, he's from the States, the site of the fight, with many Americans in the audience. Strutting with an easy confidence, Bradley entered the ring of the MGM Grand Garden Arena. The crowd met the announcer's introduction of this phenomenal American boxer with only faint encouragement. Encouragement barely audible over a chorus of jeering. Jeering. *Boos*. Oh, the roar of this merciless assembly. He bounced, light on his feet, and you could see his gaze roving over the people. Vocal abuse. Taunting. Whistling. Bradley is an American. In America. Getting booed. Taunted. Cursed at. By other Americans.

Manny walked in, a more shuffling gait. The crowd went crazy. Absolutely nuts. "Eye of the Tiger" screamed from the sound system. Everyone bolted to their feet, jumping, waving, ablaze.

I mean damn, homes, that's kinda fucked up. This man comes into your country and steals all the love? Come on, dude. They can barely even understand the words rolling out of Manny's mouth, and they're erupting for this man. They love him more than they love you, a lot more than they love you, actually, and this is your home turf.

I mean damn, homes.

Bradley later said the Pacman Mania didn't rag him, but sure it did. Somebody says they hate you and they're pulling against you, and you say, "Yeah, whatever man. Go climb a bush." Somebody else says they hate you and they're pulling against you, and you cover your ears and say, *La la la la, I'm not listening*. But then more and more people show up at your door armed with hate. And more. Vegas has you as a 7-2 underdog. And then you realize that nobody outside your apartment really believes in you and that everybody—everybody!—is cheering against you. This is the kind of reception that makes a man think twice about his own abilities. *I've worked hard, but am I in over my head here? Am I good enough to be in this conversation?*

Of course Bradley told reporters that he was prepared. He wasn't mean or engaged in hyperbole, was rather matter-of-fact. He stared into the camera eyes with a calm, level gaze. "I don't care what [Pacquiao's trainer, Freddie Roach] says, I'm ready to go . . . Manny Pacquiao hasn't seen a fighter like me in a long time . . . I'm right in my prime. I'm very quick, very good reflexes . . . I get in the ring, and [other boxers] say I don't have any power, but then they feel me and feel my strength. As soon as they get hit they want to hold me . . . You look at all [Manny's] fights—he doesn't fight well inside . . . If you miss this fight you are going to miss some greatness. He has to deal with me on June ninth and that's going to be a tough task." Bradley leaned forward a little, his expression completely still. "Pacquiao's worn-out, tired. I can see it in his eyes, the wrinkles. This boy's not ready for me."

Pacquiao's response? ABC asked him whether he had a special message for Bradley before the fight. He replied with that same friendly smile. "I send wishes of good luck. And God bless us."

Sportswriters and promoters tossed out the word *upset* a few times but only to intensify anticipation. Everyone knew who would leave the ring a winner, and every time Manny's mug in the locker room flashed onscreen, his countrymen and women in the theater around me gasped or clapped or both. After the anthems played out their final notes and the appropriate sponsors had been recognized, there came a moment's pause. That moment you hold your breath just before the fight starts. The energy in that tiny Filipino theater roused the hairs on my forearm. I shivered and sat up straight in my seat.

The bell rang. Both fighters darted forward, dancing light on their feet and throwing some slight punches—at first, just light taps glancing against skin without real impact—testing the waters. Then they started playing for real. Some nice body combinations by Bradley and a couple of counters by Pacquiao.

Bradley blocked a powerful left.

A powerful left by Manny landed on Bradley's cheek. He tried to twist to avoid the devastating blow, but you could see how it vibrated through him. Folks around me shouted, "Ahhhhh!"

Another hard body combination, a series of quick jabs from Bradley. The hate had amped up Bradley's roar. On the edge of my seat now, I could see his revved-up concentration, focus, the speed of his movements. He *was* ready.

I spared a glance over at Ivana. She'd fixed her gaze on the screen; nothing would pull her away.

I turned back in time to see a big left by Pacquiao.

A flurried assault from Pacquiao. Bradley wobbled, clearly shaken by the battering his ribs and face had taken.

Pacquiao hooked Bradley, and the crowd around me exploded. Their emotions were tethered to every punch.

The ref warned Bradley about a blow delivered below the belt. The little man next to me sat down to nervously stuff his face with popcorn between rounds.

The rounds rolled on. Bradley landed a short, snappy jab, and Manny smiled and nodded. "Good one."

I was caught up in this moment, too. The energy. The fervor. I cried out to Ivana over the chaos in the theater, "Why do I care so much! This is craziness!"

A short left inside by Pacman, who dominated the sixth round. Every moment of a main-event boxing match is as exciting as the last 3.8 seconds of a basketball game, the final drive in football, the bottom of the ninth in baseball. A knockout hangs in the balance.

And I thought: *In the States, sport matters, but it doesn't really matter. In the Philippines, Pacquiao defines these people around me in this theater.* Pacman stepped out into the world and conquered it in the name of his countrymen.

A short right by Manny, and Bradley countered with a left of his own. Both men panted as they kept up the shimmy, sweat rolling over their muscled torsos.

A drop of blood beaded on Manny's lip. The lady sitting on the center aisle two rows ahead of us yelled at the screen, though I couldn't tell whether out of rage or joy.

A sharp uppercut by Bradley, and Manny countered with a left of his own.

The pace slowed.

A one-two by Bradley, followed by a furious exchange. It didn't look as if any of this was hurting Pacquiao; an easy smile flashed over his face between rounds. Despite the blood on his lip, his movements remained light and quick. He bounced back from each blow as if it had glanced off instead of rocking through him. Still, his trainer wasn't happy about round ten. A nearby mic caught his voice—"You let that round go," he said.

Bradley landed a solid right on Pacman's jaw, but the wiry Manny responded with a splendid left that sent Bradley reeling. Ivana smiled. The guy on my left let out a spontaneous, "Hey!"

In the twelfth round, Bradley needed a knockout so that the decision wouldn't go to the scorecards. He started quick, a hard hook to the ribcage and a couple of combinations throughout, but he didn't get it, didn't have enough power for Pacquiao's chin.

The vitality around me dampened slightly, progressively. The crowd's energy slowly drained from one round to the next, despite the still-cheery faces. We watched before us an older, less dominant Pacquiao. Two years before, Bradley would have been staring at the ceiling of the arena, toes pointing to the sky. That day, though, Pacquiao had probably lost round one, perhaps round two, but regained control early and then cruised through until the end. He lost round ten, and arguably won rounds eleven and twelve. Both fighters slumped in their corner seats, panting with exhaustion. I turned to Ivana. "Well, there was that. The crowd didn't get the knockout they wanted, but at least their man won."

"I don't understand exactly what just went on," she said. "And you shouldn't even try to explain it to me, but this was fun."

"Cool. What do you want to do now?" As I shot the last two gulps of water from my bottle, something crazy happened. Without a knockout, the judges' scorecards call the fight. The announcer blared over the loudspeaker at the MGM Grand Garden Arena, and Bradley's arms lifted to the sky. Battered but triumphant. I turned to the screen. Everyone in Manny's corner turned to one another in disbelief.

Manny knelt and prayed, while Bradley danced and hugged. The audience booed with ferocity. Both fighters finally made their way through the rabble to pat the other on the back.

Around me, inside the theater, the assemblage roused. Everyone gasped, shouted, and jeered. Mouths hung open. Some collapsed back into their seats in disbelief. Others mumbled about corruption to the fellows sitting next to them. No one threw a drink at the screen. Not a single shriek rang out. Instead, the mood deflated. People began to meander out, discussing the unbelievable news and just sort of staring blankly up at the screen. One by one, they shook their heads and wandered out.

"SHOCKER!" a local Filipino paper screamed the next morning. Another showed a photo of Pacquiao's mother, Dionesia, passed out on the ground after having heard the verdict.

Bradley later deflected the criticism: "There are three judges out there. That's the way they judged it. What do you want me to do?"

Pacquiao was confused but unaffected. He shrugged a little as he offered the reporters a response to the chaos following his apparent loss. "I don't even remember if he hurt me with even one punch. One hundred percent I believe I won the fight. But the decision has already been done. So you have to give credit to Bradley."

Pacquiao's trainer called for an investigation, saying, "I think the judges had their eyes closed."

CompuBox, a computerized scoring system that records punches landed, showed that Pacquiao connected on 253 of 751 total punches, while Bradley landed 159 out of the 839 he threw. Pacman landed more hits in ten out of twelve rounds. He struck seventy-two more power punches than his opponent, and that's a high number for a twelve-round bout between two well-trained warriors. *Every* percentage favored Manny. He outboxed Bradley according to *every* statistic.

Something wasn't right. Sportswriters and sportscasters unanimously tallied the fight in Pacquiao's favor, most by wide margins. Harold Lederman, a legendary former boxing judge and current analyst, scored it eleven-to-one for Manny.

The World Boxing Organization reviewed the controversial verdict with a panel of five judges. All five of them saw the fight in Pacquiao's favor.

Back in Manila, no one really seemed to know how to react in this situation.

In an e-mail a few days prior, Pops told me to watch my ass if Manny lost. The mere thought had never occurred to me.

I stepped outside, blinking against the bright sun. With the crime rate dropping to zero during a Pacquiao fight, I expected riots and pillaging afterward. And stones in the air. And burning cars. Maybe some debauchery. At least a couple scared little naked kids standing around crying for their mothers.

But the town fell under an impenetrable hush. I stood outside the theater and let my gaze stray up and down the street. Groups huddled in peace to discuss the conspiracy—lips tightened into thin frowns, many shaking their heads. But there was no outrage, no flailing hands and red faces.

A legend had fallen, and inside the mall, men sipped coffee and women examined dresses on sale. Outside, the markets reopened. People hailed taxis.

A Penny Saved Yields a Journey Yearned

When I stepped off the plane and into Asia, I instantly became wealthy. In Indonesia, my ATM receipt alerted me that I was down to my last 117 million; I was buying avocados with fifty-thousand-rupiah notes. In the Philippines, my pockets bulged with fat stacks, and I slung hundred-note bills around like a University of Miami booster at a high school football game. "What do you want? A necklace? A dress? New shoes? A miniature wooden boat for the mantle? What does my baby want? A banana shake? Yeah? Does my baby want a banana shake? *Bam.* Here's a five hundred. Get yourself a jumbo. No worries, mate. Don't even need the change."

If you wonder whether an odyssey like mine is financially realistic for you, I answer with a resounding yes. My family was never destitute, but we've often struggled. My pops will live the rest of his life on a lean retirement allowance, and my mom works as a hostess at Applebee's. So how did I make this trip happen?

First, as I began my research, and as I started working my way around the world, it surprised me to learn how far an American dollar will go abroad. I departed on this trip in the heart of a recession, arguably the greatest financial crisis since the Crash of '29, and I still had a year's worth of rewarding experiences.

The trick is to figure out which countries fit your travel budget. A hamburger in Copenhagen costs four times as much as in Prague, and Prague is one of the coolest cities in all of Europe. For the average price of renting a one-bedroom apartment for one month in Raleigh, North Carolina, I could rent my own private room on Ometepe Island overlooking Lake Nicaragua or a full two-bedroom apartment on Útila Island (in the Caribbean) for two months. I could do even better on a white-sanded beach in Thailand. I saved money in inexpensive countries (Honduras), and let my bank account loose in more expensive ones (New Zealand). Japan is pricey, as are Singapore, Taiwan, Norway, England, Australia, and many other countries, so one either figures out how to travel there creatively or dodges them altogether. Forget Switzerland until your rich aunt dies.

Interesting enough, though, I spent less money on this yearlong trip than I would have spent back home during the same year. That is, if I take all my expenses—flights, ground transportation, food, drink, lodging, entertainment, language classes in Guatemala, and hydrogen peroxide to cleanse my bovine-probe finger—and line them up against what I would have spent at home on my car, gas, insurance, apartment, food, entertainment, and two weeks of vacation. I hopped through seventeen countries on four continents for less money than it would have cost me to commute, vacation, play, eat, board, and buy a few cool new technological gadgets back in the States.

A trip like this requires sacrifice. You must sacrifice while you save for your trip and sacrifice while you are spending on your trip. *What are your priorities?* I essentially had two simple rules before I left, two means of keeping my spending in check: One, no souvenirs. Perhaps a wild idea for you on your own travels, but I already had a bulging backpack that burped something out every time I opened it. I also don't have a permanent home to start hanging paintings, laying rugs, or displaying hand-carved wooden boats. Besides, more often than not, buying souvenirs is like picking somebody up at a bar at 2:30 A.M.: you get home and wonder, *Good Lord. What was I thinking?*

Two, moderate spending on alcohol. Alcohol can kill a travel budget. That "one more beer" you just had to have offers a sad substitute for admission to hot springs or an ATV rental up a volcano the next morning. So many people I met—too many people—were passing on fun side excursions because they were "watching their money" while buying drinks by the armful. Alcohol never got in the way of me doing what I wanted to do. I kept my intake manageable and mostly bought bottles from the store rather than in rounds at the bar.

I used disposable razors for five weeks at a time. I checked books out from the library on my Kindle. I slept on whatever surface happened to be available at the time—from bunk beds in hostels, to the beach house in Honduras, to a resort in the Philippines, to tile floors in eight airports, to any of a wide variety of (free!) landing spots via Couchsurfing.

My eating varied, too. In Guatemala, Beatríz offered that, "If people can afford to only eat street food, maybe they shouldn't be traveling." I disagree. You can find some of the best—and least expensive—food in the world at open-air corner stands. When I wanted to sit down and have a more formal meal, I did. But I knew I couldn't eat out every day, so I often cooked, although usually with haste and without ingenuity. Maybe one day I'll be selecting from an extensive wine list, but right now I'm just as happy ordering empanadas from a lady on the street corner with a fryer and a cooler full of cow that got split open over the weekend.

There are two tricks to spending money on the road.

First, be simple. I packed minimal clothes and only those that would wash in the shower and dry quickly, a week's worth of drawers and socks, a quality pair of shoes, sandals, a sleeping bag, soap, a towel, a washcloth, a water bottle, ibuprofen, Band-Aids, Neosporin, diarrhea medicine, tweezers to keep my eyebrows tidy, a toothbrush, toothpaste, dental floss, Q-tips, a laundry bag, a journal, three pens, a headlamp, a digital watch, a pocket knife, my debit card to keep on me, a credit card to keep separate in case of emergency, a Kindle, my passport, a copy of my passport, and a camera. Everything else, I reasoned, could be found along the way.

Second, be creative. Ultimately, this trip cost me less than staying at home only because I was creative with my planning and execution. In Honduras, tuna orzo Alfredo became a staple because the supermarket in La Ceiba marked the ingredients down on an almost permanent basis. In Granada, I met Evu, who had been on the road for just over thirty years—since age sixteen—earning his money from paintings he sold. Ugly paintings, too.

I shopped around: bungee jumping in Slovakia offered jumps from a higher platform, a more scenic view at one-fourth the cost of the jump at A. J. Hackett's company in New Zealand.

I also saved money shopping around for flights. To wit:

For weeks I kept my eye on a flight from Costa Rica to New Zealand, because my research showed it would be—by three times—the most expensive leg of my trip. Any over-water flight is expensive, and there's nothing but a vast emptiness of water between Costa Rica and New Zealand. For eight weeks, starting five months before I was set to take off, I watched this flight, waited for it to go down. I clicked the box noting my travel time as flexible in order to find a lower price. All eight weeks those numbers held firm without any signs of retreat. This flight was going to cost me $1,604, and ready to concede defeat and be put out of my misery, I contemplated buying the damn thing, lest it could go up.

Then an idea popped in my head, born of my previous traveling experience. I once flew from Raleigh down to Atlanta to get over to Charlotte, a ludicrous move, just so I could save the equivalent of dinner money. I considered the application of this same wisdom to my current predicament. What if I flew a little out of the way?

San Jose, Costa Rica is not an airline hub. It's not a thriving metropolis of the Americas. People don't fly through there on their way to get anywhere; it's where they end up or it's where they begin. It's a tourist destination for flights coming from the north and the south, sure, but the population isn't nearly what it is elsewhere in Latin America—Santiago, Chile; Buenos Aires, Argentina; Mexico City, Mexico. Surely one of these places would have a cheaper flight to New Zealand.

Nothing. All flights from South America filtered through Santiago, while the flights up north went through Mexico City and cost just as much. Most were far more expensive than $1,604. Then I checked Los Angeles: $551 to New Zealand. My heart fluttered as I readjusted my seat. I checked the flight to Los Angeles from San Jose: $263. By combining two segments on my own, I cut the flight price nearly in half in exchange for an extra nine hours in the air and a flyby in Fiji to pick up a few additional passengers.

Too easy. Extra air time meant extra frequent-flyer miles, and since Ivana and I were creating our own itinerary in New Zealand anyway, our flight schedule wasn't pressing. The extra time meant I had to spend money on two extra sandwiches, but it also meant time to read *Twenty Thousand Leagues Under the Sea*.

The second way I was able to manage this trip is that I made saving for it habitual and fun, an easy lifestyle change. I sacrificed four fundamental things in the two years that I hustled to save for my journey: food, lodging, car, and clothes. I ate out once or twice a week, otherwise opting to cook my own food at home or at a friend's house. I lived in a four-bedroom apartment with three roommates, each of us with our own bathroom and a common living and kitchen area to share. I drank Tony's booze at his apartment before going out, and then bumbled from bar to bar drinking Diet Cokes on the rocks. I drove a seventeen-year-old Plymouth Sundance that coughed fumes when driving under twenty miles an hour and wouldn't kick out air-conditioning when going up an incline. I tended bar at the Hilton Garden Inn and promptly deposited all my tips in the bank. I sought inexpensive local entertainment—movies at the dolla-fitty, tennis, games of pool—but splurged for occasional weekend trips with friends. And when necessary, I shopped for clothes at Walmart or Target.

None of these were real sacrifices, though. Being a miser is not a sacrifice; cooking your own food is not a sacrifice; driving an old car is not a sacrifice. Leaving a wife and newborn to go fight for your country is sacrifice; two jobs while raising a son and a daughter without assistance is sacrifice; donating a kidney is sacrifice; handing out ramen noodle flavor packets to trick-or-treaters after the bag of candy is empty is sacrifice.

Saving for this trip was simple. Delayed gratification. It's simple to favor your own cooking or pass on a shiny car when you're surveying with wanderlust the world map on your wall. Your roommates aren't *that* bad; the dolla-fitty shows the same movies as the real movie theater, just a month or two later. The anticipation of your trip is very real, as is the prospect that this could actually happen, so you tolerate those niggling forfeitures while visions of daiquiris and the sunset on a Thai beach appear in cloud bubbles over your head. "Just six more months to save," you say.

Meeting Raf

Imagine what it might be like to reach through the computer screen to confront a person on the other side.

Years ago, I read some articles and a couple of books on outsourcing, and it changed the structure of my life. Every time the media mentioned outsourcing or a presidential candidate shunned contracting work overseas, I assumed this only affected big dogs, major corporations rather than little guys like me. Manufacturing a shirt is cheaper in China; so is routing customer service calls to India or accounting work to Bulgaria.

But I'm not in manufacturing, my handful of customers can ring my cell phone for service, and Brian does my taxes over his lunch break.

The Internet changed all this, bringing virtual assistance to the commoner on a digital silver platter. Individuals can now (easily) shuffle their menial duties abroad, freeing up time to expand their businesses or cut their work hours in favor of extra time with the fam. Regular people—you and I—with a local lawn care business or a side project trying to sell homemade reversible purses can find someone elsewhere in the world to handle every task that makes us want to rip our hair out. The little guy can now research affordably, manufacture affordably, and market affordably. A recent Google search lists limitless tasks available for outsourcing: sales lead development, website management, software upgrades, article submission, fact-checking, travel research, slideshow creation, meeting preparation, party planning, online-dating profile management, wake-up calls, and shopping.

Attending a wedding soon? Don't write the toast yourself, silly! Let us do it for you!

I read an article about some fella who experimented with literally outsourcing everything in his life. Everything. He sent work-related tasks abroad, sure, but he also farmed out tasks like ordering books online, arguing with his wife, calling his parents to wish them a happy anniversary, and reading a bedtime story to his son. Honey, his personal assistant, whom he would never meet in person, was up early and eager to work for him.

If you can somewhat coherently list instructions in an e-mail, assignments will be completed for you overnight, finished by the time you sit down at the table for your bagel in the morning. Globalization allows for a collaborative effort to be affordable and efficient for everyone.

"But wait! Sending jobs abroad is an abomination for the American worker!"

"But wait! Investing abroad allows room for sharper creativity and increases profits Stateside!"

Reality dictates that you're losing a competitive edge if you aren't exporting uncomplicated tasks that can be completed online. Having your website built in a foreign country is going to cost you half the price (or better) and much less time. There are many, many jobs—old ones and new ones—that must be completed in the States, but there are other tasks that can be sent abroad.

So, a couple of years before my world adventure began, I had plopped down on my sofa and flipped my laptop open. A few clicks and I began my search. India grew expensive for outsourcing, so the Philippines became the new *it* place. John Jonas, the foremost expert on outsourcing to the Philippines, said: "They speak American English in the Philippines, and, unlike some other countries in the world where you might outsource tasks, Filipinos are loyal. They aren't going to spend a hundred hours working for you and then run off to become your competitor. They just want to support their families with a stable paycheck."

A Rafael Apolinario III's credentials spanned my screen. I had spent half an hour sifting through many others to get to him, those quoting a higher rate and those less expensive, when I settled on him due to his glowing enthusiasm. "Yes, sir!" he wrote. "I can get that done, sir!!! And I can do it quicker than your deadline!!!"

Well, okay then, Raf. Let's see what you got.

Here's the thing. Not only is my boy Raf logging hours for half the cost of America's burger-flipping minimum wage, he's doing some pretty advanced computer work for me: lead generation, search engine optimization, linking, submitting articles to various websites. I can send him a list of one thousand colleges and universities and say, "Uh, Raf, I need the names and e-mail addresses of the vice provosts at these universities. You think you can do that in forty hours?"

He says, "Yes, of course, Sir Adam, but I will try hard to do it in thirty!"

I asked him once whether he knew how to put together a video from a file of pictures, and he wrote, "Not today, Sir Adam. But I can learn by tomorrow!"

Also, the advantage here falls one hundred percent in my favor. If I find Raf's work unsatisfactory, I move along to the next Filipino. If he takes too long to complete a task, I move along to the next Filipino. If he's too busy working for other people, I move along to the next Filipino. I can always simply move along to someone else. I'm not obligated by explanation or reason. He's fired; another is hired. I don't pay for health care or Social Security or sick days or a stipend for gas. I don't match his 401(k) contributions. There are no company retreats to the mountains or appreciation luncheons or snacks in the break room. He pees when he has to, and then he's back to work. Raf is responsible for his own training and for buying all his own computer equipment.

I send him money; he sends me quality work. It's a very simple relationship.

And he loves it. Consider this. I'm no bully—Raf and I have developed an e-friendship and mutual respect over the last two years, which he has spent building valuable databases for me—but these practices wouldn't fly with American workers. Raf's hustle, though, plays to a different tune. He lives a week-to-week life, balancing five or ten different employers. Some days he works twelve hours; some days he goes to the beach; some days he goes to the beach with his laptop and works twelve hours. Some days he tells me he worked twelve hours when he probably went to the beach instead. No matter to me. When it comes time for a spreadsheet of contacts to show up in my inbox, he is Right. On. Time. And when I say, "Sorry, Raf. I don't have any work right now," he writes back, "Okay. No problem, Sir Adam. Maybe next week possibly. Talk to you then."

This, without a doubt, has lifted my professional life to another level. I can spend a hundred hours generating a list of sales leads or I can spend one hour writing instructions and ninety-nine hours writing or speaking or anything else that doesn't lend itself to delegation. And this list that Raf has built is going to be better than the one I would create, more content rich and more valuable. I take that list and I work it. Raf heads to the bank to collect a fat paycheck.

From the outback, Ivana wanted to go to a beach. One with powdery sand and few people. One where we could lounge by the shore and eat filet mignon and drink a bottle of chardonnay. One where she could swim without concern for sanitation.

I e-mailed Raf and inquired about a cool place to hit up in the Philippines. "Trying to be easy on my bankroll," I said. "But I still want to get credit for spoiling my girl a little." Trading my American dollar for forty-five pesos sounded good.

He replied almost instantly. "Adam . . . you are welcome anytime! I am excited to finally meet you personally. You can fly into Manila, and I can come meet you there. Or you can take a transfer to Kalibo. I live just an hour and a half ride from Boracay, the most beautiful beach in the world."

He was exaggerating, kind of. Just this year, TripAdvisor touted Boracay as the second-best beach in the world, just after Providenciales in the Caicos Islands. This is somewhat remarkable, considering Boracay's glorious white beaches are still relatively undiscovered by the New World (I met exactly one American under thirty during eighteen days there), and that back home, my boy Korey needed four tries to even pick out the Philippines on a map. We speak of sunning in California or the Caribbean or Australia or Brazil or Thailand. But never on Philippine beaches.

Never mind. There was Raf at my condo at the Nirvana Resort. How awesome to be standing next to this young man!

Around five feet tall, he weighed in at 115 pounds. I was almost literally two of him. He sported a Fisher Price My First Mustache and had curled the top of his hair into a minimohawk, the style of the decade among Filipino men. He was, remarkably, just as he looked in the picture on his Gmail profile.

"Adam, sir! You made it!"

I've been less nervous walking out to speak to a thousand people. What was I supposed to say?

"My man Raf. What. Is. Happenin'?" We hugged. I gave him a signed Manny Pacquiao shirt I bought for him in Manila. I insisted we do away with this *sir* business.

I learned that he was two years from thirty, though he looked to be between fifteen and seventeen years old. I'd never known his age.

If you've ever contracted work overseas, perhaps even developed a bit of a friendship with your workers, you can appreciate the eeriness of this experience. It's quite similar to an in-person encounter with a romantic prospect you met through an online-dating website. "In person? Oh, man. Didn't think we'd ever actually meet in person." *What are we supposed to say?* With my fingers resting on the keyboard, I have so much time to think these things through over the Internet. I'm witty and articulate online; I have a firm presence and identity. I have the time and resources to feign legitimacy by infusing my prose with trivia or creative metaphors. I'm clean-shaven in all images, and the edited sound bites on YouTube portray me as charismatic.

The tide shifted when I met Raf. I was no longer in charge. Raf, the Raf who always apologized for simple, meaningless errors and always asked me twice whether I found his work sufficient, morphed into a man in control. All five feet of him. He showed Ivana and me to the cool spots on the beach, he took us to buy fresh spices and produce, he gave us a tour of the creaky but clean office he worked out of, he introduced us to his family, and he helped us to avoid getting swindled. "No, man, don't buy that one," he advised when we passed by souvenir shops.

He cooked. Sauteed prawns and pork adobo. He combined shrimp, spinach, string beans, tomatoes, onions, peppers, fish sauce, and a tamarind base to make a tangy traditional Filipino soup. I bought ingredients, he cooked them.

Ivana—the Ivana who can serve you a gourmet meal when provided only with ground beef, honey, ginger, garlic, and a bay leaf—scribbled down notes in a worn-out notepad. "Hm. What is that taste? Is that balsamic?"

"Nope," Raf replied. "Red wine."

"Hm." She squinted as if trying to rationalize this new possibility: red wine. Her pen scratched away.

And then we went wakeboarding. Raf spit out Tagalog, the native language, all over that island until we arrived at the only place with the equipment to offer wakeboarding.

"Asgoias7gdata ascpo ia∑jsg9dkin sa."

"Viearigi wepoΔicgit Zagatafreu denshnei Nede rhavenako."

I blinked. "What was that?"

"He said they can take us out for eighty dollars for a half hour."

"Well, tell that man he can go ahead and go take a dive in a ravine full of crocodile shit."

"Maasd¥ goiawan—"

"No, don't tell him I said that. Jesus." I snorted. "Ask him about eighty bucks for the hour."

"Uuuuu gh!ananaraw masjjjjea3keavich anovhaven™arahova hour?"

"Haep7oiasd ñgheiiiiau manh©÷anuna parama kkeri Jehovah's Witness."

"He said a hundred."

I forget where we settled. It wasn't in my favor but far better than a white man would have been able to negotiate on his own in Boracay. I really didn't have a choice anyway. This man owned the only wakeboarding equipment on the island. I spent pocket change to fight bulls in Nicaragua, and I was ready to go to the ATM in order to wakeboard, with Boracay's lounging green hills and rough cliffs as a backdrop. Boats were zipping this way and that under the sun's full gleam. A few white tufts littered a mostly cloudless sky. It's irresponsible to spare expense for these once-in-a-lifetime experiences.

A half hour later, I was sitting next to this dude, this guy I'd known for two years, but really only a few hours. We were relaxed out there, under the sun, on the boat together. This guy was so different from me, yet so knitted to the fabric of what I'm trying to become. This was wild. I steadied myself on the board, riding in ten- or fifteen-second segments, while he took pictures.

"Did you get that one?" I asked, surfacing from a spill after one of my jumps. I shook my head to fling water from my shaggy hair.

"Hm. Yes, man. But I tell you it might be a better picture if you can get off the water a little bit."

Back home, I often mix business with pleasure. When the work is done, I'm usually off to dinner or to the tennis courts with the person on the other end of the contract. I keep in touch online, even though I know we might not ever do another deal.

Meeting Raf in such a beautiful atmosphere was an interesting blend of business and pleasure. We have nothing in common, and there wasn't a whole lot to talk about. He was nice; I was nice. We spoke very little about current political happenings and a lot about Manny's fight.

Raf lives a world away from me, literally and metaphorically. The people of his country are almost as poor as the people of Honduras. Raf lives in a cramped one-bedroom apartment and cooks his meals—mostly rice and bits of fish. He deposits most of his earnings into his nineteen-year-old brother's college education fund or into a savings account for the business he wants to open one day. He walks around town, whether his destination lies one block or a couple dozen away.

I wouldn't be able to have an assistant if I hadn't found Raf. Others in the world are far less efficient and always looking for you to sign a month-to-month contract. They call you *sir* or *ma'am,* but they don't mean it. Raf means it, though, and finding him was like finding treasure.

In a way, he and I are living off of each other. His pockets stay full and my business gets a boost to the next level.

And in between home-cooked meals and time on the boat, it felt good to be able to step out of the virtual world, establish a real connection, look him in the eye, shake his hand, and thank him personally.

A Hut for Two

B oracay Island is a romantic place that skirts a poverty-stricken community, where improvised shacks are crunched up against one another. Like all vacation destinations, visitors are intruders, a nuisance greeted with a smile. "You want a massage?" "Kitesurfing? Best price on the island." "All-you-can-eat buffet! Aren't you hungry this evening? Great food. Great fish." Natives outfit their livelihood with pesos hustled from tourists.

The pristine island stretched out before us, full of craggy inlets and coves and caves and green hills, all surrounded by white sandy shore. The water, a clear bluish-green as it should be in these scenarios, gives way to the darker waters of the coral not fifty meters from shore. Ivana and I meandered, fingers entwined, on a quiet stretch of Puka Beach, reasonably removed from the flurry of the center of the island. A few booths offered necklaces, and an occasional guy chugged by with a cooler of ice cream on his back, but the rabid, insistent commercialism of the island's main drag doesn't exist at Puka. Peace replaced the bustle, bare sand the crowds. Divers and kitesurfers and Jet Skiers assaulted other corners of the island but left this stretch for the sunbathers and swimmers. This place is the ghost of tourism's past.

It was the start of the low season, the rainy season, and a typhoon blustered about, still miles out at sea, but threatening to soak the region. Tourists faded with the sun behind the clouds, but Ivana and I lingered. When it rains in Vermont, you're miserable without a jacket and an umbrella; when it rains in the Philippines, you're rejuvenated.

The wind picked up, whipping Ivana's hair and pelting our bare ankles and calves with sand. I glanced up and down the abandoned shore just as the leaden clouds began to dump swollen pellets of soft raindrops. Ivana laughed and pulled my arm forward. Thankfully, every hundred feet or so at Puka, there are bamboo huts with roofs thatched from nipa-palm leaves—and cheers to whoever built those. They sit on the edge of the sand, back against the hills of trees, and they serve as little picnic areas or as relief from the sun or foul weather.

We ducked inside one such hut, our clothes already plastered wet to our skin.

"Whew," I remarked, wiping the rain out of my eyes. "That was close. Some storm."

"We should put the camera in a Ziploc bag," Ivana said. She reached into my backpack.

"Good call." The wind buffeted the hut and shook its thin shell.

In the distance, the layer of clouds broke a bit. They seemed to crumple, allowing brilliant rays of orange light to streak through, splitting the deluge. With a sigh, I lowered myself to sit on a bench at the front of the hut. The structure was makeshift but sturdy. Ivana sank down beside me, our arms and legs brushing. At our backs was a wall of green. The air around us was warm. I leaned back against the bamboo and inhaled the scent of sand and sea and the lingering scent of sunshine on our skin. Five minutes, we sat there when, finally, the rain stopped.

I scanned the scene. "Look at that. Everybody has gone home. I mean, *every*body."

"Yeah, it was flowing pretty good." She'd pulled her hair back in a ponytail, but a few strands of blonde slipped free and fell over her face.

I'm not going to say that we were both thinking the same thing, but there was suspense in the air. I stared at her for a moment, wanting to brush the hair out of her eyes. She just stared back at me.

"Yeah," I said, stating the obvious. "Came down pretty fierce. No people out here."

"Yeah, no people." She had slid on a bright-red pair of shorts; sand clung to her bare feet and ankles. Already the sun had left its mark on her; a smooth tan covered every inch of her exposed skin, with a few streaks of white peering from around the edge of her bikini top.

"How about all those idiots that have sex on the beach?" I asked with a clear sarcastic tone, as if to say, *Ah yes, an empty beach. That reminds me of getting naked.*

"Yeah, I mean, come on," Ivana replied. She looked to my face and then back out to white waves cresting in the still choppy sea. "Go find a bed, right? Go inside, at least."

"Ha. Yeah. Idiots."

Ivana isn't conservative. *Afternoon delight* was among the first slang phrases I taught her in English, and I'd already been through various sexual situations with her—shopping for birth-control pills, the Night Adam Couldn't Get It Up. I had little to lose. "Inside," I added. "Enjoy a little privacy."

A faint laugh broke out through her lips. Full lips, slightly chapped from all our adventures. "Where there are no people."

"Yeah, no people. Sure. Right. But I mean, really, there aren't any people left out here." We were both playing a game, but a casual observer to the conversation couldn't detect who was playing whom. I had a clear motive, but maybe she did, too.

"True," she agreed, rubbing the sand off her calves.

I've done it in some public places. Cars in parking lots. A picnic table at Lake Johnson Park in Raleigh. In college, my girlfriend and I went at it in most of the buildings on campus and once got caught with our shorts at our ankles in the basement laundry room of Monican. I tell you that the excitement lives strong when sneaking around and dies hard when exposed.

"This might be the wine talking," I said to Ivana, "but it's not so crazy to, y'know . . ." I made a motion with my fist, if she had any doubt what *y'know* meant.

She laughed. Laughing always makes her eyes glitter. "You had, like, one glass of wine. Two hours ago."

"Sure, sure. Right, well, would you ever give it a shot?" I hid my intentions behind a joking voice.

Silence. She looked away. I swear I saw a smirk play at the corners of her lips.

My face perked up in confusion. "Wait. Would you?"

More silence.

Well, I'll tell you that a man doesn't require a third round of silence as a cue. I ripped off my swimming trunks as if I had recently discovered that they were on fire. Ivana wasn't far behind and required little assistance.

There was a beach. It was empty. And we were naked.

The pace slowed. We took a moment to stare at each other. Waves twirled and burst like a sparkler on the Fourth, then dribbled to shore. Clouds puffed. One could sense rain lingering in the distance. Boats, caught in the first shower, scattered to avoid the next. Distant islands started to fade in the darkness. The sun burned through, though, and Ivana and I were the only ones who could see it. The salty aroma of the sea, delivered by a fluffy breeze, tickled my nose.

Ha, I thought. *Eight months prior, I was home and happy, but not like this.*

"This doesn't happen all the time," Ivana had said as she removed her undergarments, and I agreed. But, my goodness, it should! Every human should exercise with regularity and then take a day off to dispatch his or her clothes on a beach.

Sometimes you make slow, sweet, tender, quixotic love. And sometimes you go in there and get rowdy. One day, soft affection, the next day, toys and slapping. I'm a poor evaluator of when each of these applies, but on the beach, I know there's only one approach. You don't *fuck* on the beach, and you don't *get laid* on the beach. Every love song in the world has carried you to this moment, so save the aggression for the next round.

The waves continued to roll and kiss the sand, the clouds continued to puff. I closed my eyes, slid my hands around Ivana's hips, and leaned my head back.

And I realized: this was going somewhere. Anyone can have sex on the beach, and again I tell you, they should. Stay at Nirvana Resort, hail a tricycle, and ask for Puka Beach. The name itself begs, "Come shed your apparel upon my shore."

Ivana wasn't just anyone, though. The physical act of sex was just as good as every other time with Ivana. Bed, couch, bathroom, beach. Location changes can be fun, but it's still the one you're with that matters. A beautiful woman is a beautiful woman, and as I said, the streets of this world are teeming with them. But this one was different. There is this idea that, *my goodness, I must be the luckiest son of a bitch this side of Jupiter. What a wasted experience this would be with any other girl. This may never happen again, and I'm okay with that because this memory will last forever.* Each touch was joyful. Each kiss mattered. I was racing up the cleared lane of a mountain, one that kept going and going and going, where each scene rolled into the next. No sight of the summit. And that was okay. Welcome, even. I needed to lose myself in that moment; I needed it to never end.

But it did. The scene exploded before me. The light brightened and the world around us—the little bamboo hut, the beach, the gentle slaps of water, the sun shining through the clouds—focused to its sharper resolution. The setting consumed me, overtook me. It was exceptional, supernatural. The waves and the sun and the white sand and, Jesus, fluffy breezes tickling my nose? Experiences like that last forever.

Reluctantly we pulled our clothes back on. We lingered on the beach. The sun had bent over the horizon, and the moon glowed brightly. I swore that if I had a net and a length of string,

I could have nabbed it. I took Ivana's hand in mine, and we waded in the shallows. The cool undertow tugged the sand from beneath us. I kissed Ivana's forehead. We smiled. And we said nothing.

I, an American, met a Slovak girl in Honduras and then made love to her on a beach in the Philippines.

And that's pretty awesome.

EUROPE

A Moment of Solitude

Ivana flew home for a spell, so I spent four days with my good man Tony in Barcelona—eating tapas at outdoor cafés, taking long walks to admire the ornate architectural works of Gaudí and Montaner, and spending one very late night shouting drunkenly into microphones—and then headed south to the island of Mallorca rather than west to run in Pamplona, as I thought I might back when my year started.

From four out of seven sources, I heard that those wishing to present themselves as heroic have greatly overhyped the Running of the Bulls in Pamplona, Spain. You knock back a shot or two of tequila, you sprint for two minutes, you go drink more tequila. The bulls aren't after you—they're trying to get around you just as much as you are trying to avoid them—and accounts of injuries are limited to some drunkard who got cocky, desired to smack the ass of the beast, and proceeded to stumble along the wrong stretch of cobblestone. Besides, after fighting three bulls in Nicaragua, it didn't make much sense for me to start running away from them now.

Instead I sat for thirteen days and nights on my fourth-floor balcony overlooking the Mediterranean and listening to the sounds of the sea, watching sailboats cruise and yachts boast their supremacy. I went to Bukaro and the maître d' asked, "*Sólo uno?*" and with a content smile, I responded, "*Sí, señor.*" I packed salami, Brie, pimento-stuffed olives, and crackers, and wandered down to the beach. I crossed the street to Café Cyrano to drink sangria by the liter and munch on the best Margherita pizza I've ever tasted. Birds twittered by day, and live jazz hummed by night. Barefoot, shirtless, my hat turned backwards, I smoked hand-rolled cigars and sipped eighteen-year-old single-malt scotch. While watching the sun set into an explosion of scarlet and purple over the ocean.

I reflected on the first thirty years of my life and pondered the next thirty. I bought ice cream cones. I peered up at the night sky. I breathed deep. I drank in the luminance. And I giggled.

But mostly, I read. *The Alchemist. Bull City*. A chunk of Roald Dahl's collection. A book on the D-Day invasion. *The Green Mile* (again). I stumbled through the first eight lines of *The Canterbury Tales* before switching to Bill Bryson. I filled the gaps with a little Hemingway so I could bring him up in conversation in my e-mails home. I started *Lonesome Dove* and intend to finish it sometime early this year.

I ate and drank, bronzed my skin som'n sexy, and had my eyes in a book just about the whole time.

And life was good.

Those Less Traveled

A mericans—young Americans, especially—need to experience the world more. A mere 35 percent of Americans have a passport, and New Passports Issued is down one-third from five years ago. Even my Stateside friends who do have passports either used them just once for a specific trip or on weeklong, all-inclusive package deals to France or Italy or Caribbean beaches.

Worse, *Foreign Policy* magazine recently reported that almost one in three American teenagers doesn't pay any attention to daily news. "Another 32 percent are merely 'casually attentive,'" they write. Combined, that translates to over 60 percent of America's youth who are unaware of or apathetic about world events.

On the last leg of my trip, I considered the shame of this during a day trip to Auschwitz. I had previously read Anne Frank's *The Diary of Young Girl* and seen *Schindler's List* and watched a couple of documentary accounts, so I thought I had some perspective on these awful places where Germans herded Jews. But when the moment came, and I found myself walking where the persecuted walked and brushing my hands over the walls where their frail bodies leaned, I realized my teachings had left me short of a complete education on the devastation of Auschwitz.

People were tortured here. They were starved and beaten.

They were refused a change of underwear.

They were stuffed into that chamber and gassed.

They were hung on those gallows, displayed for the torment of their peers.

They were lined up on that wall there and shot in the head. Brothers and sisters, friends and lovers were forced to carry the dead bodies away and burn them.

Creativity died here. Talent died here. Visionaries and innovators died here. Future doctors and researchers and mathematicians and journalists—they all died here.

These were their eyeglasses and shoes and dishes. The prisoners were told they were simply being relocated, and this was the luggage they brought with them for the promising journey.

Hitler once said, "we shall regain our health only by eliminating the Jew," and I know there are a lot of angry people like him, but that kind of anger became more real once I actually stood among the effects. At Auschwitz, the most extensive murder campaign in human history had been carried out. I could sense the corpses, the souls tormented in this place. Women and children sent on arrival to the chamber, men forced to work and then sent to the gas chamber when their utility had been exhausted.

These were the gravel roads where they marched to their death, bare feet bloodied and frozen.

These were the barracks where they slept, huddled together on tiny wooden bunks as a bitter winter raged around them.

I left Auschwitz after only seven hours, my emotions still on edge. Upon returning to America, I knew I would want to tell my friends about this place, but I also knew that words would fail to describe my experiences. It's a place that must be experienced, not read about. It's a place that must be touched, not seen in blurry photographs. Yet I know that most of my friends will never visit Auschwitz, not because they feel as though they've figured it out, and not because they don't care about the horrors that took place there, but because they simply don't travel. It's an American affliction.

It's puzzling. Why don't we travel? Do we lack imagination? Are we scared? Too busy? Too skeptical? Too worried that we'll be forced to like soccer? Are we working too hard? Are we ignorant of the possibilities of world exploration? The United States has some amazing landscapes to discover, but do we just figure that's good enough and there's no need to step beyond our borders?

There's cultural diversity in the States; indeed we're one of the most culturally diverse countries in the world, but maybe that diversity still leaves us short of complete educations. Fantastic traditional restaurants populate cities big and small across the country, but we don't have chicken satay served up freshly grilled in two minutes, street side, by an Indonesian dude in Bogor. We have Irish pubs, but we don't have The O'Sullivan Brothers playing live in the corner at The Quays in Dublin. We have first-generation immigrants from Latin America—both legal and illegal—but we've never seen the plight they've escaped.

There is only one way to gain firsthand experience: firsthand.

The more we travel, the more we develop either a distaste for or an attraction to our home country. For me, it was the latter. Each day brought new adventure, and, just the same, each day hastened my arrival back to my favorite country in the world. I appreciated each place I visited, and I worked to make the most of my journey, but not once did I think, *Hm, yeah. I'd like to live here one day.* The longer I trod, the closer I drew to the traditional American values of courage and liberty and tenacity.

But I also started to see clearly my own ignorance, as well as the erroneous presumptions people make about the world. The beliefs I encountered on my travels were almost as outrageous as the ones I brought along with me. Aldous Huxley once wrote that "to travel is to discover that everyone is wrong about other countries," and after most locales visited, I've saluted this philosophy.

This is how we—everyone, everywhere—are weaned, I suppose. Parents, relatives, and friends surround us from the time we're small; they teach us what to think—and to hell with the alternative. Granddaddy was a Democrat, so I will be, too. Maw and Paw were Christians, so there must not be any other options. Society values sports over the sciences, so how can I confidently set off to investigate the mating rituals of the weaver ant when all three of my uncles insist I should be spending my time throwing a football?

And it's the same everywhere. There are so many narrow-minded and conflicting thoughts in this world that one must take a moment to go make his or her own discovery rather than sit at home in steadfast acceptance. Over the course of my travels, I've met some people who strengthened stereotypes, others who crushed them. I've heard—and often believed—that Brits are humorless; Americans are fat, greedy bullies; Japanese are tireless workers; Spaniards labor only as hard as their siestas allow; and Australians spend too much time playing. Indeed, there may be excessively hardworking Japanese, and fat Americans, and Aussies devoted exclusively to pleasure, but I've also met just as many of their opposites. Most of the Brits I've met on the road were hilarious. Many people of this world are lazy, and many more rarely crack a smile—regardless of their religion, their home country, or their skin color.

There are many Americans I don't like and many that I do. It would be ridiculous to base my regard for my own countrymen on the actions of one or two. Yet, I haven't always applied that same logic abroad.

In the Philippines, I met Olle, the only Swedish person I encountered on my travels. I didn't like him. Constantly cold and aloof, he complained an awful lot. He made plans with Ivana and me and then failed to show up. So does that mean I won't like any Swedes? Did he not like me, either? Was he a jerk that day merely because of other events and circumstances in his life? Had he recently received a bit of bad news?

In Kraków, Poland, a young man named Jeff arrived at my hostel after a long day of travel. Despite being weary and hungry, he nevertheless maintained a cordial and upbeat demeanor. Kazimiera, the receptionist, glanced down at his passport as she signed him in. "It's your birthday!" she chimed with a thick accent. "Yes, it is," he said. He'd been on the road for several birthdays and didn't mind if this one passed in the dark, as well.

Ivana and I went for a run. We came back. We showered. We pulled on clean clothes. We walked into the kitchen–dining room area to make a salad for dinner. Kazimiera entered, balancing a croissant on a plate, bridged by two candles, and tucked under her arm, a bottle of rum purchased with her own money. She sang "Happy Birthday" to Jeff in halting English. Just met this dude, didn't know him from any other traveler, hadn't exchanged more than a few hundred words with him in her life, and she made his day. We divvied up shots and laughs as Jeff declared that this was his favorite birthday ever.

And I remember thinking, at that moment, about my view of Poland. That it can get brutally cold. Wars had been waged there. Their economy festers in the dumps, much as it always has, much as it most likely always will. Nothing revolutionary comes from there, save a tasty kielbasa. And when we arrived, no one in the street really gave me much of a nod or a smile.

Yet here was Kazimiera, the warmest, most generous stranger I'd met in a year.

I used to think that Americans reigned supreme, and many of my peers have shared this sentiment with me. My friend Michael Virchow, a self-described redneck, once told me that he didn't need to ever leave the country. "All of the great people of the world are right here," he said. That seems a wild statement to me now. Traveling has heightened my understanding of the vast assimilation in America. If I've learned anything from one plane ride to the next, I've learned that no society is better than another. People all around this world are just as scummy or loveable as those found in America. Some hate homosexuals; others invite them into their lives. Some beat their dogs; others cuddle with them. Some prefer sunsets; others sunrises. You assume all this before you step outside your border, but it's humbling nonetheless to actually experience it for yourself.

As Americans we stand proud of our country—as proud as any other nation would and should be—but we usually give ourselves more credit than we deserve. This dynamic often exists with the world's superpowers. Along with China, we dominate the global economy, but that's more a result of numbers and facilities than anything else. We don't need fifty people to invent a cool new gadget—just one—and with 314 million people, fertile resources, and a sturdy infrastructure, we carry a distinct advantage toward innovation. We can have just as many shitheads as the rest of the world, and we do, but we're able to hide those shitheads, invent the computer, and think we've done something. But the shitheads are still there.

America has a broad range of talent, but so does China. Wouldn't you like to meet that talent? Exchange a few ideas? See for yourself why China resides with us at the top of the food chain? Maybe, on your way there, swing by Cambodia to investigate why they hang desperately at the bottom?

Little innovation comes out of Peru, but they have talent, too, right?

Ed Luce, the Washington bureau chief of the *Financial Times* and author of *Time To Start Thinking: America in the Age of Descent*, recently remarked on BBC News that "you're twice as likely to move up an income group—up a class—in Canada or Germany as you would in the U.S." Not only do we not realize the reason for this, but also most of us have never even met a German our age to gain insight into his or her routine and way of life. Could meeting a real, live, breathing German raise our awareness?

Also consider India. Here's a country listed as *developing*, a country with over a billion people—most of them washing clothes by hand and lacking supplies for school—and a system without the resources and support to foster individual growth. A friend of mine told me it's not uncommon to see a guy squat down to use the street as a bathroom, midday, as everyone else veers around him. Despite the country's struggles, India has a generation of computer engineers keeping pace with—and sometimes striding ahead of—their counterparts in the States.

More to the point, the people of India seem to hold a completely different idea of happiness and achievement than you or I. Gandhi lived a supreme life, yet he never owned a Mercedes. No matter where we live, it's possible to gain perspective on the Indian side of satisfaction, but isn't there a more authentic experience to be had if we drag ourselves off our sofas and go there?

From America, our reach is wide, our brands omnipresent. This is both good and bad. Apple has stratospheric earnings per share, not only due to U.S. sales, but also because it makes its products available from Indonesia to Australia to the Czech Republic. Charities in America help to reduce the world's epidemics and relieve natural disasters. Project Kesho, based in Bellevue, Washington, focuses on improving educational access for East Africa's rural youth. U.S. organizations have built entire communities in Nicaragua. Americans invent incredible gadgets, and American entrepreneurs inspire people the world over with their dedication and focus.

Just the same, our nation is excessively overweight, and people across the world see that on their television screens. Our political system is embarrassingly polarized. Our grasp of the English language grows weaker. Our divorce rate is spiraling out of control. We have the highest teen-pregnancy rate in the developed world, and second place isn't even close.

I'm fascinated by this dynamic: the American culture has spread across the world and made an impact, but just as some people dance to our music at a discotheque, or wear our jeans, or offer their gratitude for donated medicines, or otherwise benefit from our creativity, some note McDonald's negative impact on worldwide obesity or Coca-Cola's contribution to diabetes. Others go further, claiming that nothing positive has ever risen out of America: "You are responsible for the meltdown of the entire global economy," one guy railed at me in a pub in Perth, Australia. "You've brought the world to war to serve your own interests."

Conversely, back in Guatemala, I met a guy named Pablo between rum and Cokes at Café No Sé in Antigua. Café No Sé is a neighborhood bar for tourists, if there can ever be such a place. Dim butter-warm lights create a soothing atmosphere, perfect for sharing stimulating ideas. Pablo, a fellow in his early thirties with a head of wild dark hair and a chin peppered with whiskers, leaned against the bar. His button-down shirt (top two buttons undone), chinos, and shiny black shoes blended well with the attire of the rest of the bar. Pablo kept near me, allowing me to practice my Spanish. This meant that, as he translated, most of our conversation happened twice. We spoke of travel and women and Guatemalan fútbol. Finally, the smile slipped from his face, and his dark eyes grew serious. He leaned in. "I love your country," he said. "I would go to war for you right now and without hesitation." All this despite sometimes-strained military relations between my country and his.

I'll be the first to admit that I still don't really understand America's presence on the world stage; I've gathered only hints about it along the way. I can, however, say for certain that my travels have greatly improved my understanding of the world and my place in it and America's place in it. We read about it, and we talk about it, but we don't really understand that India and China and Russia stand abreast of us at the forefront of innovation. Sometimes ahead of us. *It's scary*, we say. *They're coming to steal our place at the top.* But we don't really believe this could actually happen, nor—more important—do we fully grasp the ingenuity required to maintain our place at the top, to continue to make a positive impact on a world that needs it.

One solution for this naïveté, maybe, is to get out there to see for ourselves. Ideas and compassion bloom in the unknown beyond. Creative juices flow, ears perk, eyes dilate. We— Americans—don't travel until we're old. In New Zealand, Nic, twenty-six years old and relatively well-traveled, observed that I was only the third American he'd met on the backpacker trail.

The third!

Is it arrogant of our younger generation to stay home? Lazy? Careless? Are we so pompous that we think we have the rest of the world figured out without having to investigate it? Shouldn't we be excited to meet the wonderful people of this world, to learn the history, to see the scenic places and taste the yummy food? And what about the darker side of this globe? Even if it's not practical for everyone to save their money to go travel for a year, I see no reason why everyone couldn't scrape together the change for a plane ticket to go volunteer for a little while, at the very least. There's suffering in this world, and that suffering ain't in America.

Get out there. Meet people. See places. Eat street food. Take a class or teach one. Inform yourself about the world and inform the world about you. Choose your own adventure.

- Stand in Auschwitz.
- Dig a trench.
- Muster a mob of cattle.
- Sing karaoke in an unfamiliar tongue.
- Test local beers.
- Go fishing in alien waters.
- Take a kid for a ride in an airplane.
- Play rock-paper-scissors.
- Observe the treatment of the natives.
- Hike a mountain your friends have never heard of.
- Put the moves on a good-looking stranger in a strange bar in a strange land.

Samuel Johnson was right when he said, "The use of traveling is to regulate imagination by reality, and instead of thinking how things may be, to see them as they are."

Meeting the Parents

After spending thirteen days in Mallorca, Ivana and I traveled the south of Spain for two weeks. Soon enough, though, we were boarding a bus bound for Zlaté Moravce, her hometown in Slovakia, and I was more wound-up than I'd been all year. I twisted the straps of my backpack between my fingers as we waited in line. "I can't do this," I said. "I'm not ready."

Ivana said, "My mom is going to freak out. She's so excited to meet you, and she has no idea that we're coming home this week." Looking at me sideways with a slight curve of her lips, she added, "I've planned this very well."

I said, "Good Lord. Can we delay this a couple of days? Let me catch my bearings here a little bit?"

Next minute we were on the bus. "Um, darling, are you listening to me?" I asked. She smiled and turned her face toward the window.

Next minute, we were off the bus. "Okay, how 'bout this?" I said, every minute drawing me closer to meeting her parents. "Here's what we can do. Give me an extra day, and I will take you to the fanciest restaurant you can find within fifty miles of your house. Fifty miles, I say. Wine, appetizer, main entrée, dessert, foot massage. The works. How can you say no to that?"

Next minute, our packs were slung across our shoulders. "Why so soon? I want to get around and see a little bit of Slovakia first. We just got here!" This didn't feel right. A backpack on the shoulder with a destination ahead is one of the most satisfying feelings in this world. Yet I'm not sure I've ever felt as uncomfortable as I felt at that moment (save, of course, the moment in the outback that I lost that crucial game of rock-paper-scissors).

Next minute, we were on the main street, walking toward her neighborhood. Ramshackle gypsy dwellings lounged to our left. A warped sidewalk to the right tripped up strangers, while locals stepped neatly over each crack and gap in the concrete. A few trees pockmarked the street, but their rough trunks twisted, branches gnarled up and leaves curled into a bitter brown. All these things seemed like plenty warning to me. "I can't do this, honey. What if your mom is embarrassed because we didn't give her any advance notice to clean the place up? That's not very nice of us." It's intense: living six months in a row, twenty-four hours a day, with the same person, with only momentary breaks to go to the bathroom. However, I never felt the desire to flee or put a hundred yards distance between us until that moment.

The very next minute, I stood at the doorstep of her parents' apartment building, big and more modern than the places we'd passed en route. I stared at the chocolate-brown front door and thought what a silly color choice that was. It really should have been dark green. My right hand rattled the coins in my pocket. "Seriously, Ivana, be sensible. I'm not ready for this."

Ivana beamed. If I didn't know better, I would have sworn she was enjoying my torment. "No, no. You're going to do great. I can't wait to see the look on her face. I hope she's home." And then: "Any last words before you surprise her?" She settled a hand on my arm, a light touch that eased my nerves. If she hadn't had such a cheery disposition, that contagious grin lighting up her face, I would have walked away to regroup.

"Ugh," I said. "If I don't make it out alive, I bequeath all my clothes, my dresser, and my bookshelf to my brother, and my body to science."

"Bequeath?" she asked.

She pulled out her camera and started filming. I breathed deep. She said, "You can do it." The next minute, I used her key to open the door. Her entire family started hollering *"Prekvapenie!"* The surprise had been planned all along. Mom, dad, sister, both sets of grandparents, an aunt and two uncles, two cousins and a girlfriend. Balloons bounced against the ceiling of her parents' apartment, and a huge, colorful, hand-painted WELCOME, ADAM sign stretched across the foyer, ten feet ahead of me. My face felt warm and red. I kissed her mom on each cheek as she served up a traditional shot of stiff liquor. In Slovak I said, "Uh . . . hello. I am Adam. Nice to meet you. I am hungry. Give me food now, please."

We ate and drank and were merry. Ten different parts comprised my surprise party—among them, rounds of introduction, a song of welcome, gifts of flowers and alcohol, various stages of food, a song wishing me well in the future, and two cakes. With a salute of *na zdravie*, we toasted my health, their health, everyone's health. All around me, the chattering syllables of a foreign tongue rose. I understood no one, save a phrase or two from her mom on occasion, but Ivana tirelessly zipped from one corner of the room to another to translate. We made plans for the upcoming weeks—unreasonable plans—and broke them before they could even develop fully.

"Dinner at your place . . . ? My choice of menu . . . ? Let's do it twice!"

"Bungee jumping? A beach in Croatia? I'm down."

"Absinthe? I've never tried it before, but—well, if you can assure me that you'll help me find my way home . . ."

I promised time for movies and thermal pools and workouts and then couldn't find enough hours in the day.

Ivana introduced me to Bubinko, her family's adorable, fluffy bunny rabbit. Bubinko would snoop around, nose twitching as he sniffed with the curiosity of a beagle, and then he would promptly fall off into a catatonic state, midhop. He'd sit, this little ball of black and white fur, parked by the couch. How can a party not be fun, your days not brightened, with a narcoleptic rabbit bounding about? Kind of like when your uncle passes out drunk from too many Rob Roys at Thanksgiving and still, even asleep, manages to make everyone laugh.

I met Adel and Hanka and Tomáš and all the rest of Ivana's friends whom she hadn't seen in nearly a year. Every time we made a run to the post office or to the gyro joint on Župná, we ran into another acquaintance. Cobblestone streets wind up and down Zlaté Moravce; outdoor cafés speckle the downtown, and wineries linger on the fringes; when one goes to the bank, the teller greets him or her by name on arrival; people rent movies from an actual movie store with actual shelves of DVDs and a clerk who says, "How'd you like it?" upon return. Driving out of town to watch the sun set over the hills and the lazy, stretching fields of sunflowers, there can be no other thought than, *My, now this is about as good as it gets.* It's an amiable town, a preserved and peaceful town.

But it's bloody depressing. This is a small place, Zlaté Moravce, a prosaic small town in the fashion of yesterday's Midwestern burgs; sixty years after the death of local enterprise, descendants of industry skeletons mosey about looking for something to do. Bubinko has the right idea. This is the place where inspiration goes to nap and desire to wilt, the place you'll never hear, "I've got a plan." A fantastic location to escape for a week but not two. People in the streets just kind of wander around with no particular finish line; people in their homes just kind of sit there and wait. The old folks still say the Germans are fascists. Some of Ivana's friends have left for the capital or more prosperous parts of Europe, while others stand by in a daze. It's an industrialized El Porvenir, Honduras, without the stray dogs in the streets.

Though maybe they want it that way. Maybe some people detest change. Maybe some people would rather not move forward. They'd rather wake up and know exactly what the balance of their day looks like. For me, it's depressing. For them, it could be paradise.

Finally, after the commotion of the first week, I took a breath and got to know Ivana's mom and dad and sister. We hopped in the car and drove to the High Tatras, Slovakia's famous mountain range. We hiked for hours, weaving among magnificent old trees. We ate at wonderful restaurants, lounging on patios overlooking the jagged peaks rising around and behind us. We went to three different water parks. We snapped stunning photos. I went bungee jumping, and Ivana's dad looked as if he couldn't decide whether he was impressed by my courage or skeptical about my poor judgment.

At Liptovská Mara, I went wakeboarding. While comfortably positioned on top of the board behind the boat, I removed one hand from the handle, shot Ivana's dad the hang-loose sign, smiled wide, and promptly caught an edge and planted my face in the water.

This is a curious man, Ivana's dad. Always engaged, though he mostly keeps to himself. In larger settings of six or more people, he gets lost in the chattering bedlam, but one-on-one or around a table of four, he lends his ear and then offers something to say in return. He takes a turn as the life of the party but knows to bow out before his welcome has worn.

At a huge birthday bash for a neighbor, the conversation at the table started to wane. I looked over at Ivana's dad as he leaned in toward his wife and whispered in her ear. She smiled. Seconds later, they were on the dance floor, twirling about.

A stern man with a spontaneous sense of humor, he would be quick to reel his head back in laughter, throat extended, veins loose and all. If he spoke English, he's the kind of guy who could easily lure me into a corner to tell me in a hushed, matter-of-fact tone, "If you ever do anything to hurt my daughter, I'll immediately fly to wherever you are on the planet so I can take a moment to cut one of your nuts away from your scrotum with a rusty butter knife. Just so you know where we stand." And then a pat on the back: "Right. Well, I'm parched. You ready for another beer?"

Walking through town after I'd known the family for only two days, we passed a church. Buildings looked depressed, even the ones that had recently been painted over. A destitute lady with tired eyes walked up. She requested spare change. In the States, I would have said "Sorry, no." But Ivana's dad looked at her with a kind of perplexity, as if to say, *You want money? For what . . . ? Oh, because you have been struck by tough times?* The lady's plea must have worked. He looked around, still perplexed, as he pulled out a handful of coins from his satchel and handed them over. Four times this happened while I stayed in Slovakia. Every time this confusion and compassion on his face, and *every* time he would give them his spare change and walk away without another word.

Through Ivana, I said to him, "All of your change? Really?"

He smiled, and Ivana translated his reply: "I'm not too worried about it. She needs it more than me."

Ivana's sister is cordial and playful and always in a good mood. In the morning, it was *"Dobré ráno, Adam!"* and in the afternoon, *"Adam, dobré popoludnie!"* Before a meal: *"Dobrú chuť!"* She heard about me smoking cigars in Spain, so she made me a ceramic ashtray, bumpy and a shiny shade of brown. Taupe, I think. Still, though, we had no means to talk to each other. Her mom spoke a series of broken phrases to me in English, and her dad not more than four words at a time—"Wake up time, friend!"—but Veronika preferred to deliver her "Hellos," "Good mornings," and "How ya doings?" to me in Slovak. And once she saw that I'd conquered the salutations, she seemed to forget that I couldn't go further, that I'd come from America, a land faraway, and hadn't taken the time to learn to have a conversation in her language. So while everyone else was translating through Ivana, Veronika came right at me.

"Adam, pod' sa pozrieť na zajaca."

I laughed twice and shot her a thumbs-up on my way into the living room. "Ah, yes. *Ďakujem za tortu.*"

"You two are a couple of idiots," Ivana remarked.

"What?"

"She told you to come look at what the rabbit is doing."

I chuckled. "Oh, okay. Cool."

"And you told her thank you for the cake."

But Ivana's mom was the real gem to me. Using Slovakia as our base for a month, I left with Ivana for four long weekends in Poland, then Vienna, then Budapest, then Prague. On every long return bus or train ride, I leaned back against the seat and yawned. No matter how tired, I was always excited to come back and see Ivana's mom. Always smiling, always wondering what she can do to help, always trying to engage in cheerful conversation. With silky brown hair and jasper eyes, she's beautiful, not just for forty-seven but for any age. Women in Slovakia, like the women of Eastern Europe or Scandinavia or Brazil, are exotic looking: they're either strikingly gorgeous or they have sideburns, and there's rarely an in-between. Mária Mravíková is the former, no question, and this only added to the charm of the work she put in every day.

"Ivana, come here and translate, please," I requested.

Ivana, fingers wrapped around a cup of hot tea, followed me into the living room.

"Could you please tell your mom that she doesn't need to be ironing my drawers?" I pointed to Mrs. Mravíková like a small child tattling on their sibling.

After a pause and a series of quick, amused Slovakian phrases, Ivana turned back to me. "She said that you're in her house now, and this is what she does."

"Right, but they are drawers."

Ivana shrugged. "She doesn't care. They need to be ironed."

I was trying to be logical. "Nobody will see them, no matter how rid of creases they might be. They are drawers."

Ivana's mom pressed away at my undergarments.

"She said this helps kill the bacteria."

I walked to the bedroom, returned with an armful of socks, and inquired, "These haven't been ironed in a while either. Possible bacteria. Do you have any experience with socks?" With a smile, she jokingly confessed that if she used the right setting, she was pretty sure she could loop one around my neck.

But this was only part of it. Not only did the day's worn clothes disappear from the floor and return to me folded and wrinkle-free, but I never touched a dirty dish. Ivana and I always had a ride anywhere we wanted to go day or night. I rarely touched a bottle of wine, but my glass remained filled to the brim. I had to go to the grocery store only once. There was always plenty of body wash in the bathroom and never a grain of sand on the floor. And when I requested an ibuprofen for a headache, Ivana's mom immediately scurried off to the pharmacy as if I was in the middle of a heart attack.

I was frequently on edge, wondering what her parents were talking about in my presence, and it didn't help that the tone of the Slovak language favors nothing I've ever heard.

One morning Ivana's mother poked her head in the doorway and spoke with Ivana. A moment later, she disappeared down the hallway.

I sank back into the bed, deflating the fluffy mattress and pillows. "What did your mom say? She hates me, doesn't she? Ugh, I knew she hated me." And then her mom reentered, carrying a tray of breakfast and settling it over our legs. Cereal, two sausages, eggs, fruit, yogurt, and cups of tea. Every morning. I insisted, "Seriously, you *really* shouldn't be doing this," and she just smiled and acted as if my protests didn't translate, as if she didn't understand what I was talking about.

Somehow Ivana's mom had received the wrong message and ended up on the wrong side of the interrogation. Someone must have told her that she was supposed to impress me, rather than the other way around, and after several attempts at telling her to just take a moment to chill out, I finally learned to say, "Yes, ma'am, I *am* hungry, and a plate of stuffed mushrooms sounds delicious." Champagne? "Why not?"

Then, just like that, I ran out of money. Teary-eyed, I shook hands with Ivana's father and hugged her sister.

Ivana's mom drove me to the airport in Budapest, two hours away. I said, "Thanks for everything." We hugged and exchanged pleasantries in English.

"What a trip!" I said.

"You are nice young man!" she replied. "Very nice. A good young man for Ivana."

She pulled two Tupperware containers out, each with five of her famous chicken schnitzels. "For the trip," she said. "A very long trip." I whispered my thanks, voice a little hoarse, and turned to walk down the terminal. And I wondered, as I headed for my plane, whether Mrs. Mravíková was thinking the same thing as me—that I sure hoped I would one day see her again.

HOME

We shall not cease from exploration
And the end of all our exploring
Will be to arrive where we started
And know the place for the first time.

—T. S. Eliot, *Four Quartets*

So I spent all my money, which I figured might happen, because before I left, I said to my brother, "I'm going to go out in the world and spend all my money." I flew twelve-and-a-half hours to New York's JFK from Budapest's Ferihegy via a nineteen-hour layover at Kiev's Boryspil (an airport whose inefficiency is exceeded only by the gloominess of its staff). I grabbed a shuttle into Manhattan, packed two pieces of fried chicken in my pack, and hopped on an overnight bus to Union Station in D.C. I caught the Yellow Line out to the Pentagon and then bus 7F to King Street. I hadn't showered in sixty hours, so I doused myself with body spray, and at 7:02 A.M., positioned just before the King Street on-ramp to 395, I stuck up my thumb and my NORTH CAROLINA sign.

After a patch spent on the receiving end of a series of hostile glares and entertaining gestures, I realized I might cover those last 270 miles home quicker by foot than I would hailing a ride. I caught the 7E back to Pentagon Station and took the subway back to Union Station. Undeterred and still elated to be Stateside, I busted out my Visa to purchase a small mountain of Reese's Peanut Butter Cups and a ticket for the next train steamin' south, vowing the entire time to pick up the very next hitchhiker on my path who didn't look like he wanted to stab me in my jugular.

My boy Korey picked me up at the Durham Amtrak station and came at me with a sturdy embrace before I could pause to breathe a second sniff of my home state. By seven o'clock we were with my pops at his house in Chapel Hill, and ten minutes later, I started cooking dinner. We ate outside under the crispness of an early fall evening. The Great Vacation was over, and there I was. Sitting on the brick patio behind Pops's modest residence, overlooking his elegant yet unpretentious garden, cocktails in hand, seven days before my thirtieth birthday. I had far fewer dollars but a much bigger smile than when I turned twenty.

I didn't take this trip to meet myself. I was happy before I caught that first flight to Guatemala City. I didn't take this trip so that I could grow up, become a man, and leave all those immature days behind me. I wasn't unfulfilled when I left, and I didn't reach enlightenment as a result of this trip. I didn't find God, though I was told many times that He is out there to be found.

I read seventy-one books, including nine classics and one—slowly—in Spanish; I worked with poor kids in Honduras; I discovered that *coger* means "to catch" in Spain and "to fuck" in Latin America; I fucked three buses; I bungee jumped and scuba dived; doved; doven; went scuba diving; I learned about the reproductive organs of a chicken (and if you ever see a rooster violate a hen, you'll be curious about them, as well); I spent a night with absinthe, and you'll go a long way to persuade me to do it again. I took my comprehension of Spanish to the next level; I woke up early; I slept late; I got robbed; I survived a bull in Nicaragua and a pregnancy scare in Australia; I went to *Rigoletto* at the Státní opera in Prague and danced in the cage at a gay club in Barcelona at four in the morning; in Thailand I got a tattoo, rode an elephant, and then ate the best street food in the world; I grew a mustache and a mullet, although, as mandated previously, not at the same time. I clicked a number of items off of the *List o' Good Times*, but in the end, my most memorable experiences weren't even on it. I say I'd like to run a mile along the Great Wall, for example, and that's merely a setup to get me to China to see what other kind of mischief I can dig up.

And after all of it, I still barely managed a dent in the things I'd like to do. Some things I still can't afford, others were in countries I never got to, and a few just didn't feel quite right. Firing an AK-47 in Thailand sounds awesome, but then an Aussie from Melbourne said to me: "You go in there. You pay your money. And then you're standing around with a bunch of totally random dudes who also have loaded AK-47s in their hands. They say, 'So, where are you going to go next on your trip?' and you can only think about how completely mad this situation is."

I just wanted to go investigating, and I wanted to do it before it was time to start paying down a mortgage and wiping asses. Just as my friends and family who stayed back in the States had unique experiences of their own while I was gone, this journey heightened my awareness. I visited Copán and Auschwitz and analyzed the difference between the historical treatment of the Māori and the Aborigines. Still, I don't profess to all of a sudden "get it" now that I've skipped the border for a year. Not only do I not think I'm cultured, this year proved that I'm totally bereft of culture. I don't have solutions to any of the problems that politicians and pundits and nonprofits try to solve every day. Heck, I still don't understand the function of seven of the nineteen straps on my backpack. I probably have more questions now than when I started a year ago.

What did I learn? What's the big payoff? What's the point?

I'm still figuring that out. Really, I had my little experience, and maybe I took away something completely different than you have by reading about it or than you would by taking a trip of your own. Maybe there aren't one or two or five concrete answers to those questions anyway. Maybe, there are things I will learn about this trip in five, ten, thirty years, long after its completion, things I can't conceive now but will as my education continues.

I'm grateful to have shared the company of some truly great people and witnessed the difference that one person can make in his or her own life and the life of someone else. America is the greatest country in the world, but the core reason we've fallen behind in a few places is because we chase certainty and shun nonconformity. Our aversion to risk increases every day. Fear takes over. This is a world that favors those who challenge conventional thinking rather than those who fall in line, and getting out into the world challenges us to think in different ways. It's fascinating the perspective we can gain when we step out of our cushy bubbles of comfort, even just a little bit. And I mean that both ways: I know that I made a difference volunteering in Central America, and I'm telling you that those kids and their families and Loyd Miguel and René and Pastor Gener made a difference in my life.

"If you think you're going to go out in the world to make a major impact, you're insufficiently motivated," Jim Palmer told me one sunny afternoon in Nicaragua. "But if you take it one step at a time, one family at a time, one meal at a time, one child's education at a time, one water pump at a time, it's amazing what can become of that."

I knew Marginee Callejas for fifteen minutes, and I'll never forget her. Flora I knew little more than an hour. There are good people in every town around the world who will lead you to the local swimming hole, just as there are jerkoffs who can't be bothered giving directions. I'm thankful for the good people I met this year.

I'm grateful to have gained perspective, however little of it I might have gained.

Indeed, after seeing the poverty in the villages of Nicaragua and Honduras and in the cities of Jakarta and Manila and then the simple life of the Australian outback and the tranquility of Slovakia, I have a greater appreciation for many things, but this doesn't necessarily make me more perceptive than my peers. It's simply a different perspective. It means that I won't bitch at the server the next time there is a hair in my tuna tartare and I'll have increased admiration for my friends back home who don't care what brand of watch they have on their wrists. I'm now moving forward with a heap of memories I'll not soon forget. The next time I'm having a bad day, I'll remember the happy, dimpled expressions on those kids' faces in Honduras; when I'm feeling rushed and anxious, I'll put myself on top of that platform in Slovakia, about to jump, and I'll tell myself to just relax a little; and when it's pouring rain, too yucky to go outside to play, I'll pull up the pictures of that view from the top of the Indian's Nose overlooking Lake Atitlán in Guatemala, and that will make me smile.

The one and *only* thing I've learned to be an indisputable fact is that our lives are only as satisfying as the vibe we put out into the world. Good shit is going to happen to us, and bad shit is going to happen to us. How we react to these circumstances—rather than the actual circumstances themselves—will ultimately determine our happiness.

Maybe it's not practical for you to get missing for a year, but I hope you have the cojones to do something uncommon, whether for a week, a month, or longer. The next time adventure extends an invitation, I hope you'll RSVP with a *yes, please*. And I hope you won't be deterred by the financial sacrifices you may have to make.

Critics cite years like this as playtime, an obstruction in the career climb. Wasteful, they say, asking how one will find a job when he or she returns. One of the volunteers in Honduras, Chris Hays, answered this blankly, "Even in an economic crisis, crappy jobs aren't going anywhere. I had a crappy job when I left, and— if I want another one—there'll be one waiting for me when I get back. My trip, however, won't wait." Is this irresponsible? I say no. After all, we spend a lifetime hoarding our money, and for what? Unlimited cruises in our seventies? Yes, a career is important, but don't we sometimes spend so much time with our lips on our boss's cheeks that we miss out on some primetime moments of exploration?

More than that, aren't employers ravenous for innovative candidates with the ability to think critically? A classroom education is essential, but isn't there also value in seeing the world as it really is, rather than just through a textbook or cocktail-party conversation? In this global economy, isn't it important to actually get out there to investigate the globe? Am

I not an improved American citizen now that I've spent a little time outside? Hasn't this year imparted teachings that I maybe couldn't get any other way?

Won't lessons learned with the concert tickets in Guatemala or in that taxi in Managua or examining the financial intricacies of the Australian-Indonesian cattle trade apply to the business world? Won't meeting Rafael face-to-face in a social setting, and seeing where he comes from, develop my professional relationship with him and other foreigners?

Am I now better equipped to embrace uncertainty?

At the very least, haven't I improved my potential interview patter?

I guess I'll soon see, but in the meantime, I just know that if I wouldn't have left home, it would be the next on a very short list of regrets in my life. My seventy-year-old self isn't going to look back on my twenty-ninth year and say, "Man, I wish I would have worked that year." He would, however, be upset if I hadn't caught that first flight to Guatemala City.

Everybody tells you that the BMW 6 Series is the car to have.

Awesome.

Everybody tells you that every year you delay grad school takes money out of your pocket.

Fine.

Everybody tells you that you should be buying a house.

Whatever.

Everybody wants to tell you how to be a millionaire, and the idea is a sexy one, but maybe we spend so much time chasing shiny things that we forget that happiness also shows itself among those experiences that you can't hold in your hand. I gave up a lot to take this trip, and I'm glad I did. I would love a pool in my backyard and pretty plants on the front porch and a new model in my driveway, but before I try to get those things, give me an experience I can't adequately explain with words.

Moving forward, this trip has sharpened my awareness of my own mortality. At some point, I'm going to get brain cancer. Or multiple sclerosis. Or fibromyalgia. Or pneumonia. Or gout. Or have a stroke. No doubt there is something ill and debilitating brewing discreetly in my body right now. I don't know what a pulmonary embolism is, but apparently it can strike you down without warning, young or old. There are drunk drivers and malpracticing doctors and crazy men entering movie theaters with assault weapons.

While I was in Prague, the government placed an immediate and total ban on all liquors with over 20 percent alcohol content after a wave of methanol poisonings killed twenty-four people. Twenty-four people! Just sitting in a bar, sipping their favorite cocktails. While I sat in a bar and watched their obituaries on TV, all shelves were immediately cleared. It turns out, unbeknownst to many (especially tourists), one out of every five bottled liquors in the Czech Republic—in restaurants, pubs, and shops alike—is brewed on the black market.

It's always an early demise—"too soon," they say—and in the meantime, my hair is going to continue to recede, my metabolism will continue to slow. My pace drags, my posture curls. My knees aren't getting any stronger for athletic competition, and my lower back is already starting to ache on occasion. I used to be able to stretch for three minutes to get back to 100 percent; now I need ice packs and massages.

But we move forward. Marianne du Toit trekked from Argentina to New York with two horses. Peter Jenkins walked across America. Robin Lee Graham left port at sixteen to sail around the world. Philippe Croizon swam from Spain to Morocco, and that mother is a quadruple amputee.

At a hostel in Poland, I met Paul from England. "Yeah, dude," I boasted. "I've been traveling around the world for just about a year. Been all over the place. Done some great things. Good times." I went on and on about my exploits—mostly bullfighting—and then asked him what he was up to. "Oh, I'm in the process of cycling home," he said. "From China."

Thousands of other journeys going on right now, enriching experiences and happy memories. We continue to build on those memories—to create more—for the rest of our lives.

Before I departed, the biggest questions were, *Why a year? Why not six months? Why not five years? What makes you so sure a year is the magic time?* And now I can tell people that a year was perfect. For one, I didn't miss much. I missed Dave's and Brian's weddings, but that just gives me an excuse to fly up to Boston to hang out with them for a weekend; I missed Christmas with the family, which I cherish, but I'll catch up with all of them shortly; I found out about a series of current events long after they were current (the death of Muammar Gaddafi; blackouts in India that left 620 million people without power; flash floods killing over a thousand people in the Philippines after Tropical Storm Washi; and *Curiosity*'s landing on Mars); I missed the Oscars, Grammys, Emmys, ESPYs, and every other award program that, now that I mention it, doesn't really matter anyway; I skipped out on Carolina's great year on the hardwood—underclassmen and injuries considered—and a truly mad NCAA tournament, but now I'm around to watch a new season; I've lost pounds and gained pounds along the way, and before breakfast this morning, I gazed into the mirror at a dumpy belly and fragile limbs that look as if they haven't seen a weight room in just about exactly a year.

Ultimately, one year was perfect because now I'm hungry. I lost touch with my family and friends back home, and now I'm excited to reconnect with the life I set to the side: I've missed dinner with Ma, drinks with Korey, lunch with Pops, and board games with Easy. Tony and I are going to go sit in the steam room. I want to get the guys together to go paintballing.

Maybe I didn't need to run off and find myself, but it feels good to return home armed with purpose. Before I left, my life was a little disorganized, my direction foggy. I was in a happy place, but my creative juices had run dry. No new ideas. I was just cruising. Now? I've got a couple concepts I'm eager to try out over the next five years. I've had a year to ponder and process where I do and don't belong; I'm more focused; and I'm excited to start working hard again, hone a skill, save money, launch my own business. Failing that, I'll go get a master's degree. I'm energized. This year energized me.

This was the greatest year of my life, let there be no question about that, and just the same, I'm thrilled to be home and moving toward the next endeavor. I hope you are, too.

And then, there's the girl.

I cannot overstate how completely fantastic this girl is. She is sharp and fun and funny and considerate and a hundred other characteristics.

Last September my family and friends gathered to throw me a going-away party and wish me well on my forthcoming journey. Halfway across the world, two nights before, Ivana's family and friends did the same.

Forty-two days later, I arrived in El Porvenir via the wrong Antigua to meet up with the rest of the volunteers. I looked as if I'd recently been spit out the ass end of a typhoon, and Ivana was sucking on a plastic baggie of ice water. Not exactly a scene out of a romantic movie.

A couple months after that, from Honduras, she left with a group to go north to Guatemala for a visa run, and I was a day from departing for Nicaragua. We were to be separated for two months before reconvening in Nicaragua to head to New Zealand. I woke up solo on New Year's Day and wrote her a note:

Ivana,

I want to tell you where I was last night...

I was alone, but I was not lonely.

Everyone went to La Ceiba to dance and drink and converse and be merry. They had fun. Carly, Liz, Christina, etc. So much dancing. Salsa. Meringue. Bachata. I stayed home.

I watched a movie. You know I can dance, more or less, mostly less, but I was in the mood to relax on the recliner. I made a couple of drinky drinks, one per hand—keep 'em coming. 11:55 came. I went to the bathroom to pee. I exited the house, locked the door, and walked ten meters out to the beach. Ten meters! (It's just right there, y'know.)

11:58.

11:59.

Midnight struck, and the sky was wide open. Not a cloud to be seen. A thousand stars in the sky. Okay, a million. Countless. Waves crashed to the shore. Lightning bugs flashed. Crickets chirped in the distance as they always do in these circumstances, although the wind was tranquil, rather than whirring about. No one in sight. Just me standing on a sandy beach.

And you.

Fireworks ignited behind me. I turned, head tilted back, chin to the sky. One after the other. Boom. Boom. Boom.

Pause.

Then, more. Boom. Boom. Boom. Lighting up the night sky. Vibrant.

12:03.

12:06.

The fireworks stopped. But the scene persisted. The beach. The waves. The stars. You.

I laughed. I don't know where it came from, Ivana, but I laughed. Where are you right now! Guatemala? Honduras? Ahhhhhh! Where are you! You don't understand. I know you dig me, but you don't understand how much I dig you. Do you? Maybe you do. I hope you do. Man, I hope you do.

Yes, you do.

We dig each other. And that is pretty grand.

So many girls I've dated. So. Many. Girls. Fantastic girls. But not The Girl.

You are The Girl, Ivana.

Life is great. Movies, books, kids to play with, strolling the streets of Raleigh with Korey and Tony, Easy inebriated and hollering for a taxi on a vacant road, relationship talks with Sana on I-40 from Wilmington, travel, mountains, skiing, snowboarding, pears dripping with juice, street food, gourmet food, cheap wine, fine wine (can we tell the difference?), lakes, rivers, sunsets, sunrises, no sun at all, pineapples with black pepper (if they say so), sneaking in for late-night swims in the community pools in Cary (you wanna do it?), brunch on the back porch, cookouts in the park, New England in fall, New Zealand in spring, North Carolina anytime (of course), working hard, going for broke, bungee jumping in Slovakia (you promised!), skydiving, white-water rafting. And sitting on a fluffy sofa, doing nothing at all.

But none of it means much anymore without you by my side.

I was alone, but you were there with me last night, Ivana. I raised my glass to the great year to come, and I raised my glass to next December 31, at midnight, when we'll be together (in the flesh), and I can look into your eyes, wrap my arms around you, and touch my lips to yours.

That will be the happiest occasion of my life.

Until the next one.

With you.

And it's important for you to know something: that when the newness wears off (as it soon will), when these wild notes to each other become progressively rare (as they do), when everything is normal rather than high (as it surely will be), in two years when we are simply standing in our modest kitchen together, likely in the 'hood (rent at a minimum), candles glowing, music crooning, a glass of white wine in the left hand and a frying pan in the right... I will want you just as much then as I do right now at this moment.

A

So, here I go, off to summon my girl to North Carolina for New Year's Eve; beyond, if I'm lucky. Maybe the next time I see you and we're swapping stories, she'll be on my arm.

And you? Here you go to find your own journey in this world— near or far, a month or a year, solo or accompanied. Cheers! To your next adventure.

ABOUT THE AUTHOR

Adam Shepard has been featured on NPR, CNN, Fox News, *Today*, and *20/20* and profiled in the *New York Times*, *New York Post*, *Christian Science Monitor*, and *Atlantic Monthly*. He currently spends his time empowering audiences to take initiative. His keynote speech *What Will You Do Next?* details strategies for capitalizing on both triumph and misfortune.

For book clubs, retail resale, educational institutions, gifts,
or promotional use,
One Year Lived is available for 78 percent off the cover price at
www.OneYearLived.com.

24244638R00161

Made in the USA
Middletown, DE
19 September 2015